ISBN 978-0-282-40979-1
PIBN 10850698

1 MONTH OF
FREE
READING

at

www.ForgottenBooks.com

By purchasing this book you are eligible for one month membership to ForgottenBooks.com, giving you unlimited access to our entire collection of over 1,000,000 titles via our web site and mobile apps.

To claim your free month visit:

www.forgottenbooks.com/free850698

CONTENTS.

PREFACE.

No man, conscious of his moral integrity, intellectual ability and studied efforts to benefit humanity, will ever apologize for speech or book; hence I make no apology for publishing the following pages.

The vaccination practice, pushed to the front on all occasions by the medical profession, and through political connivance made compulsory by the state, has not only become the chief menace and gravest danger to the health of the rising generation, but likewise the crowning outrage upon the personal liberty of the American citizen.

The immediate occasion which induced me to take up the pen against this great medical evil of the times, was the closing of the public schools in San Diego, Cal., (February, 1899), against all children who failed to show a certificate of vaccination. Emerging from that heated contest, with my feelings and convictions roused to their highest tension, these pages were thrown off at welding heat; and if they are pervaded with sarcasm and irony as well as sterling fact and solid argument, they will serve all the better for popular appeal to the masses, who need rousing to a realizing sense of the unmitigated scourge that lurks on the point of the vaccinator's lancet. The general public are not aware; the householders of the land have not given this subject that attention which, as parents and guardians of little children, it is their solemn duty to do. I send forth this book to open their eyes, to rouse their conscience, and to discover to them a cruel and insidious enemy where they have been cajoled into the belief they have a friend.

For the last thirty years I have made a practical study of the workings of vaccination in the various countries of the globe. I have personally investigated it in Trebizonde, Asiatic

Turkey, while there holding a Consular appointment under
General Grant; in South Africa; in New Zealand and Australia; in British India and Ceylon; in Egypt, China and the
countries of Europe; in Mexico and the Islands of the Pacific,
not omitting our own United States. I have for many years
been familiar with the heroic struggle of reformers in England
for the repeal of the compulsory enforcement of vaccination,
for resistance to which thousands among the laboring poor
have been fined and imprisoned. In all hot countries the principal mode is from "Arm to Arm" vaccination, on account of the
unruly, uncertain behaviour of the ordinary putrid calf pus.
This mode has spread syphilis and leprosy among the native
inhabitants until the indigenous populations of the Sandwich
Islands and the British West Indies are threatened with extinction. Yet the fee-hunting doctors are incessantly hounding the
legislatures for more stringent compulsory enactments, by
which they will be enabled to inflict and repeat this degrading
rite upon the defenceless natives for the enhancement of their
revenues.

Moreover, vaccination is a "civilized" practice. English,
French, German, and American physicians, by means of compulsory vaccination laws which they have lobbied through the
various governments and legislatures, have the masses of the
people, and especially the native populations of the countries
which their respective governments rule, at their mercy. The
native Hindoo and the tropical islanders know full well the ca-
lamitous results of arm to arm vaccination, but are powerless to
protect themselves. In the United States and Great Britain,
the evil assumes other and equally portentous forms which are
fully set forth in the following chapters.

Compulsory vaccination, poisoning the crimson currents
of the human system with brute-extracted lymph under the
strange infatuation that it would prevent small-pox, was one of
the darkest blots that disfigured the last century. Its pall,

though partially lifted, still rests like a deadly nightmare upon the body politic, and, sad to state, the medical profession—save a few of the most broad-minded and enlightened—have been the chief instigators. They encouraged it just as they encouraged and practiced in the past profuse bleeding—just as they encouraged catharsis, with the inflamed gums, loosened teeth and the mercurial sore-mouth. And there are medical Bourbons today that will salivate. Thirty years ago physicians would not allow their fever patients a drop of cold water to cool their parched tongues. Many died pleading—begging for water, water!

The majority of doctors are behind the times. They may have diplomas, but they are laggards. They are not students. Many of them prefer the billiard-room to the post-graduate course. They prefer the club-room to the medical laboratory, the cigar to the clinic. They are fossils and away behind in the researches that gladden this brilliant era.

While copious bleeding with much of the old "shot-gun" practice has been relegated to the dreamless shades of the past, they still compulsorily poison with cow-pox lymph; and then piteously complain that "medical practice does not pay"—that multitudes prefer psychic physicians, hypnotic practitioners, osteopathists, mental healers and sanitarium treatment to theirs. Of course they do. This is natural; for just in the ratio that the latter increase do graveyards grow lean and coffin-makers' occupations are in less demand.

It is admitted that prevention is preferable to cure. And there is not an intelligent medical practitioner in the land who will unqualifiedly risk his reputation upon the statement that vaccination is a positive preventative of small-pox. Volumes of statistics as well as the highest medical science of this country, Canada, England, and the Continent would be directly against him. The most that any physician of good standing now contends for is that vaccination modifies the disease. This is stoutly denied. On the contrary it rather aggravates the disease as there are two poisons now in the system instead of one for nature to contend against. It is sanitation, diet, pure air, calmness of mind, confidence, and cleanliness that modify the small-pox; all of which modifiers are infinitely cheaper, safer, and in every way preferable to cow-pox poison, which, if it does not kill, often marks, maims, and sows the seeds of future eczema, tumors, ulcers, carbuncles, cancers, and leprosy.

We have at our command testimonies—scores of testimonies—proving beyond any possible doubt that men unvaccinated have nursed small-pox patients in hospitals at different times, for years, and never took the disease, while on the other hand we have, with the dates and figures, the most positive proof that those who had been vaccinated—vaccinated two and three times—took the disease when exposed, and died therefrom. These facts are undeniable.

Time, at my age, is too precious to parry words with mere ordinary physicians; hence, will only add that when laymen or medical practitioners tell me that calf-lymph vaccination, however manipulated, prevents or modifies the small-pox, they most severely, painfully, try my patience. I do not tell them they are falsifiers, but do state emphatically that if I should say that cow-pox vaccination invariably prevented or modified small-pox I should consider myself either a most pitiable ignoramus or a most infamous falsifier of facts! Such is my position, and medical men, considering it, can pose upon just which horn of this dilemma—this downy couch—they find the most comfortable.

The time has come for scholarly men, for cultured, independent physicians to speak out plainly against this baleful scourge—to take a brave stand for the right and defend it though the bigot's fire be kindled, or the crimson cross again be built.

Compulsory vaccination and class legislation of all kinds in the interests of any one profession, are opposed to the genius of unfoldment, the spirit of the age, and to the Constitution of the United States. They are smitten with dry rot and stamped with the black seal of death. They are going graveward, and fee-hungering physicians are the principal mourners. This is emphatically an age of research and progress. Nature, afire with the indwelling Divinity, and voiced by the law of evolution, says, grow—grow or die, giving place to something better. The good and the true, only, are immortal.

Previous to the Reformation the state stood behind the priest and enforced his edicts, from whence thousands of victims fell before the steel and the flame of a merciless persecution. Today the state stands behind the commercialized, fee-hunting doctor, to enforce his vaccination fraud against the lives and health of millions of little children. It is especially for the removal of this disgraceful compulsory curse that I speak as with a tongue of flame, that I make my earnest, impassioned piea. Restore the American citizen to his liberty in matters medical as we have guaranteed his liberty in matters religious, and then if the medical profession have any specific of value to offer, the common sense of the people will come to know and adopt it.

J. M. PEEBLES, M. D.
Battle Creek, Michigan.

Our quotations from distinguished American physicians and laymen: Dr. Alexander Wilder, Dr. Leveson, Dr. Foote, Dr. Winterburn, Dr. E. M. Ripley, Dr. T. V. Gifford, Frank D. Blue, Esq., Hon. A. B. Gaston, W. H. Burr, Esq., Washington, D. C., the Rev. I. L. Peebles, Methodist Episcopal Conference, Mississippi, and others. From such English authorities as William Tebb F. R. G. S., W. Scott Tebb M. A., M. D., (Cantab), D. P. H., Dr. Alfred R. Wallace, Dr. Creighton, Dr. Crookshank, Dr. Ross, Dr. Hitchman, Dr. Sir J. W. Pease, Dr. William Rowley, F. R. C. P., John Pickering, F. R. G. S., E. S. S., F. S. A. etc., Dr. T. Mackensie, F. R. C. P. From members of the Parliamentary Commission, and the brainiest men of Europe, are not only copious, but convincing to demonstration. The statistics in this volume, gathered from official reports and tabulated with the greatest care,—are strictly, positively reliable.

The whole trend of the higher thought and study is against vaccination. To this end the learned Rev. I. L. Peebles, of the Mississippi M. E. Conference, says (page 28) in his crisp and stirring booklet, entitled, "Opposition to Vaccination:" "If I had ever suggested to a legislator to enact a law enforcing vaccination, I should repent of it as long as I lived, either for being so cruel or so ignorant. Physicians and legislators who are parties to this filthy, poisonous butchery, and who practice it without having studied it most thoroughly and prayed over it most earnestly, should be ashamed of themselves. Let us remember that it is cruel enough to maim, scar, or butcher a person when he wants us to, but how much more cruel to butcher him by force!"

CHAPTER I.

A BRIEF SKETCH OF VACCINATION FROM JENNER TO THE PRESENT.—PRELIMINARY.

Since the dawn of history the most dreaded scourge of mankind has been the prevalence of Zymotic diseases—small-pox, plague, yellow fever, typhus, scarlatina, diphtheria, etc. In certain years, at particular recurring periods, these diseases contribute a very large percentage to the total death rate, especially among urban populations. They are contemplated in the popular mind as being so swift and merciless, that whole communities stand in helpless terror at their approach! The desolation which has sometimes been reported from distant cities is apprehended to be as complete as that left in the path of a cyclone, or like the cindered remains of a great conflagration. The most dreaded among these zymotic diseases is small-pox, because it is equally present and at home in all climates. But the popular notion that small-pox was a veritable plague until inoculation and vaccination provided a "sure and infallible defence" against it, is altogether erroneous. It is certainly taken far greater account of since the days of Jenner than during the eighteenth century, and there are strong reasons for concluding that the special prominence given to it of late years, is due to the clamor of doctors who desire to have the state guarantee an unfailing resource for fees by making vaccination compulsory.

The people cannot be too often reminded that the native

soil wherein small-pox most thrives and fattens, is "filth." It
ever follows close upon flagrant violations of the law of cleanliness. Where large populations are crowded in the midst of
wretched surroundings, reeking with filth and vicious in their
dietetic and drinking habits, there expect a fearful fatality when
once the small-pox has entered their foetid precincts. The individual or the community that has a wholesome diet, pure
blood, sanitary surroundings, immunity from poverty and freedom from blood poisoning incident to vaccination, need have
no more fear of small-pox than from a mild attack of measles.
Until scientific sanitation began to engage the attention of state
and municipal authorities, the plague returned as punctually to
the cities of Europe as small-pox has during the last century.
Now the percentage of fatality, not only in small-pox but in all
zymotic diseases, is steadily declining, as sanitation becomes
more rigidly enforced in crowded districts, in spite of vaccination and other silly and reactionary devices which the doctors
from time to time, aided by legislation, continue to inflict on
mankind. Alfred Milnes, M. D., M. A., of London, well remarks—"What About Vaccination?" page 17:

"Small-pox is one of a group of allied diseases, called the
Zymotics. The name means that the disease is due to a process
of fermentation. But for common-sense purposes, it is better
to call these diseases by the plain English name of filth diseases.
They are diseases which take their rise in filth, which are nature's punishment for filth, which are both frequent and virulent
where filth prevails, and which can be cleared away by the clear-
ing away of filth. Now, in the eighteenth century, in the latter
part of which Jenner liv,d, it must be confessed that the English
people had not yet awoke to the beauty and the necessity of
cleanliness. Filth was universal, and small-pox was terrible.
Not so terrible as many persons want to make out, but still a
formidable danger."

A. M. Ross, M. D., in his vigorous pamphlet, "Vaccination

a Medical Delusion," writes:—

"Wherever the streets are narrow, the lanes and courts filthy; where cesspits abound and filth is allowed to accumulate and ferment; where the weak, intemperate and unclean congregate together, and where the children are ill-fed and badly clothed—there small-pox makes its home and riots in filth and death."

The modes of treatment which have from time to time been invented to combat small-pox, have been for the most part empirical experiments and make-shifts, without any rational foundation in science, which have been abandoned, one after another, but not until thousands of lives were destroyed and hundreds of thousands were cursed with grievous and incurable ailments; not until self-sacrificing reformers had spent valuable lives in assailing the petrified superstitions of doctors and politicians. Once committed to an error, it is amazing with what conservative persistence public bodies will continue to defend it. To repeal a measure once adopted would seem to be a tacit confession of fallibility, and fallibility is a human defect which legislative bodies are slow to admit.

The earliest form of treating small-pox in Europe seems to have been imported from the same region the disease came from, namely, from the far East, which reached England by way of the Saracens at the time of the Crusades, or by way of the Moors who reached Spain. This earlier mode of dealing with small-pox was styled "the red cloth treatment." A priest and physician of the fourteenth century, John of Goddesden, England, wrote a treatise on this form of cure. The patient was wrapped in red cloth, while window curtatins and drapery of red were also provided for the sick room. It was thought this treatment conduced to throw the morbid symptoms out to the surface; and as matter of fact, it was sinless and harmless in comparison to the thrice accursed practice of vaccination.

SMALL-POX INOCULATION.

About eighty years before Jenner's discovery—1721—a
practice was introduced in England, called Inoculation, which
was accomplished by taking pus matter direct from small-pox
patients and introducing it into the blood of healthy individuals. Sometimes the virus was introduced into deep incisions,
but more often from the point of the lancet just under the skin.
The milder method was introduced by Gatti, a French physician,
and adopted by Sutton and Dimsdale in England about 1763.

Small-pox inoculation, the forerunner and parent of vaccination, like its successor, was derived from a superstition
practiced by the common people, which has come to be styled
"the tradition of the dairy maids." Jenner derived his earliest
idea of vaccination—while yet a student of medicine—from a
young country woman who had contracted cow-pox. Small-
pox inoculation was derived, not from scientific experimenta-
tion, but from a superstition practiced by the common people
in India since the sixth century. The fad having once become
the fashion, the doctors adopted and bowed to it as a fetish
which must not be questioned; and after the people had thoroughly learned by sad experience that it was a public curse and
not a blessing, rose in revolt against it, still the doctors—who
were now reaping a fat revenue from the practice—continued
in the vigorous defence of the superstition, and in the persecution and misrepresentation of the reformers who had arisen to
overthrow it. Mr. Porter, who was English ambassador at
Constantinople in 1755, informs us, (Gentleman's Magazine, for
October of that year): "It is the tradition and opinion of the
inhabitants of the country that a certain angel presides over
this disease. That it is to bespeak his favor and evince their
confidence that the Georgians take a small portion of variolous
matter, and, by means of scarification, introduce it between the
thumb and the forefinger of a sound person. The operation is

supposed to never miss its effect. To secure beyond all uncertainty the good will of the angel, they hang up scarlet cloths about the bed, that being the favorite colour of the Celestial inhabitants they wish to propitiate."

We may well inquire: how did this superstition reach England, obtain royal patronage, receive sanction by the Royal College of Physicians, and dominate all classes of society for more than half a century before it was finally overthrown and superceded by another superstition that has not discounted one whit the mischief which the earlier superstition had accomplished? The story may be briefly told. One Timoni, a Greek physician in Constantinople, in a letter addressed to Dr. Woodward, professor of physic, first brought the subject to English notice. This letter was printed in the Philosophical Transactions for 1714. But the real credit—or discredit—of the introduction of the practice into England, was due to Lady Mary Wortley Montagu, whose husband was ambassador to the Porte in 1716. Lady Montagu wrote a friend in England, detailing the process of "ingrafting" as a preventative against small-pox. This famous letter was written in 1717, but the inoculation craze was not fairly inaugurated in England until 1721. In 1724 Steele congratulated Lady Mary for having "saved the lives of thousands of British subjects every year." Voltaire was in England about this time, and became an ardent worshipper of the newly imported fetish. He knew well how to reach the feminine portion of the population of his native France. He assured them that the charms of the ladies of Circassia were due to this ingrafting practice, and that thousands of English girls had adopted this method of preserving their health and beauty. So it was not long before inoculation also became the rage in the kingdom of Louis XV.

In the same year that inoculation reached England (1721), 244 persons were inoculated in Boston, Mass., by Dr. Boylston, of whom six died. Numerous deaths also followed the practice in England, and by 1728 it became quite generally discredited; but in 1740 it again revived, and for thirty years held full sway. This revival was largely due to the luck of two doctors, Robert and Daniel Sutton, who gave minute attention to hygiene, by which their inoculated patients generally went through with a very mild form of small-pox, which all would invariably do under a thorough system of sanitation. But this simple secret was not generally understood in those days, and so the brothers Sutton not only received great credit, but reaped a very handsome profit through their device of cleanliness. Their practice became very popular, receiving patronage from the nobility who paid them immense sums for their services. As small-pox induced by inoculation was infectious, the same as when taken in the natural way, enterprising inoculators persuaded whole parishes to submit to it, so that all having it at once, none would be expected to catch it by subsequent exposure. The rich harvest of money accruing from the practice, therefore, became a powerful motive in the defence and perpetuation of the system, precisely as vaccination today, enforced by legislators and boards of health, gives lucrative employment to a class whose self interest prompts them to every specie of subterfuge and special pleading to perpetuate the compulsory clause in vaccination legislation.

After the fruitless trial of nearly a century, it was discovered that inoculation was sowing the seeds of a long train of diseases, in their most fatal form, communicating infectious complaints from one person to another—cancer, scrofula, consumption, and other more loathsome diseases were spreading to an alarming extent. It was seen and confessed by hundreds of physicians that the net result of this practice was a multiplication of ailments and an enormous increase in the total mortality. Dr. Winterburn, of Philadelphia, writes,—"The Value of Vaccination," page 18:—

"From the most trustworthy sources, however, it is evident that just as now we have epidemics of measles, and other of the zymoses, varying greatly in intensity and fatality, so in the pre-inoculation period there were epidemics of small-pox of great fatality and others of very moderate intensity. But after the introduction of inoculation, the ravages of small-pox increased, not only directly as the result of inoculation, but each new case became, as it were, a centre of disease, from it spreading in every direction, often with great virulence. It spread small-pox just as the natural disease did. It could be propagated anywhere by sending in a letter a bit of cotton thread dipped in the variolous lymph. In this way, not only the number of cases, but, also, the general mortality was very greatly increased. But so hard is it to alter the ideas of a people after they have crystallized into habit, that although it was evident that epidemics of small-pox often started from an inoculated case; and although the most strenuous efforts were made to supersede it by vaccination, inoculation continued to flourish for nearly a century and a half. It was found necessary in 1840 to make inoculation in England, a penal offense, in order to put an end to its use. Even that has not prevented its secret practice by the lower orders, where ideas die hardest, and the rite is even now probably more than occasionally performed."

SMALL-POX INOCULATION.

Some knowledge of the history of small-pox inoculation is important at this time, since it furnished so many exact parallels to the history of vaccination. With few exceptions medical men defended it, made light of its multiform dangers, and held it up to public attention as the great desideratum of the common security and welfare. They juggled with statistics the same as vaccinators do today to defend their practice, pointing out that 18 per cent. of small-pox patients died who took the disease in the natural way, while only one in ninety-one of the inoculated died. But at last the real facts—tragic and unwelcome though they were—confronted both doctor and layman in such a signal and alarming manner, that Parliament was invoked to put an end once and forever to the inoculating rite.

Nevertheless, as we shall presently see, no sooner was this superstition abandoned, than the medical profession adopted another which was destined to curse the world in a ten-fold greater ratio, and while they petitioned Parliament to make the earlier practice a penal offence, they likewise made their new fad obligatory and compulsory. Hence the last estate of the people was made far worse than their first, for now the liberty of the citizen to defend the health of his family was cancelled.

The first Compulsory Vaccination Act passed by Parliament also contained this clause, retiring inoculation to the limbs:

"Any person who shall after the passing of this Act produce in any person by inoculation with variolous matter, or any matter, potency, or thing impregnated with variolous matter, or wilfully by any other means whatsoever produce the disease of small-pox in any person shall be guilty of an offence, and shall be liable to be proceeded against summarily, and be convicted to be imprisoned for any term not exceeding one month."

Arthur Wallaston Hutton, M. A., makes the following significant observation,—"The Vaccination Question," page 14:—

"In the early years of the present century, when medical men, with almost complete unanimity, were seeking to replace the variolous inoculation by the vaccine inoculation, they confessed, or rather urged, that the earlier practice had destroyed more lives than it had saved. And this was undoubtedly true. For not only did the practice inflict the disease on the person inoculated, but that person became a new center of infection, from which small-pox could be and was occasionally 'caught' in the natural way. * * * * * * * We talk of small-pox inoculation, as if it were an uniform practice; whereas it really varied as much as vaccination does now. It might communicate the disease in its most deadly form, or it might do just nothing at all, beyond making a slight sore, which proved, if tested, no defence against subsequent exposure to the infection of small-pox. Disastrous, however, as the practice was— and so clearly is that now recognized that for the last fifty years the practice has been penal—it may be admitted that there was 'something in it,' and that, in the special cases of medical men and of nurses, it might still be resorted to with advantage, if performed in isolation hospitals. For although some constitutions are so susceptible of small-pox (as others are of other fevers) that one attack does not afford security against a second or even a third, the general rule is that one attack does confer subsequent immunity; and a person inoculated when in good health, and when there is no severe epidemic about, might conceivably pass through the ordeal with less risk than if a natural attack of the disease had been waited for and incurred."

JENNER AND VACCINATION.

As we have seen, the inoculation superstition was the chief medical curse of the eighteenth century. It sent multitudes to untimely graves, and permanently impaired the health of other multitudes, since the septic poisoning from within reached the very fountains of life and laid the foundations for a long train of incurable diseases. In the final summing up its pledges were broken and its flattering promises were unfulfilled. Yet vicious as it proved, it was superseded at the hands of Jenner by a fallacy still more monstrous, until the nineteenth century, which, notwithstanding its boasted civilization, has been more cursed by the doctors than was the eighteenth.

Edward Jenner, born in 1749, at Berkley, introduced vaccination in England in 1798. He is credited with the fanciful discovery that by poisoning the blood with cow-pox, a future attack of small-pox would be prevented. This delusion has been so completely disposed of by Dr. Creighton and Prof. Crookshank that I need devote but little space to the Jenner episode. In the first place, Jenner was far from being a learned man. In the department of exact research he was a blunderer, yet his personal qualities were amiable and attractive. He was in the habit of writing verses and had a faculty of making fast friends. His medical degree was confered with the simple preliminary, not of an examination, but the payment of a fee of fifteen guineas to the University of St. Andrews. And his Fellowship in the Royal Society—according to the admission of his latest biographer, Dr. Norman Moor, by a procedure which amounted to a fraud. In the field of natural history, where he made some pretensions, his knowledge was scanty and empirical. His published observations on the cuckoo,—Phi. Trans. Vol. LXXVIII —read in 1788, called out a witty and critical tract entitled, "The Bird that Laid the Vaccination Egg."

In strict truth, Jenner was not the discoverer of vaccination. Many of the common folk in his time, chiefly dairy maids, had already noted the fact that those who took the cow-pox were less susceptible to small-pox; and years before Jenner took the matter up, a Dorsetshire farmer, named Jesty, inoculated his wife and two sons with the cow-pox, in the conviction that this would prove a preventive.

THE COW-POX.

This is a filth disease, a "bad disease" whose original source is in the human degenerate; a disease communicated to the cow's teats by stable boys who not only suffer from the "bad disease," but whose hands are soiled by grooming the greasy heels of diseased and ill-kept horses. Bear in particular remembrance, that the cow-pox is not natural to the bovine species. Bulls and steers are never troubled with it; neither are heifers without the voluntary and conscious agency of man. It is only milch cows that catch the disorder. Dr. George W. Winterburn, whom I have already quoted, writes:—

"This disease which is called cow-pox in cows, is known as grease in the horse. Grease is a disorder resulting from inflammation of the sebaceous glands of the skin, about the heels of a horse, and is properly called eczema pustulosum. The disease originating from a scrofulous condition, supervenes from exposure to wet, and from subsequent lack of cleanliness, and is always the result of carelessness on the part of the groom. The discharge from these vesicular pustules is often profuse, very irritating to the surface over which

it flows, and foetid. * * * * This purulent matter, carried on the dirty hands of farm-laborers to the teats or other
sensitive parts of the cow, produced the disorder which has
been misnamed cow-pox."

And these are the vile forms of corruption, charged with a
deadly virus—sometimes horse-grease, sometimes small-poxed
cow virus, but more frequently syphilized cow-pox—which Jenner pronounced "a sovereign remedy against small-pox," and
who declared to the British Parliament when he applied for his
£30,000 reward: "Whoever is once vaccinated with cow-pox
is forever afterward protected from small-pox." Yet in spite
of Jenner's promises, and notwithstanding the civilized world
has been vaccinated and re-vaccinated ad nauseum, the world
continues to suffer from small-pox epidemics, just as it did during the inoculation times, while such mitigation as we really enjoy is due--in spite of vaccination--to an increased sanitation observance of more rational habits of living. Following up Jenner's observations, Arthur Wallaston Hutton remarks,—"The
Vaccination Question," page 19:—

"His theory was that the disease of the horse's hoof, known
as 'horse-grease,' was the source of human small-pox and also
of cow-pox; and in this way the relationship was established to
his own satisfaction. Neither proposition is true; nor indeed
did Jenner care to maintain the truth of either proposition when
the merits of vaccination had once become established in people's minds; but the theory justified or seemed to justify him
in describing cow-pox as variolae vaccinae or 'small-pox of the
cow;' and it is really this theory which has mis-directed pretty
nearly all the observations that have been made on vaccination
right down to the present day. Sir John Simon, a living authority on the subject, explains that persons vaccinated cannot take
the small-pox, because they have had it already; and this belief is still shared by hundreds and thousands of people."

Again the same high authority says:—

"But what is in truth the nature of cow-pox? It is an ail-
ment, not of cattle, but of the cow, as its name implies, exclu-

sively, and of the cow only when she is in milk; and it is further a disease of civilization. It does not occur when a cow
suckles her own calf; nor, for that matter, does it occur where
cow-stables are kept decently clean. Jenner observed that it did
not occur when the milkers were women only; and hence his
theory that the disease originated in 'horse-grease,' his assertion being (first stated as an hypothesis, and then, a little lower
down, as a thing which 'commonly happens') that the disease
was communicated to the cow's teats by a man-milker who had
just dressed the diseased horse's heels. Other observers also
professed to have noted that the disease only occurred where
there were both men and women milkers; but they drew another inference as to its origin, for which they found confirmation in the disease's popular name. Apparently it is in some
way due to the friction of the teats by the milker's hands; it occurs spontaneously (i. e. apart from inoculation) only where
cows are milked; and its name had reference not to small-pox
but to "great-pox," with which its analogy was popularly and cor-
rectly discerned. Presumably it is a consequence of its partly
human origin that it is so easily (and ordinarily without danger)
inoculable on man, which other diseases of animals are not.
That, however, is mere conjecture; what is now certainly established beyond all reasonable doubt is that cow-pox bears no
pathological relation to small-pox. The similarity in name is
the only connection; for, though there is a superficial resemblance between the vaccine vesicles and the variolous pox, the
two diseases are really quite distinct. The definite establishment of this fact, which of course upsets the whole alleged
scientific basis of vaccination, is due to the labors in recent years
of Dr. Creighton and Professor Crookshank, though the real
character of cow-pox had long ago been suspected."

In an article communicated to the Academie de Medicine
in 1865, by Auzias-Turenne, I quote the following language:
"Between syphilis and cow-pox the analogy may be a long way
followed up, * * * but, happily, for the vaccinated, cow-
pox passes through a rapid evolution, and does not leave virulent remains for so long a time or so frequently as syphilis."

In that thorough and carefully written work of Dr. Creighton, published in 1887, he was the first to demonstrate Jenner's

mistake. He set out to find some explanation for the complaints that were continually multiplying of the communication
of syphilis by vaccination. The results of his investigations
were embodied in the volume, "Cow-pox and Vaccinal Syphilis."
His early judgment was that the communication of two diseases
by one and the same act was improbable; but as the evidence
he accumulated became overwhelming, he at last gave up every
doubt that these syphilitic symptoms are part and parcel of the
cow-pox itself, which is sure to make its presence felt if inoculated in the system through the ordinary process of vaccination.

In the same year that Creighton published his book, estab-
lishing the connection between syphilis and cow-pox, Prof.
Crookshank was pursuing independent investigations into the
micro-pathology of a cow-disease that had broken out in Wilk-
shire, which the Agricultural Department of the Privy Council
thought might bear some relation to scarlet fever in man. In
this investigation, Crookshank also critically examined the nature and origin of cow-pox, with the result that his researches
fully bore out and confirmed Dr. Creighton's conclusions. "In
fact," says Hutton, "the syphilitic nature of cow-pox is the
theory which now holds the field; and it is hardly contested by
the advocates of vaccination, who are content to rely solely on
the evidence of statistics." How horrid to contemplate!

We are therefore face to face with the gravest, and at the
same time the most disgusting, aspect of the whole vaccination
problem. Note that the cow-pox is not a natural bovine disease; that only milch cows contract it, and this invariably
through human agency. Long before Creighton and Crookshank wrote, it had been suspected by high authorities, that
man is not only the medium of transmission of horse-grease to
the cow's udder, but that he communicates a loathsome virus
from his own person as well. Therefore the horse-grease disease in the cow, is a very different malady from the cow-pox,
which is derived from man and from man alone! Let us be

frank. A large percentage of vaccination practice has inoculated whole communities with the thrice accursed syphilitic taint, according to the brand or stock of vaccine used; for be it known, that vaccine corruption has now become an ordinary article of commerce, the same as baking powders and "embalmed" beef. I shall hereafter show that the vaccinator can rarely be certain of the quality of his stock, or of the extent of harm that will result from his practice.

The identity of cow-pox and syphilis was first definitely pointed out by Dr. Hubert Boens-Boissan in 1882; and Dr. J. W. Collins in his "Sir Lyon Playfair" pamphlet gives 478 cases of "vaccino-syphilis," details of which have been published by various medical authorities, both in England and on the continent.

When these facts shall be fully realized by a much crucified and long suffering public, it will not take long to put a stop to the compulsory feature of this infamous crime. We shall then no longer submit the bodies of our defenceless children to the assaults of salaried, place-hunting doctors, nor longer tolerate the flagrant usurpations of parliaments and legislatures over our personal liberties and the sacredness of the family circle.

Now, to return to Jenner. His first vaccination was on a boy named James Phipps, who later died of pulmonary consumption. This was in 1787. Two years later he vaccinated his own son, then a year and a half old, with swine-pox, which at that time was considered as protective as cow-pox; and had not this mode been considered too disgusting for popular approval, it would in all likelihood have taken precedence over cow-pox vaccination. Thereafter Jenner repeatedly inoculated his child with small-pox. But being delicate in health he died in his twenty-first year.

Dr. John Hunter, the noted physiologist in Jenner's time, expressed a wise judgment on the de-merits of Jenner's system. He wrote:—

"The introduction by inoculation of mineral or vegetable poisons into the blood is hazardous, and in certain quantities may be destructive; but the introduction of animal products from another living body, be it a man, a cow, or even an ass. is infinitely more pernicious, because allied to it in being vitalized."

In 1797 Jenner made an abortive effort to get his treatise incorporated into the transactions of the Royal Society.   Then he turned his attention to the feminine portion of English society, and soon enlisted the enthusiastic support of many ladies of the aristocracy, a number of whom became amateur vaccinators in their respective parishes.   In this way the practice was soon made so fashionable, so popular, and lucrative withal, that it soon became the rage among the English people.   Even the clergy took it up, one of whom vaccinated three thousand persons in three years.   Indeed, vaccination came so near being converted into a religious rite, that christening and vaccination of children were performed on the same day.

After vaccination had been on trial for three years, before people or Parliament had any means of knowing whether Jenner's promise that vaccination would number the days of small-pox, the king signified to his prime minister his wish that Parliament should award to Jenner a benefaction, and the Commons cheerfully responded, voting him £30,000.

When Jenner was confronted with a large number of glaring failures in high life—of cases he had pronounced as "successfully vaccinated," who came down with small-pox, in the confluent form, he came forward with a new doctrine to repel his opponents, viz: "that as cases of small-pox after small-pox were not uncommon, vaccination could not be expected to do more than small-pox itself."   Remember, this pitiful plea was not brought forward until the failures of cow-pox to protect had become multiplied and notorious.   Dr. W. Scott Tebb, of London, in his valuable and exhaustive work, "A Century of Vaccination," writes, page 16: —

"On all these grounds, I demur to the theory of identity, and hold that small-pox and cow-pox are antagonistic affections—that cow-pox, instead of being, as Dr. Barton maintains, of a variolous, is, in fact, of an anti-variolous nature—that it alters and modifies the human constitution so as to render some individuals wholly, others partially, and for a time, unsusceptible of small-pox.

"At the end of 1798, six months after the publication of Jenner's 'Inquiry,' the case for vaccination stood thus: Most of the children's arms had ulcerated, and the variolous test, in the few cases in which it had been applied, had produced equivocal results. Moreover, all Jenner's stocks of lymph had been lost, so that no further experiments could be made. Dr. Beddoes, of Bristol, in writing to Professor Hufeland, of Berlin, said: 'You know Dr. Jenner's experiments with the cow-pox; his idea of the origin of the virus appears to be quite indemonstrable, and the facts which I have collected are not favorable to his opinion that the cow-pox gives complete immunity from the natural infection of small-pox. Moreover, the cow-pox matter produces foul ulcers, and in that respect is a worse disease than the mildly inoculated small-pox."

NO IDENTITY BETWEEN COW-POX AND SMALL-POX.

In the course of vaccine practice much confusion has arisen from the careless manner of diagnosing the cow disease. A variety of opposing symptoms have long been known to follow in cases of vaccination with pus taken from the cow. Thence it came to be asserted that there was a genuine cow-pox and a "spurious cow-pox." In cases of failure the spurious variety was made to do duty. Jenner held that cow-pox was small-pox of the cow, hence the misleading name he gave it, variolae vaccinae. Dr. George Pearson, a cotemporary of Jenner, objected to this designation, asserting that "cow-pox is a specifically different distemper from the small-pox in essential particulars, namely, in the nature of its morbific poison, and in its symptoms." More recently Dr. George Gregory—quoted by Dr. Tebb—opposed the identity theory.

Winterburn says—"Value of Vaccination," page 41 :—

"Experimenters, entitled to respectful attention, have shown that it is a delusion to suppose that the inoculation of cows with small-pox has ever produced cow-pox; it produces small-pox and nothing else. The small-pox may be induced on the horse or cow by variolation, but the variolous inoculation is never transmuted into grease in the horse, or cow-pox in the cow." This is undeniable.

Dr. Seaton, a high authority, says: "It is quite out of the question that cow-pox on the human subject should have been transformed into small-pox." The two diseases, therefore, being specifically different, neither can have any effect to ward off the other. Why not inoculate with erysipelas to prevent small-pox? It would be just as rational, just as scientific, and to my mind, just as efficient.

Dr. George Wyld, whose acquaintance I made in London, and whom I know to stand very high as author, physician, and scientist, endorses the conclusions of the French Academy. He says :—

"I find that many medical men are under the false impression that all that we require to do is to inoculate the heifer with small-pox matter, and thus get a supply of vaccine lymph. This might become productive of disastrous consequences. Small-pox inoculation of the heifer produces not vaccinia, but a modified small-pox capable of spreading small-pox amongst human beings by infection."

It will hence be seen that a large share of modern vaccination is really only a modified form of inoculation. It is neither cow-pox nor horse-grease, but small-pox propagated from human beings, through calves, to human beings again. This fact, horrible as it is, admits of no denial.

We must therefore accept it as proven: Cow-pox is not small-pox in the cow, but it is "horse-grease" in the cow, whose udder often becomes secondarily infected with syphilis. Therefore when we submit to the official vaccinator, or we shall be treated to inoculation of virus from a small-poxed calf, or to the cow-pox virus often taken from a syphilized calf. Think of it, fathers and mothers, when the "Health Board" closes the door of the schoolroom you are taxed to support, requiring your children to present a certificate of vaccination; requiring that their bodies be submitted to the dangers and degradation of vaccine corruption! May your souls rise up in indignant protest against the sacrilegious invasion of the home which the American constitution has sanctified to liberty; aye, in protest against this infernal rite, becoming the hag of the pit! Think of it, mothers, who would bring your daughters up to be healthy, and clean, and chaste, that your state and city should have delegated the privilege to fee-hunting doctors, to break down the protective walks you have builded about your little ones, and poison the fountains of their life blood with a virus of contagion which may mock your solicitude and disappoint the fondest hopes you have cherished for the future of your posterity. Think of it, ye fathers and mothers of daughters, that your state and municipality should put you under compulsion to observe a rite which is liable to taint those daughters with the virus of the scandalous disease, the out-lawed disease, the disease whose home is the polluted den of the "Stingaree," the disease against which civilization revolts—aye, the disease too loathsome to name, except in whisper! Is it not quite time the curses of the vaccine dispensation were numbered?

SMALL-POX HABITAT.

Small-pox is a disease of towns, of the crowded, filthy quarters of towns. It is a disease of the poor, and particularly of the children of the poor. The average small-pox death rate in towns is fifty to seventy-five per cent. greater than in the country , while towns that have a large proportion of park space are greatly favored over those where this important feature is lacking. The epidemic in England of 1871-72 was notably severe in the mining districts where population is over-crowded.

In the miserable dwellings of the poor, air and light—two most important essentials of health—are woefully deficient. In the beginning of the eighteenth century the government pursued the self-destructive policy of putting a premium on these prime-essentials by taxing the windows of the poor. Every aperture that would admit air or light into a dwelling had to pay for the privilege to exist. Even a window to light a stairway, garret, or cellar, was rated among the luxuries and had to be taxed. So windows could not be afforded by the poor, and which thousands who lived in filth and squalor, did not care to afford. We should hence feel no surprise when we learn that small-pox has always been chiefly confined to the lower strata of society. In Austria it is fitly named the "beggar's" disease, and in all countries it is most at home in crowded and unclean quarters. Concerning the epidemic of 1852, Dr. Rigden writes—"Medical and Surgical Journal, Dec. 22, 1852,—"The most severe cases, and the greatest number, existed, generally speaking, in the districts most thickly populated by the lower orders, and most badly drained."

In the debate on the Compulsory Vaccination Bill in 1853, Lord Shaftsbury pointed out "that the small-pox was chiefly confined to the lowest class of the population, and he believed that with improved lodging houses the disease might be all but exterminated."

After the Warrington epidemic in 1873, the Royal Commission pointed out, that all but eleven of 445 infected houses were rated at less than £16 per annum, and 406 of them at £8 or lower; and Dr. Coupland found at Dewsbury the disease was confined almost exclusively to the filthy working class.

Again, small-pox is a disease of children, like measles and whooping-cough, and predominantly, as already stated, the children of the poor. In the eighteenth century, small-pox mortality in the manufacturing towns fell almost entirely among children under five years of age. In Kilmarnock, from 1728 to

1763, the infant small-pox mortality was 90 per cent. In Man. chester, from 1769 to 1774, it was 94 per cent. In Warrington, for the same period, 94 per cent., Chester, in 1774, 89 per cent., and Carlisle, from 1779 to 1787, 95 per cent. Hence, in the eighteenth century small-pox was predominantly a disease of infants. This continued to be the case until the 1837 epidemic, when the average percentage fell to about 50 per cent. Since 1873 there has been a marked shifting in the small-pox death rate in England and Wales. Here are the figures from the forty-third annual report of the Registrar General (1880, page 22), quoted by W. Scott Tebb:—

England and Wales.—Mean annual deaths from small-pox at successive life-periods, per million living at each life-period.

	Under 5.	5.	10	15	25	45 up
Vaccination optional, 1847-53..	1,617	337	94	109	66	22
Vaccination compulsory, 1872-80	323	186	98	173	141	58

This increase in the adult mortality, we shall hereafter see, is principally due to compulsory vaccination, and was therefore considered a sufficient ground for the repeal of the law.

SPREADING OF SMALL-POX.

The history of small-pox in Leicester, England, has furnished conclusive testimony that this disease can be kept within narrow limits without any assistance from the hungry army of vaccinators. In 1872 Leicester was a much vaccinated town; but the large small-pox mortality during the epidemic of that year, generated such an emphatic protest against vaccination that the percentage of vaccinations to the number of births began to rapidly decline. By 1885 they dropped down to 39 per cent.; in 1886 to 23 per cent.; in 1887 to 10 per cent.; then to 6 per cent.; and since 1891 has almost entirely ceased. From 1872 to 1895 only 23 deaths from small-pox were recorded for Leicester.

Now in defence of the Leicester system—which is simply a system of thorough sanitation—the report of its medical officer for 1893 tells a story which should be dinned into the ears of every health board throughout the civilized world,—a story of cleanliness as the preventive par excellence of small-pox. Addressing his townsmen, the Leicester health officer said:—

"You are entitled to great credit—more especially in the case of small-pox, which, by the methods you have adopted, has been prevented from running riot throughout the town, thereby upsetting all the prophecies which have again and again been made. I need only mention such towns as Birmingham, Warrington, Bradford, Walsall, Oldham, and the way they have suffered during the past year from the ravages of small-pox, to give you an idea of the results you in Leicester have achieved, results of which I, as your medical officer of health, am, justly, I think, proud." Sanitation is the all-potent watchword.

Writing on the relative value of vaccination, Dr. Scott Tebb remarks,—page 93 of his great work:—

"Not only may well-vaccinated towns be affected with small-pox, but the most thorough vaccination of a population that it is possible to imagine may be followed by an extensive outbreak of the disease. This happened in the mining and agricultural district of Mold, in Flintshire. * * * * Leicester, with the population under ten years of age practically unvaccinated, had a small-pox death rate of 114 per million; whereas Mold, with all the births vaccinated for eighteen years previous to the epidemic, had one of 3,614 per million."

Here is one among hundreds of demonstrations that can be given of the utter worthlessness of vaccination as a preventive of small-pox. If protection is good for anything it should be effective during the prevalence of an epidemic; but we see that is just where the unvaccinated enjoy the greater immunity from an attack of the disease.

Besides filth and overcrowding, hard times and war are prominent factors in the spread of small-pox. In 1684 there were very severe frosts over Europe, followed with a general failure of·crops. The poor suffered great privations and discoragement. This was followed the next season with a vast in-

crease both of epidemic fever and small-pox. Then the great
small-pox mortality among the weavers in the east end of London in 1719 followed upon a season of great scarcity and loss
of employment among these same weavers. Bad harvests in
England were also encountered in 1794 and 1795, causing such
widespread distress among the poor that Parliament had to take
some measures for its temporary relief. The year following—
1796—the small-pox fatality swelled to an unprecedented figure,
being the largest within the London Bills. Then the harvest
failure in 1816 was followed with small-pox and typhus in epidemic form.

War may be set down as another active cause of small-pox,
and of zymotics generally. War is always attended with hard-
ship, exposure, over-crowding, anxiety, and an abnormal mental
tension. Our losses in the Civil War, on the Northern side,
footed up to about 360,000, of whom 110,000 were killed, and
250,000 died of disease; which—in round numbers—62,000
were cases of typhoid; 62,000 died of bowel complaint; 62,000
from throat and lung trouble, and 62,000 from small-pox.

Small-pox in eastern France, among the peasantry in the
earlier part of 1870, was only an average amount but late in the
year, immediately following the terrible slaughter by invasion
of the German army, it broke out with unusual violence. Dr.
Robert Spencer Watson took notes on the field round Metz.
He writes:—

"November 6, 1870. Then I went to Lessy and Chatel St.
Germain, hearing everywhere the same state of distress. All
the crops gone, all the winter's firewood gone, many houses destroyed, and numbers needing help in every village. * * *
When the mare's hoofs sunk deep, she knocked up bits of flesh,
and the stench was so sickening that I should have fainted but
for my smelling salts.

*   *   *   *   *   *   *   *   *   *   *

"In one place there were fifteen long streets of railway
vans, filled with typhus patients; in another as many streets of

canvas tents, also filled with sick. I visited these places, and found them in the filthiest state; but the Germans had begun to put them into order. At first, you might see soldiers, in full small-pox, walking about the streets, but this was soon forbidden.

* * * * * * * * * * *

"The main body were encamped outside the walls of Metz, on low ground near the Moselle, the wetness of the season having converted the camping-ground into a morass. In some places the impress of the men's bodies was left as a cast in the mud in which they had lain. Their clothes and their blanket were saturated with mud. Their food for weeks had only been a biscuit and a bit of horseflesh without salt. Dysentery was universal, and typhus and small-pox raged. Over a wide area around the camp the carcasses of dead horses were left to rot and contaminate the air."

Mr. William Jones was in Metz when Bazaine's army surrendered:—"The constant cry of the wretched sufferers for water was distinctly heard outside the square in which they were isolated. All these black typhus patients perished, and were buried in huge trenches outside the walls of the city. * * *

Mr. Allen, who was vaccinated, and, he believes, re-vaccinated, took the small-pox, and his own sister, who came over to nurse him, caught the disease from him and died there, and was buried in the cemetery at Plantieres outside the walls of Metz."

Dr. Scott Tebb observes: "There is, indeed, some reason to believe that this war was the starting-point of the great European pandemic of small-pox in 1871-72."

The same high authority has furnished the following table, showing the decline in small-pox from 1838 to 1895:—

England and Wales.—Average annual deathrate per million living, from small-pox, fever, typhus fever, and scarlet fever, in five-year periods from 1838-95.

Years.	Small-pox.	Fever.	Typus Fever	Scarlet Fever.
1838-42	576	1,053	—	—
1847-50	292	1,246	—	—

Years.	Small-pox.	Fever.	Typus Fever.	Scarlet Fever.
1851-55	248	983	—	—
1856-60	198	842	—	—
1861-65	219	922	—	982
1866-70	105	850	—	960
1871-75	408	599	81	759
1876-80	82	380	34	680
1881-85	83	273	23	436
1886-90	16	202	7	241
1891-95	24	185	4	182

"Over the whole period it will be found that the small-pox death rate declined 96 per cent., while fever declined 82 per cent. But the most extraordinary feature of the table is the large small-pox death rate in 1871-75, twenty years after vaccination had been made compulsory." Thus from 1838 to 1871 death from small-pox had only abated 29 per cent. while fever diminished 43 per cent.; hence, since the commencement of registration, there was practically a very slight decline in small-pox until 1871-72 epidemic, while the death rate from fever very materially diminished. The cause of this abatement is very plainly stated in the forty-second annual report of the Registrar General (1879) :—

"Had the deaths from one or more of this group of causes fallen, while those from others in the same group had risen, or had the fall been trifling, or the totals dealt with insignificant in amount, it might have been suspected that the alteration was a mere alteration in name. But as the deaths under each heading have declined, as the fall in the death rate from them has been enormous—62.4 per cent. in the course of ten years—and as the totals are by no means small, it may be accepted as an indisputable fact that there has in truth been a notable decline in these pests, and it may be fairly assumed that the decline is due to improved sanitary organization."

Here is common sense: "improved sanitary organization," and no class in any community understand this better than

members of the medical profession. The only rational explanation, therefore, that can be assigned for the dogged persistance
with which they continue to push their accursed vaccination
practice to the front is, that it pays.

In Oriental countries—China, India, Egypt,—where sanitation is almost wholly neglected, we have illustrated the utter
futility of vaccination to check the fatal strides of small-pox.
In the "Report on Sanitary Measures in India in 1879-80," page
142, we read:—

"The vaccination returns throughout India show the same
fact, that the number of vaccinations does not necessarily bear
a ratio to the small-pox deaths. Small-pox in India is related
to season, and also to epidemic prevalence; it is not a disease,
therefore, that can be controlled by vaccination, in the sense
that vaccination is a specific against it. As an endemic and epidemic disease, it must be dealt with by sanitary measures, and if
these are neglected small-pox is certain to increase during epidemic times."

Again, in the "Memorandum of the Army Sanitary Commission for the Punjab" (1879), we read:—

"Vaccination in the Punjab, as elsewhere in India, has no
power apparently over the course of an epidemic. It may modify it and diminish the number of fatal cases, but the whole Indian experience points in one direction, and this is that the severity of a small-pox epidemic is more closely connected with
sanitary defects, which intensify the activity of other epidemic
diseases, than is usually imagined, and that to the general sanitary improvement of towns and villages must we look for the
mitigation of small-pox as of cholera and fever."

On this branch of the problem Dr. Scott Tebb sums up as
follows:—

"At the present time, compulsory vaccination, by paralyz-
ing efforts in other directions, blocks the way towards sanitary
reform. When the laws are abrogated vaccination must, like
all other medical prescriptions and surgical operations, rest
upon its own merits, or, in other words, on its inherent persua-
siveness, unaided by the arm of the law. The practice will then,

in my opinion, in the not very distant future be surely abandoned.

"This will prepare the way for a new era of improved health and human happiness, the result of scientific sanitary amelioration in all departments of our social, domestic, and municipal life."

We should not forget that all zymotic diseases run in periods of greater and lesser intensity. This is true of yellow fever, of scarlatina, of typhus, and diphtheria, as well of small-pox; and it is during periods of epidemic intensity that the complete worthlessness of vaccination is brought home to us. In the London Lancet, July 15, 1871, we read :—

"The deaths from small-pox have assumed the proportions of a plague. Over 10,000 lives have been sacrificed during the past year in England and Wales. In London, 5,641 deaths have occurred since Christmas. Of 9,392 patients in the London Small-pox Hospitals, no less than 6,854 had been vaccinated, i. e., nearly 73 per cent. Taking the mortality at 17 1-2 per cent. of those attacked, and the deaths this year in the whole country at 10,000, it will follow that more than 122,000 vaccinated persons have suffered from small-pox! This is an alarming state of things. Can we greatly wonder that the opponents of vaccination should point to such statistics as an evidence of the failure of the system? It is necessary to speak plainly on this important matter."

ZYMOTICS A CONSTANT QUANTITY.

In the history of zymotic diseases we are confronted with the very important fact, that though small-pox seemed to abate after vaccination came into fashion, other forms of zymotic diseases cropped up and swelled the death rate to the same uniform proportions. When one epidemic predominated—as typhus, scarlatina, or diphtheria,—small-pox would be found to be in abeyance; then one after another would manifest epidemic violence, so that the death rate went on with singular uniformity. Given the same conditions the death rate of a people will display the same uniform percentage from year to year, and nothing will vary this number except a change in these conditions. When a whole people improve their sanitary regulations the death rate diminishes and the average duration of life advances. Aggravate these conditions, either by war, famine, or intemperance in its multiform phases, and the death rate infallibly rises to a larger sum total.

This compensatory law is well illustrated in Sweden, where deaths from small-pox in 1825 were 1,243, and from typhus, 3,962; but four years later small-pox only claimed 53, while deaths from typhus rose to 9,264. Then again, in 1846, the small-pox fatality was only 2, while deaths from all causes were 72,683. In 1851 small-pox became epidemic again, notwithstanding very thorough vaccination, when the small-pox fatality rose to 2,448, but the total death rate was almost precisely that of 1846, being 72,506.

The statistics of other countries reveal the same law. In Prague, from 1796 to 1802, the total mortality was 1 in 32, when small-pox fatality was very high; but from 1832 to 1855, when small-pox fatality was extremely low, still the total death rate was 1 in 32 1-3.

Dr. Robert Watt, in 1813, considering the vast number of deaths from small-pox among children, says:—

"I began to reflect how different the case must be now; and to calculate the great saving of human life that must have arisen from the vaccine inoculation. At this time (1813) above 15,000 had been inoculated publicly at the Faculty Hall, and perhaps twice or thrice that number in private practice."

In eight years (1805-13) little more than 600 had died in Glasgow, of small-pox; whereas in 1784 the deaths by that disease alone amounted to 425, and in 1791 to 607; which, on both occasions, exceeded the fourth of the whole deaths in the city for the year. To ascertain the real amount of this saving of infantile life, I turned up one of the later years, and, by accident, that of 1808, when, to my utter astonishment, I found that still more than a half perished before the tenth year of their age; I could hardly believe the testimony of my senses, and therefore began to turn up other years, but I found it amounted to nearly the same thing. To make the facts clear, let us bring the results of the past three decades together, thus :—

GLASGOW MORTUARY STATISTICS. 1783-1812.

Decade.	From Small-pox.	Measles.	Whooping-Cough.
1783-1792	3,466	211	854
1793-1802	2,894	398	914
1803-1812	1,013	1,655	1,151

Decade.	Children Under Two.	Children Under Ten.	Total Deaths All Ages.
1783-1792	7,293	9,919	17,607
1793-1802	6,277	9,050	16,685
1802-1812	7,120	10,913	20,175

To ascertain how a low small-pox mortality was compensated by other diseases, Dr. Watt divided the years 1783-1812 into five periods, of six years each, and in this way set forth the proportionate mortalities :—

GLASGOW MORTUARY STATISTICS. 1783-1812.

Years.	From Small-pox.	Measles.	Whooping-Cough.
1783-1788	19.55	.93	4.51
1789-1794	18.22	1.17	5.13
1795-1800	18.70	2.10	5.36
1801-1806	8.90	3.92	6.12
1807-1812	3.90	10.76	5.57

Years.	Children Under Two.	Children Under Ten.	Total Deaths All Ages.
1783-1788	39.40	53.48	9,994
1789-1794	42.38	58.07	11,103
1795-1800	38.82	54.48	9,991
1801-1806	33.50	52.03	10,034
1807-1812	35.89	55.69	13,354

—"Diseases of Children," Glasgow, 1813.

Now put these facts by the side of the idiotic—the false assertions of Sir Spencer Wells, that:—

"It may not be generally known, but it is true, that Jenner has saved, is now saving, and will continue to save in all coming ages, more lives in one generation than were destroyed in all the wars of the first Napoleon."

The fluctuations in the death rate between plague and small-pox is strikingly similar:—

MORTALITY FROM PLAGUE IN LONDON, 1604-1651.

Year.	Deaths.	Year.	Deaths.
1604	896	1628	3
1605	444	1629	0
1606	2,124	1630	1,317
1607	2,352	1631	274
1608	2,262	1632	8
1609	4,410	1633	0
1610	1,803	1634	1
1611	617	1635	0
1612	64	1636	10,400
1613	16	1637	3,082
1614	22	1638	363
1615	37	1639	314
1616	9	1640	1,450
1617	6	1641	1,375
1618	18	1642	1,274

1619...............	9	1643...............	996
1620...............	21	1644...............	1,412
1621...............	11	1645...............	1,871
1622...............	16	1646...............	2,635
1623...............	17	1647...............	3,507
1624...............	11	1648...............	611
1625...............35,417		1649...............	67
1626...............	134	1650...............	15
1627...............	4	1651...............	23

In 1878 Sir Thomas Chambers said in the House of Commons:—

"You cannot show that vaccination has reduced deaths or saved a single life. There may be no small-pox, but the disappearance of small-pox is by no means equivalent to a reduction of mortality."

Thus I might indefinitely multiply illustrations of the truth of this law of constancy which variations in the intensity of specific diseases does not affect. The practice of vaccination therefore is utterly opposed to the plain teachings of sanitary science. It is the most untenable dogma in the whole category of medical theories, which has never been demonstrated to be sanctioned by any ascertained law or principle in the healing art. No precious lives have been saved as the outcome of the vaccine delusion, while just in proportion as it has modified the symptoms of the contagion it professes to save us from, has other and more disgusting forms of zymotic disease multiplied upon the race. Aye, more. It has become an added factor for the wider diffusion of cancer, erysipelas, eczema, carbuncles, tumors, leprosy, and last but not least, to relegate the "bad disease" from its dark, infernal den, domesticate and make it common in the households of the land!

CHAPTER II.

VACCINE STOCK AND COMMERCIAL VACCINATION.

No vaccine stock used since the days of Jenner is entitled to the designation "lymph." Lymph is a natural and healthy fluid that circulates in the lymphatic vessels. All so-called lymph—which is simply vaccine pus—is a collection of blood corpuscles in process of destructive fermentation. The various frauds of vaccine pus are charged with the same specific quality, their chief differences consisting in their relative degrees of rottenness. They are each and all a species of septic poison, no matter how or where they were brewed. The fermenting cells in this vaccine substance abound with pathogenic globular bacteria, of which they are both the active element and chief factor in conveying filthy diseases of the blood and skin to the human body. Through this blood-poisoning ichor, into which the ruthless lance of the vaccinator is daily dipped, the germ of a legion of diseases assault the citadel of health, enters the peaceful precincts of home, and with the connivance and assistance of the politician and legislator, inflicts upon the little children of the land the barbarous and degrading rite whose curse will spread and multiply through generations yet unborn. I now remember, the prophet predicted a "time of trouble" for the last days. He must have had his eye on the vaccinator, and knew full well when he would arrive. Lo! the last days are here, and the trouble predicted is upon us!

That all so-called vaccine lymph contains blood cells has been well known to the medical profession since 1862. Dr. Heron Watson writes (Edinborough Medical Journal, March, 1862): "There is no vaccine matter, however carefully removed from the vesicle, which, on microscopic investigation, will not be found to contain blood corpuscles." Upon this point the statement of Dr. Husband before the Royal Commission said in its report: "The evidence given by Dr. Husband, of the Vaccine Institution of Edinborough, established the fact that all lymph, however pellucid, really does contain blood cells." (Sec. 430.) Dr. Scott Tebb writes, (A Century of Vaccination, page 307): "There is nothing necessarily in the appearance of the vaccine vesicle to lead one to suspect syphilis;" while Dr. Ballard informs us (Prize Essay) that "the perfeet character of the vesicle is no guarantee that it will not furnish both vaccine and syphilitic virus."

Let us see how much the guarantee to furnish "pure" vaccine pus is worth. Mr. Farn, director of the National Establishment in England, when put under examination before the Royal Commission, furnished some details that would be well to reflect upon:

"Q. 4,130. You are a medical man, are you? No.

Q. 4,133. Have you made any special study of microbes? No.

Q. 4,154. With such (microscopic) power as you are able to employ would you be able to recognize or distinguish any micro-organisms which might be present? No, I should not.

Q. 4,155. Have any micro-organisms been identified, or stated to have been identified, for such a disease as erysipelas and so on? I am afraid you are going rather out of my depth as a non-medical man.

Q. 4,159. Is there any disease within your experience whose cause you can identify with such microscopical power as you employ? Not that I am aware of.

Q. 4,173. Having regard to what you have told us, do you think it would be possible, from the microscopical examination you made, to guarantee that any lymph was pure? No; I should not undertake to say whether it would be a guarantee that the lymph was pure. I do not know that you could do it.

Q. 4,200. Are we to understand that, as a matter of fact, you have ever guaranteed lymph? No.

It seems, therefore, that there is no such thing known or obtainable as pure vaccine lymph, and it is very significant that as long ago as 1883 the Grocers' Company, by reason of the numerous disasters following vaccination, offered a prize of £1,000 for the discovery of any vaccine contagium cultivated apart from an animal body, but up to the present time the award has not been made. The matter has, however, been settled beyond all dispute by the Royal Commission itself. They say: "It is established that lymph contains organisms, and may contain those which under certain circumstances would be productive of erysipelas." (Sec. 410).

—"A Century of Vaccination," page 269.

It will hence be seen that the commercial sharks who advertise to furnish vaccine lymph "absolutely free from all organisms except the pure vaccine germ," are either as ignorant of the microscope as Mr. Farn, or else through motives for lucre they deliberately deceive the public. Probably both these allegations are true.

"If it be asked, with what shall we vaccinate? the answer would seem to be simple enough—why, with vaccinal virus, of course. But if we ask, what is vaccinal virus? the answer is not readily found; nor is there, even now, after nearly a century of vaccination, any concord in the profession as to the proper material to be used.

* * * * * * * * * * *

"When Jenner first performed the rite, he used cow-pox virus. We have already seen what was the origin of this dis-

order in the cow, viz., that it was a contagious disease transferred, by careless manipulation, from the heels of the horse to
the udder of the cow. Jenner believed that small-pox, swine-
pox, cow-pox, and grease were merely varieties of the same
disease, as he implied by the name variolae vaccinae. He vacinated his own son with swine-pox. He employed the grease-
virus (horse-pox) in a large number of cases, and furnished it
to other vaccinators. Acting on his suggestion, the king of
Spain, in 1804, ordered all the children in the Foundling Hospi-
tai at Madrid to be vaccinated with goat-pox. Jenner claimed
that the virus of these and various other animals were all
equally efficacious with cow-pox in warding off small-pox. He
also used arm-to-arm vaccination, derived both from the cow
and from the horse. He therefore practiced five distinct things
under the one name of vaccination: (1) Cow-pox vaccination;
(2) cow-pox-child vaccination; (3) horse-pox (grease) vaccination, which he denominated as the equination of the human
subject; (4) horse-pox-child vaccination; and (5) swine-pox
vaccination.

"Although he asserted that grease, cow-pox, and small-
pox were all one disease, he made no attempt to prove it by inoculating the cow with variola. But, as early as 1801, Gassner,
of Gunsburg, inoculated with variolous virus eleven cows, producing on one of them vesicles having all the characteristics of
vaccinal vesicles, and from which 'a stock of genuine vaccine
lymph was obtained.' With this small-pox-cow vaccine four
children were inoculated, and from them seventeen other children were in turn vaccinated. In the following year (1802) a
number of cows were successfully variolated at the Veterinary
College at Berlin.

 * * * * * * * * * * *

"Beside this variola-vaccine lymph, as it is called, another,
and as it is asserted, a new variety of lymph or virus has been
imported. This is the celebrated Beaugency stock, which is
claimed to be a spontaneous case of cow-pox, untainted with
variolation on one hand, or horse-grease on the other.

Thus there are a number of strains of vaccine material:
 a. The original cow-pox of Jenner;
 b. Equine-pox stock;
 c. Swine-pox stock;

d. Goat-pox stock;

e. Variola cow-pox of Ceely, and others;

f. Spontaneous cow-pox of Beaugency.

"Each of these have passed through many transmissions, and to a certain extent have become crossed or intermixed, and with the exception of what is now called 'calf-lymph,' it is impossible for anybody to tell what he is using. This so-called 'calf-lymph' is offered in two varieties. One of these is claimed to be inoculation from the Beaugency stock, which it is confessed, is of unknown origin, and which from the mildness of the vaccine-disorder which it sets up, is of dubious value.

"The other variety of 'calf-lymph' is derived from small-poxing a heifer, and from the vesicles thus produced calves are inoculated; these in their turn furnishing the 'lymph' or virus for the human subject.

"T s furnishes two more varieties of vaccine material:

g. Calf-Beaugency stock;

h. Calf-small-pox-cow-pox."

—"The Value of Vaccination," pages 37-39, Winterburn.

"When the Royal Commission on Vaccination was reluctantly conceded by the late (Conservative) government in April, 1889, the medical profession was (and still is) in a state of hopeless confusion as to the merits of the various vaccines introduced and recommended by rival purveyors. One variety is used in Germany, another in France, a third in Belgium, and in England all have been tried more or less. It was suggested by the medical press that the Royal Commission should deal with this much vexed phase of the vaccination embroglio; and after the evidence of Dr. Cory, Dr. Gayton, Mr. Farn, and other vaccine experts, it was anticipated the commission would have made a pronouncement on the subject. This professional expectation has not been realized. To illustrate the extent of this medical confusion, and for the information of those who contemplate subjecting their children to the vaccine operation, the writer subjoins a list of some of these vaccines:

(1) The original Jennerian Virus, or Horse-grease Cow-pox.

(2) Woodville's spontaneous Cow-pox Virus, contaminated with small-pox.

(3) Swine-pox with which Jenner inoculated his eldest

son. 'Swine-pox' has no relation to a pig's disease; but is only an old name for the mildest form of small-pox, called also the white small-pox, or pearl-pox. (Crookshank, 'History and Pathology of Vaccination,' Vol. I, page 287.)

(4)   Horse-pox or horse-grease passed through the cow.

(5)   Spontaneous Cow-pox—the Gloucestershire brand.

(6)   Ceely and Babcock's lymph — small-pox passed through the cow.

(7)   The Beaugency Virus.

(8)   The Passy Virus.

(9)   Dr. Warlomont's Calf-lymph, in points, tubes or pots of pomade as supplied to the Royal Family in England.

(10)   The Lanoline vaccine or vesicle pulp invented by Surgeon-Major W. G. King, and used extensively in India and Burmah.

(11)   Donkey-lymph, the discovery of Surgeon O'Hara, and strongly recommended to municipalities in India.

(12)   Buffalo-lymph, recommended in India as 'yielding more vesicle-pulp than calves,' but chiefly conspicuous for its abominable odor.

(13)   To these must be added the lymph passed through numberless more or less diseased human bodies, which has been shown by high authorities to be capable of spreading leprosy, syphilis, and other loathsome and incurable diseases."

—Anti-Vaccination League Circular.

Dr. Warlomont, of the Government Vaccine Depot, Belgium, advises medical practitioners, when families apply for vaccination, to require such families to furnish their own vaccine material, thus making the family take the risk while the doctor pockets the fee.

————

THE TRUE CHARACTER OF ALL ANIMAL "LYMPHS."

Since one form of vaccination after another has been tried and then abandoned because of the evil effects which followed, still the doctors and vaccine-farm firms have found the practice far too profitable to think of abandoning it; and so from time to time they announce the discovery of a new brand of vaccine material, which they guarantee a gullible public to be double proof against the remotest possibility of danger, and an absolute safeguard against small-pox. "Pure Calf-lymph" is at present the harmless elixir which vaccination promoters offer in the market. Just how this "lymph" is manufactured is one of those mysteries which the vaccine firms never impart to their patrons; and whether the secret is out or not, I know the nature and habits of the species, and propose to throw a search-light upon it long enough to allow the general reader to note a few items regarding its behavior.

We have already seen that all vaccine material is animal pus, which is animal tissue in process of decomposition or retrograde metamorphosis—but a small remove from absolute rottenness. In other words, it is the serum of a particular disease thrown out upon the skin, and this putrifying serum invariably contains a specific virus, a putrefactive or septic poison, no matter in what way the putrefaction of animal tissue has been induced. The vaccine pus may be charged with one or a dozen forms of septic poison, according to the nature of the putrifying tissues which have contributed to its production. Nor is the danger lessened, but rather augmented, by subsequent transmissions, as every additional channel through which it passes will contribute its own taint of involved disease.

Dr. T. V. Gifford, of Kokomo, Ind., in an address before the Anti Vaccination Congress in Paris (1889), professes to have learned at least one method of producing vaccine calf-lymph. He says:—

"A Boston medical student, whom I had long known as a reliable gentleman, voluntarily informed me how they produced bovine virus at the Boston vaccine farm, where students are permitted to see the whole operation. He said they shave

the hair from the udder of the heifer with a razor, then scratch
or bruise the udder with a steel-tined instrument and leave it to
fester simply from the bruising. Now put this with the following which I have already quoted form Dr. Spinzig—'Vaccination is tantamount to inoculation and is septic poisoning'—and
this from the little Philadelphia book afore mentioned—'that
vaccine virus has no special properties inherent to it'—and this
from another scientific writer—'All pus of animal organisms
has the same specific quality and differs only in strength and degrees of rottenness or development'—and you have a solution
of the whole question, which is simply this: It makes no difference how the pus is produced, whether by bruise, wound or
introduction of other pus or other foreign poison. The degree
of virulence of the pus is governed by the character of the tissue out of which it is formed and the length of time it remains
in the sore."

Again, "Animal lymph is admitted to be too active, especially in tropical countries, to be used direct; and in general, therefore, it is available only after one or two removes,
when it carries with it diseases both animal and human, as has
been shown in evidence before the Royal Commission on Vaccination."

—"Leprosy and Vaccination," page 181, Wm. Tebb.

On this important phase of the vaccination question I will
cite a number of authorities who are at the very summit of the
medical profession, most of whom will be found quoted in Dr.
Scott Tebb's excellent work, "A Century of Vaccination."

The London Lancet (June 22, 1878), in a criticism of Dr.
Henry A. Martin, observes:—

"The notion that animal lymph would be free from chances
of syphilitic contamination is so fallacious that we are surprised
to see Dr. Martin reproduce it, and so contribute to the perpetuation of the fanciful ideas which too commonly obtain on
the origin of vaccino-syphilis.

"Dr. Henry M. Lyman observes: 'It is certain that the
disturbances, produced by the use of a virus which has been
newly derived from the cow, are generally much more marked
than the effects which follow the use of a more perfectly hu-

manized lymph.'"

—"American Medical Times" for March 8, 1862.

"But there is a special vesicular vaccine eruption attending the acme and decline of the vaccine disease. The Germans have called it 'Nachpocken.' I have often, nay almost always, seen it as a secondary eruption on the teats and udders of the cows immediately before and after the decline of the disease in them. The same I have repeatedly seen in children, especially in the early removes from the cow; and still continue at times to wit-ness it, to the great temporary disfigurement and annoyance of the patient, and the chagrin and vexation of the parent. It is essentially a genuine vaccine secondary eruption. I have witnessed it in vaccinating the dog. I have colored illustrations of this secondary eruption in man and animals, and have seen some severe and a few very dangerous cases in children where the skin and visible mucous membranes were copiously occupied with it."—Dr. Scott Tebb, page 367.

"Vaccination with bovine lymph has brought to light a series of phenomenal symptoms, except to those medical men who have kept fresh in their minds the descriptions of Jenner and the early writers. Jenner described the disease caused by early removes from the cow, and he consequently gave a picture of only the intensest forms of it, in his 'Inquiry' and 'Further Observations.' A glance at the colored engravings in Jenner's great work, in Woodville's, Pearson's, Bryce's, Willan's, and all others, shows that the vesicle was larger and the areola more intensely red than in the cases familiar to us up to the time of the introduction of the Beaugency lymph. The reader of the early vaccinographers can hardly believe there was not some exaggeration in their descriptions of the serious constitutional symptoms, and the bad ulcers which sometimes succeeded vaccination; ulcers so bad, indeed, that they had to be treated with solution of white vitrol."

—Dr. Thomas F. Wood, New Jersey.

"In the report of the Oxford Local Board to the New Jersey Board of Health, Dr. L. B. Hoagland, in referring to an epidemic of small-pox, says: 'About fifteen hundred persons were vaccinated during its prevalence, one-third of them with humanized virus, and the remainder with non-humanized bovine virus, the constitutional effect being much the more marked when the latter was used. One child, of five years, lost its life by taking cold in her arm; gangrene set in, and she died from septicaemia. Some of the sores were three or four months in healing."

"In my use of bovine lymph it was observed that the vaccine vesicle resulting was much larger, the areola and inflammatory induration were more extensive, the crust large, flat, and thin, generally ruptured, and came away before the sore was cicatrised. In two instances the inflammatory action was so high that the vesicle sloughed out en masse, leaving a deep ulcer."—Dr. E. J. Marsh, Board of Health, Patterson, N. J., 1882.

Dr. George B. Walker, of Evansville, Ind., writes: "The bovine lymph was more violent and caused troublesome ulceration and sometimes eruption over the body."

In the Journal of Cutaneous and Venereal Diseases Dr. Morrow bears out the almost universal opinion of medical men in the United States when he says: "The experiences of the profession in this country with bovine lymph shows that it is slower in its development, more intensely irritant in its local and constitutional effects, and more prolonged in its active continuance."

Dr. Alexander Napier, assistant to the professor of Materia Medica, Glasgow University, and physician to the skin department, Anderson's College Dispensary, calls attention to a certain remarkable group of skin eruptions, which he finds reported in the American journals, and with scarcely an exception they related to cases where animal lymph was used. He first refers to instances reported by Dr. Rice in the Chicago Medical Journal and Examiner for February, 1882, in which that gentleman states that "about one in ten of all vaccinated have bad arms, with a high grade of fever, and eruption resembling somewhat that of Roseda or German measles."

—Dr. Scott Tebb, page 373.

Dr. Pierce, quoted by Scott Tebb, writes: "Judging from the number of times I have been questioned by anxious parents on the meaning of these eruptions, I believe with Dr. Holt that the fact of their liability to follow vaccination should be widely known."

"In nearly every instance I have mentioned in which spontaneous generalized eruptions followed vaccination, the lymph used was animal lymph, not humanized lymph. What does this indicate? That, as Dr. Cameron, M. P., once argued before this society, the nearer the virus to its original source in the days of Jenner, the stronger it is, and the more efficient the protection it affords? Without venturing to give any opinion as to the greater efficacy of calf lymph vaccination as a prophylactic against small-pox—a matter which can only be settled on the basis of a wide statistical inquiry—it seems very clear that in animal lymph we have a more powerful material, one which more deeply and obviously affects the system than our ordinary humanized lymph, if the degree of constitutional disturbance is to be taken as an index of the effectual working of the virus."

—Dr. Napier, Glasgow Medical Journal, June, 1883.

More recently we find in an article on "Small-pox in San Francisco," by Dr. S. S. Herrick, the following remarks: "Besides the uncertainty of the bovine virus, there are other features of common occurrence, which are not pleasant and which are not found in the human product. The sores are apt to be quite serious in character; a considerable eruption on the body is liable to take place; and the points of vaccination frequently develop a raspberry-like excrescence (sometimes a true ecchymosis) which may remain for weeks, and is often mistaken by the inexperienced for the normal result of vaccination."

GLYCERINATED LYMPH.

When the "pure calf-lymph" was found to be uniformly harsh in its effects, and to be attended with extensive eruptions and ulceration, a new device was invented by the manufacturers of the vaccine stock for commercial purposes—a device to still further mask its insidious and destructive work. This was to add glycerine to the so-called lymph, which, it is claimed, destroys all micro-organisms except the vaccine germ that is wanted. In the first place, this is an admission that the lymph without the glycerine, which had already been in use for years, really contained micro-organisms in addition to the vaccine germs, which therefore embraced a real element of danger; and in the second place, the virtues claimed for glycerine are pure assumption, without a shadow of evidence to sustain it.

"The perennial cry of public vaccinators (when they are confronted with the results) is that the lymph is 'unsatisfactory.' Animal lymph is often attended with excessive inflammation, and the practitioner is obliged to dilute it with glycerine, lano-line, and other substances, and its use is much more expensive. Moreover, a good deal of the so-called animal lymph in vogue is only arm-to-arm vaccine, inoculated into calves, buffaloes, sheep, and donkeys, and partakes of the diseases both of man and of animals. Of the many cases of ulcerative and of fatal vaccination which have come under my notice during the past twenty years not a few have been due to the use of carefully selected animal vaccine."—"Leprosy and Vaccination," page 381. Wm. Tebb.

"Dr. Lurman, of Bremen, gives an account of an epidemic of catarrhal jaundice in 1883-84, in a large ship-building and ma-chine-making establishment in that town, which is of interest from the fact that the patients had been re-vaccinated with glycerinated lymph. One hundred and ninety-one persons were attacked. The disease began with symptoms of gastric and in-testinal catarrh, which persisted a week or more, until jaundice appeared. The symptoms comprised epigastric oppression, anorexia, vomiting, faintness, and there was usually constipa-tion. Yellow vision occurred in a few instances. In one case the patient suffered from general dropsy with cerebral symp-toms, but none of the cases were fatal. Eighty-seven persons in the establishment, who were re-vaccinated by other surgeons and other lymph, remained unaffected. Dr. Edwards, who re-lates these cases in the London Medical Record of April 15, 1885, (Vol. XIII, page 142), remarks that the epidemic 'was causally connected with the re-vaccination, in some way or other."

"A feature of glycerinated lymph appears to be that, when it takes, great intensity of action is observed, both local and general. Thus Dr. James Cantlie refers to 'much constitutional disturbance' produced by Japanese lymph. I may also allude to an article by Dr. Robert J. Carter. He details the results of 319 re-vaccinations with glycerinated calf-lymph. He observes that in 106 of the patients the axillary glands were 'large, hard, and tender, and in some instances exquisitely painful;' in three of the cases the glands above the collar-bone were also affected.

In nine cases lymphangitis was present, the lymphatic vessels being felt as hard, swollen, tender cords along the course of the axillary vessels. In ninety-eight of the patients there was œdema and induration of the arm, and these manifestations were of a 'curiously persistent character.' Dr. Carter remarked that they were apparently dependent on the intensity of the local inflammation at the site of the vaccination."

"Abundant evidence of the danger of glycerinated lymph is adduced in Appendix IX to the Final Report of the Royal Commission. The cases are, of course, mostly erysipelas or of a septic nature; and, without including those of a less severe character, they number 84, and of these no less than 24 were fatal."—"A Century of Vaccination," Dr. Scott Tebb, page 382.

"I emphasize the point, that no lymph, whether human or animal, or adulterated with other substances, can be guaranteed as free from danger."—Ibid., page 386.

"Glycerine is a nutritive medium for the growth of putrefactive and other germs and being fluid, the germs soon pervade it throughout; and, as a fact, this preparation (glycerinated lymph) in India soon becomes putrid and septically dangerous."

Indian Lancet, March 4, 1897.

Dr. T. S. Hopkins, of Thomasville, Ga., wrote a communication concerning the results that followed the use of "patent solid lymph:"—

"Our town authorities have employed a physician to vaccinate all persons who present themselves for the purpose. The virus was procured from the New England Vaccine Company, Chelsea, Mass., as 'bovine matter.' The result has been fearful. Nearly every one vaccinated has suffered severely from erythema or erysipelas, the arm swollen from shoulder to wrist, and the point of puncture presenting the appearance of a sloughing ulcer, discharging freely sanious pus. Many of the sufferers have been confined to bed, with high fever, from five to ten days, requiring the constant application of poultices to the arm, and a free use of morphia for the relief of pain. I deem it my duty to inform you of the result here from the matter used and from whence it came. It came in cones, each one said to contain enough to vaccinate one hundred persons, at a cost of one dollar per cone. Those who have tried it tell me they would much prefer to have small-pox."—From the National Board of Health Bulletin, Washington, D. C., March 4, 1882.

"We have no known test by which we could possibly distinguish between a lymph which was harmless and one which was harmful to the extent of communicating syphilis."—Dr. Crookshank, Professor of Pathology and Bacteriology.

Thus I might multiply testimonies indefinitely regarding the wide-spread injury which has followed the use of all forms of animalized and humanized grades of vaccine material. Glycerinated lymph and all modern brands of vaccine stock are only new devices to make an old discredited virus acceptable; and the chief reason why they continue to be inflicted on the long suffering public, is because that public have no intelligent understanding of the insidious effects or the grave dangers that result from this ruinous practice.

Neither the parent or the doctor has any means of judging the quality of the vaccine virus used, since it is an article of commerce; and its production is not only associated with mercenary motives, but with empirical science as well. Commerce has usurped the field here as everywhere else, and the doctor— who is merely a "middle man" between the vaccine dealer and the vaccinated—knows no more about the composition of his stock, either in its occult properties or vital chemistry, than he does about his baking powders or canned beef; whether the former are free from alum adulteration, or whether the latter has passed through the hands of the embalmer. We know at least that from first to last the whole consignment of horse-grease-cow-pox-syphilized-vaccine pus is now, has been, and is destined to continue the most damnable stuff that was ever admitted into the category of commercialized medical practice. We may soon expect that the various vaccine farms will be massed into one gigantic trust, with a lobby at Washington and money to secure federal enforcement of a more stringent compulsory vaccination act for the entire country!

"And the beast causeth all * * to receive a mark on their arm * * and no man might buy or sell, save him that had the mark * * and there fell a noisome and grievous sore upon such as had the mark of the beast."—Rev. xvi-2.

Every child successfully vaccinated will carry on its body the scar—the brute-caused scar, the grievous sore, the scar of the "beast" till death.

CHAPTER III.

VACCINATION FAILS TO PROTECT.

The flattering promises made by Jenner and other advo
cates of his school, that cow-pox is an absolute and infallible
protection against small-pox, we have repeatedly seen is contradicted by the concurrent testimony of the highest medical authorities in all civilized countries, as also by the facts with which
we are daily confronted, but more especially in seasons of small-
pox epidemic. During the last twenty years all the leading
countries of the world have expended every effort to render
vaccination general and complete. Compulsory laws have been
enacted, an army of vaccinators put into the field, tens of thousands of prosecutions have been brought, together with fines and
imprisonments, against those who refused to comply with the
provisions of arbitrary legislation, and millions of dollars have
been expended to make vaccination universal. And I ask, what
beneficent result has been accomplished by this unparalleled
vigilance and expenditure? None. The average death rate
from zymotics has not diminished, except where improved sanitary regulations have been adopted, and even there small-pox
has not diminished in a greater ratio than scarlatina or diphtheria, as it should if the claims for vaccination had any valid
basis or justification in recorded facts. Just in proportion as
vaccination has modified the symptoms of small-pox it has aggravated other forms of infection. as will be amply shown in

the course of this discussion. And had not improved sanitation gone forward as a counteractive cause, the destructive effects of vaccination would have been far more manifest than what has already been recorded, bad as that record has been. Sanitation has acted as a powerful check to the otherwise rapid multiplication and spread of zymotic diseases.

Jenner himself found that those whom he vaccinated were not only subject to small-pox, but that they were sometimes attacked twice with the disease. Then he advised re-vaccination, and finally re-vaccinated his patients once a year. He made a marked distinction between efficient and non-efficient vaccination. Its potency was not regarded as proved until the constitution was unmistakably affected with the vaccine disease. Finally "due and efficient" vaccination meant great in amount and distinct in quality, i. e., often repeated, and vitally disturbing. As a matter of fact, if people had the small-pox under similar conditions that they usually have the swine, horse-grease, or cow-pox, it would be scarcely less disturbing, but like all zymotic diseases, the soil for small-pox is prepared by filthy living, intemperance, over-crowding, poverty, war, etc., until the populace is charged with infection to the point of explosion; then it breaks out with epidemic intensity as small-pox, typhus, or plague, according to the preponderating quality of the infection accumulated. Then a miracle is expected from the performance of a degrading rite, but the miracle is never performed, since during an epidemic small-pox ruthlessly treads down its victims without taking any note of the "vaccine-mark" on the arm, so much relied on as a talisman or magic charm against the disease! Florence Nightingale combined experience and common sense in this domain far better than nine-tenths of the doctors. She says:—

"I was brought up both by scientific men and ignorant women to believe the small-pox, for instance, was a thing, of which there was once a first specimen in the world, which went on

propagating itself, just as much as there was a first dog, or
pair of dogs; and that the small-pox would not begin itself any
more than a new dog would begin without there having been a
parent dog. Since then I have seen with my eyes small-pox
growing up in first specimens, in close rooms or over-crowded
wards, where it could not by any possibility have been caught,
but must have been begun. Nay more; I have seen diseases
begin, grow up, and pass into one another; with over-crowding,
continued fever; with a little more over-crowding, typhoid;
with a little more, typhus, and all in the same ward or hut."

COMPARISON OF SMALL-POX DEATHS.

YEAR.	NEW YORK. NO VACCINATION.	LONDON. VACCINATION THE FASHION.
	PER HUNDRED THOUSAND LIVING.	
	DEATHS.	DEATHS.
1804	169	61
1805	62	163
1806	45	110
1807	29	122
1808	62	103
1809	66	106
1810	4	106
AVERAGE	63	111

In 1820, that is, before Jenner's death, it was said: "Cases
of small-pox after vaccination have increased to such an extent, that no conscientious practitioner can recommend vaccination as affording a certain security against the contagion of
small-pox."—"Gazette of Health," London, 1820.

In 1828 there was a severe epidemic in Marseilles where
2,000 were attacked with small-pox, who had been vaccinated.
In the epidemic of 1831, in Wirtemburg, 955 persons were attacked with small-pox—all vaccinated.

"The matter has been looked into by Dr. Creighton and
by Prof. Crookshank as far as its pathological aspect is concerned; and the conclusions towards which we are pointed in

this, that while vaccination is not, and from the nature of the case cannot be, a specific prophylactic against small-pox, yet a severe attack of cow-pox, or, in other words, vaccination followed by considerable constitutional disturbance, is likely to prove, while the febrile symptoms still last, antagonistic to the small-pox infection, and, so far, affords a temporary protection against it. Probably the same is true of any other disease that produces constitutional disturbance with febrile symptoms. We must, moreover, bear in mind that many persons, apart from vaccination, had been known to show constitutional insusceptibility to the variolous inoculation, and that inoculation itself was often enough a mere formality, producing no results; and this was extremely likely to be the case when the operators were anxious that no results should be produced. Add to this the enthusiasm for the cause, which, unless Jenner and his fellow-workers had been more than human, would lead them, without conscious dishonesty, to make no record of experiments that failed, and we have perhaps a fair explanation of the whole business; but it is not altogether a satisfactory one; and it is difficult not to regret that similar experiments cannot be repeated now under conditions involving publicity, as that would really settle the whole controversy."—"Vaccination Question," Arthur Wallaston Hutton.

"The small-pox is making still greater havoc in the ranks of the Prussian army, which is said to have 30,000 small-pox patients in its hospitals."—"London Morning Advertiser," Nov. 24, 1870.

" The United States frigate Independence, with a ship's company of 560 persons, there were 116 cases of small-pox, seven fatal. The crew of this ship almost universally presented what are regarded as genuine vaccine marks. The protection, however, proved to be quite imperfect."— U. S. Navy Department Reports, 1850.

"In a cruise of the North Carolina up the Mediterranean, she shipped at Norfolk a crew of 900 men, most of whom had been vaccinated, or had the small-pox, but were nevertheless twice vaccinated prior to the ship sailing, a third time at Gibraltar, and a fourth time at Port Mahon. Dr. Henderson, who reports these facts, states that notwithstanding this ultra vaccination under such various circumstances of virus, climate, etc.,

157 of the crew had varioloid."—Ibid.

In New York (1870-71) the health department reported:

"This extraordinary prevalence of small-pox over various parts of the globe, especially in countries where vaccination has long been efficiently practiced; its occurrence in its most fatal form in persons who gave evidences of having been well vaccinated, and the remarkable susceptibility of people of all ages to re-vaccinations, are new facts in the history of this pestilence, which must lead to a re-investigation of the whole subject of vaccination and of its claims as a protecting agent."—Dr. Winterburn, page 73.

In 1882 small-pox was epidemic in Baltimore. The victims were principally foreigners, crowded together in the most filthy quarter of the town. In a crowded tenement from fifteen to twenty cases were often reported. In a single month (January) over 162,000 persons were vaccinated by the city physicians. There were 4,930 cases, of which 3,506 were children. The deaths amounted to 1,184, of which 959 were children— about 78 per cent. This, together with hundreds of other instances that might be cited from crowded centers of population, proves vaccination a complete and glaring failure in times of small-pox epidemic—the only time when such protection is needed.

When the great London epidemic raged (1871-72), 96 per cent. of births were registered as vaccinated, yet there were 11,-174 cases of small-pox in the London hospitals. At the same period 17,109 cases were reported in Milan, of which but 278 were classed as unvaccinated. In the French army during the Franco-Prussian war, 23,469 cases were recorded, every one of which had been vaccinated, and a large proportion re-vaccinated. Dr. Bayard, of Paris, says: "Every French soldier on entering a regiment is re-vaccinated; there are no exceptions."

Sir Henry Holland reluctantly admits that "The circumstances, of late years, have greatly changed the aspect of all that relates to this question. It is no longer expedient, in any sense, to argue for the present practice of vaccination as a certain or permanent preventive of small-pox. The truth must be told as it is, that the earlier anticipations on this point have not been realized."

"From childhood I have been trained to look upon the cowpox as an absolute and unqualified protective. I have, from my earliest remembrance, believed in it more strongly than in any clerical tenet or ecclesiastical dogma. The numerous and acknowledged failures did not shake my faith. I attributed them either to the carelessness of the operator or the badness of the lymph. In the course of time, the question of vaccine compulsion came before the Reichstag, when a medical friend supplied me with a mass of statistics favorable to vaccination, in his opinion conclusive and unanswerable. This awoke the statistician within me. On inspection, I found the figures were delusive; and a closer examination left no shadow of doubt in my mind that the so-called statistical array of proof was a complete failure."—Dr. G. F. Kolb, Royal Sta. Com., Bavaria.

The Registrar General (England), in his official report for 1880, points out some very important facts, namely, that the reduction in the sum total of zymotic diseases for the previous decade, should be put down to the credit of improved sanitation. The death rate from fever fell nearly 50 per cent.; that of scarlatina and diphtheria, 33 per cent., while small-pox alone increased 50 per cent., and this when vaccination was general and thorough. This proves that vaccination has no appreciable effect to check the progress of small-pox when it becomes epidemic. We also have here an illustration of the law, already pointed out, that when one zymotic disease is epidemic the others are in abeyance to the extent that the total death rate is not sensibly affected.

The "London Lancet" (1871) says, editorially: "Those who have been building up in their imagination a great and beneficent system of state medicine, under which the great causes of diseases were to be controlled, must abate their hopefulness. It must be admitted that the existing system of public vaccina-

tion has been sadly discredited and almost mocked by the experience of the present epidemic."

In a speech in the London Vaccination Conference (1881),
Dr. Bullard—with a salary of $3,500.00 as public vaccinator—
said: "If it were not for the interference of such small-pox epidemics as that of 1871, the records of vaccination would be perfectly satisfactory." Dr. Robinson retorted: "Dr. B. reminds
me of a bankrupt who avowed he would be perfectly solvent, if
it were not for his confounded losses." Aye, it is during a
money-crisis that the solvency of a bank is tested; and it is
likewise during a small-pox epidemic the value—or total lack
of it—of vaccination is tested. If at this critical period it fails
to protect, it is thereby not only proved to be utterly useless,
but an unmitigated curse; for it not only fails to yield any benefit, but it charges the bodies of its unnumbered victims with a
virus, the effects of which the most thorough sanitation will
only partially counteract.

Here are some figures:

SMALL-POX DEATHS IN LONDON.

1851-60	7,150
1861-70	8,347
1871-80	15,551

The deaths in England from the last three great epidemics
of small-pox were:

	Deaths.
1857-9	14,244
1863-5	20,059
1870-2	44,840

This is vaccinated London; this is vaccinated England, and
observe that the last curse was far more grievous than the first
—twenty years earlier.

Florence Nightingale writes that "Every one who knows
anything of public health questions, will agree as to the practical unity of epidemics and their determining causes, and that ex-

emptions from all alike must be sought, not by any one thing, such as vaccination, but by inquiring into and removing the causes of epidemic susceptibility generally."

HARD BLOWS BY PROFESSOR WALLACE.

One of the ablest writers and thoroughly scientific men in England—Prof. Alfred R. Wallace—has enrolled himself on the side of reform, and has recently written and published (1898) one of the best books on the vaccination controversy which has appeared within the history of the agitation—"Vaccination a Delusion." This has been published both as a separate volume, and also embodied in his latest work—"The Wonderful Century," where it is receiving a wide circulation. Prof. Wallace has made a thorough study and analysis of the statistical problem as it relates to vaccination and to small-pox, and arranged the results in diagramatic form—twelve diagramatic maps— the only form in which statistics show the exact truth at a glance. I am more than pleased to have access to such an ample and thoroughly reliable source of information, and shall embody some of Prof. Wallace's results in these pages:

He critically examined the early tests employed by the advocates of vaccination to prove the protective influence of the practice, and points out the fallacy and complete inefficiency of these tests. Moreover, he urges that the real test would have been to inoculate with small-pox virus two groups of persons of similar age, constitution and health, one group having been vaccinated, the other not, and none of them having had small-pox. Then have the results carefully noted and reported by independent experts. But such practical tests have never been instituted by the apologists and defenders of the practice.

The Board of the National Vaccine Establishment, appointed in 1808, consisted of the president and four censors of the Royal College of Physicians, and the master and two senior wardens of the College of Surgeons. Speaking of this board, Prof. Wallace observes:—

"The successive annual reports of the National Vaccine Establishment give figures of the deaths by small-pox in London in the eighteenth century, which go on increasing like Falstaff's men in buckram; while in our own time the late Dr. W. B. Carpenter, Mr. Ernest Hart, the National Health Society, and the Local Government Board make statements or give figures which are absurdly and demonstrably incorrect. * * * The unreasoning belief in the importance of vaccination leads many of those who have to deal with it officially to concealments and mis-statements which are justified by the desire to 'save vaccination from reproach.'"

Next Prof. Wallace cites two cases which shows the unscrupulous special pleading of members of the National Vaccine Establishment—the recklessness in making assertions which scorns the slightest attempt at verification:—

"In the first edition of Mr. Ernest Hart's "Truth About Vaccination" (page 4), it is stated, on the authority of a member of Parliament recently returned from Brazil, that during an epidemic of small-pox at the town of Ceara in 1878 and 1879, out of a population not exceeding 70,000 persons there were 40,000 deaths from small-pox. This was repeated by Dr. Carpenter during a debate in London, in February, 1882, and only when its accuracy was called in question was it ascertained that at the time referred to the population of Ceara was only about 20,000, yet the M. P. had stated—with detailed circumstance— that 'in one cemetery, from August, 1878, to June, 1879, 27,-064 persons who had died of small-pox had been buried.' Gazetteers are not very recondite works, and it would have been not difficult to test some portion of this monstrous statement before printing it. Jenner's biographer tells us that he had a horror of arithmetical calculations, due to a natural incapacity, which quality appears to be a special characteristic of those who advocate vaccination, as the examples I have given sufficiently prove.

"Another glaring case of official misrepresentation occurred in the Royal Commission itself, but was fortunately exposed later on. A medical officer of the Local Government Board gave evidence (First Report, Q. 994), that the board in 1886 'took some pains to get the figures as to the steamship Preussen,' on which small-pox broke out on its arrival in Australia. He made the following statements: (1) There were 312 persons on board this vessel. (2) 4 re-vaccinated, 47 vaccinated, 3 who had small-pox, and 15 unvaccinated were attacked —69 in all. (3) The case was adduced to show that 'sanitary circumstances have little or no control over small-pox compared with the condition of vaccination or no vaccination.'

"This official statement was quoted in the House of Commons as strikingly showing the value of vaccination. But, like so many other official statements, it was all false! The reports of the Melbourne and Sydney inspectors have been obtained, and it is found: (1) That there were on board this ship 723 passengers and 120 crew—823 in all, instead of 312; so that the 'pains' taken by the Local Government Board to get 'the figures' were very ineffectual. (2) There were 29 cases among the 235 passengers who disembarked at Melbourne, of whom only 1 was unvaccinated. The crew had all been vaccinated before starting, yet 14 of them were attacked with small-pox, and one died."

—Page 81 of "Vaccination a Delusion."

Again, officials of the Vaccine Establishment have no motives why a record of small-pox mortality should not be correct; but they have a motive to charge the record up against the unvaccinated all that the state of the public health will bear. Of fatal cases none are returned as vaccinated unless distinct and visible vaccine marks are found, which often lead to error. Besides, official vaccinators have an admitted practice of giving vaccination the benefit of any doubt that may arise as to whether the victim of the disease was ever vaccinated. Hence, while statistics are sure to embrace the full number of the unvaccinated, they rarely reveal the number of the vaccinated.

Sweden is often quoted by advocates of vaccination as bearing out their contention that vaccination really protects. They point out that vaccination was introduced in Sweden in 1801.

and that from that time to 1810 there was a great and sudden
decline of small-pox mortality.   But Prof. Wallace, taking the
report of the Swedish Board of Health, and the statements of
such authorities as Sir William Gull, Dr. Seaton and Mr.
Marsen before the Commission of Inquiry in 1871, constructed
a complete diagramatic table of Swedish mortality statistics.
I will here attempt nothing more than a brief summary of a portion of the facts.

In the first place, only 8 per cent. of the population were
vaccinated in Sweden down to 1812.   The first successful vaccination in Stockholm was at the close of 1810.   And here it is
important to note that the decline in small-pox mortality was
between 1801 and 1812, while only 8 per cent. of the population
was yet vaccinated, and even this small percentage was mostly
confined to the rural districts.   From 1812, for sixty years there
was a continuous increase in the small-pox death rate.   The
Stockholm epidemic of 1807, before a single inhabitant in that
city was vaccinated, and the epidemic in 1825, were far less severe than the six later epidemics when vaccination had become
general.   By referring to Prof. Wallace's diagram, we see that
vaccination had nothing to do with the reduction of small-pox
mortality, which was all brought about before the first successful vaccination in the capital, Dec. 17, 1810.   As vaccination increased among the population, small-pox increased also.   In
1874 there was a small-pox mortality in Stockholm of 7,916 per
million, reaching 10,290 per million during the two years in
which the epidemic prevailed.   This was a higher mortality
than the worst epidemic in London during the eighteenth century.

Prof. Wallace sums up the case as it relates to Sweden :—

"There has evidently been a great and continuous improvement in healthy conditions of life in Sweden, as in our own
country and probably in all other European nations ; and this
improvement, or some special portion of it, must have acted

powerfully on small-pox to cause the enormous diminution of the disease down to 1812, with which, as we have seen, vaccination could have had nothing to do. The only thing that vaccination seems to have done is, to have acted as a check to this diminution, since it is otherwise impossible to explain the complete cessation of improvement as the operation became more general; and this is more especially the case in view of the fact that the general death rate has continued to decrease at almost the same rate down to the present day!

*   *   *   *   *   *   *   *   *   *   *

"This case of Sweden alone affords complete proof of the uselessness of vaccination; yet the commissioners in the Final Report (par. 59) refer to the great diminution of small-pox mortality in the first twenty years of the century as being due to it. They make no comparison with the total death rate; they say nothing of the increase of small-pox from 1824 to 1874; they omit all reference to the terrible Stockholm epidemics increasing continuously for fifty years of legally enforced vaccination and culminating in that of 1874, which was far worse than the worst known in London during the whole of the eighteenth century. Official blindness to the most obvious facts and conclusions can hardly have a more striking illustration than the appeal to the case of Sweden as being favorable to the claims of vaccination."

In May, 1871, the Pall Mall Gazette expresses the medical opinion that:—

"Prussia is the country where re-vaccination is most generally practiced, the law making the precaution obligatory on every person, and the authorities conscientiously watching over its performance. As a natural result, cases of small-pox are rare." Never was there a more glaring untruth than this last statement. It is true that re-vaccination was enforced in public schools and other institutions, and most rigidly in the army, so that a very large proportion of the adult male population must have been re-vaccinated; but, instead of cases of small-pox being rare, there had been for the twenty-four years preceding 1871 a much greater small-pox mortality in Prussia than in England, the annual average being 248 per million for the former and only 210 for the latter. A comparison of the

two cases shows the difference at a glance.   English small-
pox only reached 400 per million (in 1852) while in Prussia it
four times exceeded that amount.   And immediately after the
words above quoted were written, the great epidemic of 1871-72
caused a mortality in re-vaccinated Prussia more than double
that of England."—Ibid, page 48.

If we compare Berlin with London in 1871, we find the
small-pox mortality for Berlin 6,150 per million—more than
twice that of London; and this, remember, is where vaccination
and re-vaccination were most thoroughly performed.

Again, vaccination was made compulsory in Bavaria in
1807, and was so maintained down to the epidemic of 1871,
when 30,742 cases of small-pox were reported, of which 95 per
cent. had been vaccinated.

Prof. Wallace truly remarks: "In Bavaria as in all other
countries we have examined, the behavior of small-pox shows
no relation to vaccination, but the very closest relation to the
other zymotics and to density of population. * * Ninety-
five per cent. of small-pox patients having been vaccinated is
alone sufficient to condemn vaccination as useless."

"One point more deserves notice before leaving this part
of the inquiry, which is the specially high small-pox mortality
of great commercial sea-ports.   The following table, compiled
from Dr. Pierce's "Vital Statistics" for the continental towns
and from the Reports of the Royal Commission for those of
our own country, is very remarkable and instructive:—

NAME OF TOWN.	YEAR.	SMALL-POX DEATH-RATE PER MILLION.
Hamburgh	1871	15,440
Rotterdam	1871	14,280
Cork	1872	9,600
Sunderland	1871	8,650
Stockholm	1874	7,916
Trieste	1872	6,980
Newcastle-on-Tyne	1871	5,410
Portsmouth	1872	4,420
Dublin	1872	4,330
Liverpool	1871	3,890
Plymouth	1872	3,000

"The small-pox death rate in the case of the lowest of these
towns is very much higher than in London during the same ep-

idemic, and it is quite clear that vaccination can have had nothing to do with this difference. For if it be alleged that vaccination was neglected in Hamburgh and Rotterdam, of which we find no particulars, this cannot be said of Cork, Sunderland, and Newcastle. Again, if the very limited and imperfect vaccination of the first quarter of the century is to have the credit of the striking reduction of small-pox mortality that then occurred, as the Royal Commissioners claim, a small deficiency in the very much more extensive and better vaccination that generally prevailed in 1871, cannot be the explanation of a small-pox mortality greater than in the worst years of London when there was no vaccination. Partial vaccination cannot be claimed as producing marvellous effects at one time and less than nothing at all at another time, yet this is what the advocates of vaccination constantly do. But on the sanitation theory the explanation is simple. Mercantile seaports have grown up along the banks of harbors or tidal rivers whose waters and shores have been polluted by sewage for centuries. They are always densely crowded owing to the value of situations as near as possible to the shipping. Hence there is always a large population living under the worst sanitary conditions, with bad drainage, bad ventilation, abundance of filth and decaying organic matter, and all the conditions favorable to the spread of zymotic diseases and their exceptional fatality. Such populations have maintained to our day the unsanitary conditions of the last century, and thus present us with a similarly great small-pox mortality, without any regard to the amount of vaccination that may be practiced. In this case they illustrate the same principle which so well explains the very different amounts of small-pox mortality in Ireland, Scotland, England, and London, with hardly any difference in the quantity of vaccination.

The Royal Commissioners, with all these facts before them or at their command, have made none of these comparisons. They give the figures of small-pox mortality, and either explain them by alleged increase or decrease of vaccination, or argue that, as some other disease—such as measles—did not decrease at the same time or to the same amount. therefore sanitation cannot have influenced small-pox. They never once compare small-pox mortality with general mortality, or with the rest of the group of zymotics, and thus fail to see their wonder-

fully close agreement—their simultaneous rise and fall, which
so clearly shows their subjection to the same influences and
proves that no special additional influence can have operated in
the case of small-pox."—Ibid, pages 51-52.

Prof. Wallace then proceeds to give two remarkable test
illustrations of the utter worthlessness of vaccination:—

"The first is that of the town of Leicester, which for the last
twenty years has rejected vaccination till it has now almost van-
ished altogether and small-pox is almost unknown. The
second is that of our army and navy, in which, for
a quarter of a century, every recruit has been re-vaccinated, unless he has been recently vaccinated or has had small-
pox. In the first we have an almost wholly unprotected population of nearly 200,000, which, on the theory of the vaccinators,
should have suffered exceptionally from small-pox; in the other
we have a picked body of 220,000 men, who, on the evidence
of the medical authorities, are as well protected as they know
how to make them, and among whom, therefore, small-pox
should be almost or quite absent, and small-pox deaths quite
unknown. Let us see, then, what has happened in these two
cases. In both it has been clearly proven that small-pox increased with the increase of vaccination, and decreased by sani-
tatiou, cleanliness, and hygienic living.

"Then commenced the movement (in Leicester) against
vaccination, owing to its proved uselessness in the great epidemic, when Leicester had a very much higher small-pox mortality than London, which has resulted in a continuous decline,
especially rapid for the last fifteen years, till it is now reduced
to almost nothing. * * * * * * * *

"The first thing to be noted is the remarkable simultaneous
rise of all four death rates to a maximum in 1868-72, at the
same time that the vaccination rate attained its maximum. The
decline in the death rates from 1852 to 1860 was due to sanitary
improvements which had then commenced; but the rigid enforcement of vaccination checked the decline owing to its producing a great increase of mortality in children, an increase
which ceased as soon as vaccination diminished. This clearly
shows that the deaths which have only recently been acknowledged as due to vaccination, directly or indirectly, are really so
numerous as largely to affect the total death rate; but they

were formerly wholly concealed, and still are partially concealed, by being registered under such headings as erysipelas, syphilis, diarrhoea, bronchitis, convulsions, or other proximate cause of death."

The small-pox history of Leicester presents one of the best object lessons of the past thirty years, for since the small-pox epidemic of 1871, the city not only rose in revolt and rid itself of the incubus of vaccination, but also instituted as thorough a system of sanitation as its crowded population of 180,000 would admit of. It therefore stands out clear and distinct above all the other cities in England, both as a rebuke to the vaccine practice, and as a testimony that salvation from zymotic infection lies in the direction of hygienic habits and surroundings. In 1894 Leicester had only seven vacinations to 10,000 of the population, while Birmingham had thirty times that proportion; and between 1891-94 Leicester had less than one-third the cases of small-pox and less than one-fouth the deaths in proportion to population, than well vaccinated Birmingham; whence it is readily seen that for both numbers and severity the facts are decidedly against vaccination.

"Now let us see how the commissioners, in their Final Report deal with the above facts, which are surely most vital to the very essence of the inquiry, and the statistics relating to which have been laid before them with a wealth of detail not equalled in any other case. Practically they ignore it altogether. Of course I am referring to the majority report, to which alone the government and the unenlightened public are likely to pay any attention. Even the figures above quoted as to Leicester and Warrington are to be found only in the report of the minority, who also give the case of another town, Dewsbury, which has partially rejected vaccination, but not nearly to so large an extent as Leicester, and in the same epidemic it stood almost exactly between un-vaccinated Leicester and well-vaccinated Warrington, thus :—

Leicester had 1.1 mortality per 10,000 living,

Dewsbury had 6.7 motality per 10,000 living,

Warrington had 11.8 mortality per 10,000 living.

"Here again we see that it is the unvaccinated towns that suffer least, not the most vaccinated.

* * * * * * * * * * * *

"What they urge is (the minority report), that sanitation and isolation are the effective and only preventives; and it was because Leicester attended thoroughly to these matters, and Gloucester wholly neglected them, that the one suffered so little and the other so much in the recent epidemic. On this subject every inquirer should read the summary of the facts given in the minority report, paragraph 261.

"To return to the majority report. Its references to Leicester are scattered over 80 pages, referring separately to the hospital staff, and the relations of vaccinated and unvaccinated to small-pox; while in only a few paragraphs do they deal with the main question and the results of the system of isolation adopted. These results they endeavor to minimize by declaring that the disease was remarkably 'slight in its fatality,' yet they end by admitting that the 'experience of Leicester affords cogent evidence that the vigilant and prompt application of isolation * * * * is a most powerful agent in limiting the spread of small-pox.' A little further on they say, when discussing this very point—how far sanitation may be relied on in place of vaccination—'The experiment has never been tried.' Surely a town of 180,000 inhabitants which has neglected vaccination for twenty years, is an experiment. But a little further on we see the reason of this refusal to consider Leicester a test experiment. Paragraph 502 begins thus: 'The question we are now discussing must, of course, be argued on the hypothesis that vaccination affords protection against small-pox.' What an amazing basis of argument for a commission supposed to be inquiring into this very point! They then continue: 'Who can possibly say that if the disease once entered a town the population of which was entirely or almost entirely unprotected, it would not spread with a rapidity of which we have in recent times had no experience?' But Leicester is such a town. Its infants—the class which always suffers in the largest numbers —are almost wholly unvaccinated, and the great majority of its adults have, according to the bulk of the medical supporters of vaccination, long outgrown the benefits, if any, of infant-vaccination. The disease has been introduced into the town twenty times before 1884, and twelve times during the last epidemic (Final Report, par. 482 and 483). The doctors have been asserting for years that once small-pox comes to Leicester it will run through the town like wild-fire. But instead of that it has been quelled with far less loss than in any of the best vaccinated towns in England. But the commissioners ignore this actual experiment, and soar into the regions of conjecture with, 'Who can possibly say?'—concluding the paragraph with—'A priori reasoning on such a question is of little or no value.' Very true. But a posteriori reasoning, from the cases of Leicester, Birmingham, Warrington, Dewsbury, and Gloucester, is of value; but it is of value as showing the utter uselessness of vaccination, and it is therefore, perhaps, wise for the professional upholders of vaccination to ignore it. But surely it is not wise for a presumably impartial commission to ignore it as it is ignored in this report."—"The Wonderful Century," pages 276-7.

"Although the commission makes no mention of Mr. Bigg's tables and diagrams showing the rise of infant-mortality with increased vaccination, and its fall as vaccination diminished, they occupied a whole day cross-examining him upon them, endeavoring by the minutest criticism to diminish their importance."

The second test illustration referred to a few pages back—that of the army and navy—is made complete and crucial by a comparison with Ireland, which is practically unvaccinated, while the army and navy are the most thoroughly vaccinated and re-vaccinated of any class in the whole population. In Dr. MacCabe's evidence before the Royal Commission, it appears but avery small proportion of the population in Ireland have been vaccinated, and in a thorough comparison which Prof. Wallace makes between Ireland, Scotland, England, and with the army and navy, he reaches the result that unvaccinated Ireland shows a smaller small-pox mortality than Scotland, enormously less than England, and overwhelmingly less than London. With seemingly little or no regard to vaccination, this graduated series of increase in small-pox mortality is in exact correspondence with increased density of population; while in these crowded centers we find that small-pox behaves in the same general manner as all the other zymotic diseases. One pays no more regard than the other to vaccination, but all have respect for cleanliness and hygienic living.

After discussing these features of the question, and after paying his respects to the Royal Commission, Prof. Wallace continues :—

"Now if there were no other evidence which gave similar results, this great test case of large populations compared over a long series of years, is alone almost conclusive; and we ask with amazement,—Why did not the commissioners make some such camparison as this, and not allow the public to be deceived by the grossly misleading statements of the medical witnesses and official apologists for a huge imposture? For here we have on one side a population which the official witnesses declare to be as well vaccinated and re-vaccinated as it is possible to make it, and which has all the protection that can be given by vaccination. It is a population which, we are officially assured, can live in the midst of the contagion of severe small-pox and not suffer from the disease 'in any appreciable degree.' And on comparing this population of over 200,000 men, thus thoroughly protected and medically cared for, with the poorest and least cared for portion of our country—a portion which the official witness regarding it declared to be badly vaccinated, while no amount of re-vaccination was even referred to—we find the less vaccinated and less cared for community to have actually a much lower small-pox mortality than the navy, and the same as that of the two forces combined. * * * *

"It is thus completely demonstrated that all the statements by which the public has been gulled for so many years, as to the almost complete immunity of the re-vaccinated army and navy, are absolutely false. It is just what Americans call 'bluff.' There is no immunity. They have no protection. When exposed to infection they do suffer just as much as other populations, or even more. In the whole of the nineteen years, 1878-1896 inclusive, unvaccinated Leicester had so few small-pox deaths that the Registrar General represents the average by the decimal 0.01 per thousand population, equal to 10 per million, while for the twelve years, 1878-1889, there was less than one death per annum.' Here we have real immunity, real protection; and it is obtained by attending to sanitation and isolation, coupled with the almost total neglect of the curse of vaccination. * * *

"Now if ever there exists such a thing as a crucial test, this of the army and navy, as compared with Ireland, and especially with Leicester, affords such a test. The populations concerned are hundreds of thousands; the time extends to a generation; the statistical facts are clear and indisputable; while the case of the army has been falsely alleged again and again to afford indisputable proof of the value of vaccination when performed on adults. It is important, therefore, to see how the commisssioners deal with these conclusive test cases. They were appointed to discover the truth and to enlighten the public and the legislature, not merely to bring together huge masses of undigested facts.

"What they do is, to make no comparison whatever with any other fairly comparable populations, to show no perception of the crucial test they have to deal with, but to give the army and navy statistics separately, and as regards the army piecemeal, and to make a few incredibly weak and unenlightening remarks. Thus, in par. 333, they say that, during the later years, as the whole force became more completely re-vaccinated, small-pox mortality declined. But they knew well that during the same period it declined over all England, Scotland, and Ireland, with no special re-vaccination, and most of all in unvaccinated Leicester! Then with regard to the heavy small-pox mortality of the wholly re-vaccinated and protected troops in Egypt, they say, 'We are not aware what is the explanation of this.' And this is absolutely all they say about it! But they give a long paragraph to the post office officials, and make a great deal of their alleged immunity. But in this case the numbers are smaller, the periods are less, and no statistics whatever afe furnished except for the last four years! All the rest is an extract from a parliamentary speech by Sir Charles Dilke in 1883, stating some facts, furnished of course by the medical officers of the post office, and therefore not to be accepted as evidence. This slurring over the damning evidence of the absolute inutility of the most thorough vaccination possible, afforded by the army and navy, is sufficient of itself to condemn the whole Final Report of the majority of the commisssioners. It proves that they

were either unable or unwilling to analyze carefully the vast
mass of evidence brought before them, to separate mere beliefs
and opinions from facts, and to discriminate between the statistics which represented those great 'masses of national experience' to which Sir John Simon himself has appealed for a final
verdict, and those of a more partial kind, which may be vitiated
by the prepossesssions of those who registered the facts. That
they have not done this, but without any careful examination
or comparison have declared that re-vaccinated communities
have 'exceptional advantages' which, as a matter of fact, the
report itself show they have not, utterly discredits all their conclusions, and renders this Final Report not only valueless but
misleading."—"The Wonderful Century," pages 285-6.

In addition to the above quotations, Prof. Wallace devotes
an entire chapter to a criticism of the Royal Commission on
Vaccination, in which their special pleading, their covert concealments, and their flagrant betrayal of the trust of the people
through Parliament committed into their hands are unsparingly
held up to view. But in this, as in nearly all similar bodies,
there were a few men of conscience and integrity, who put the
facts which were brought before them in their proper relation
and embodied them in a minority report. The commission as
a whole, however, conducted their investigations throughout
as though they regarded the Vaccine Establishment as their
clients, whom it was their duty to defend—even as a lawyer de-
fends a client by suppressing or disparaging the testimony that
bears on the other side.

A further word of comment relating to this Royal Commission may properly be inserted here. One redeeming feature of
the medical profession is found in the fact that a fair percentage
of its ablest members are loyal to the truth and have a large
measure of regard for the public welfare. A certain residue are
greedy and unscrupulous, and these are always plotting for
place and privilege and power; and as these—through the co-
operation of politicians—are opened and made accessible, they

are usually the foremost in securing official positions and places of responsibility. Now in the early history of vaccination this class secured state interference with a Compulsory Vaccination Law; but as the more conscientious and experienced physieiaus became fully convinced that vaccination was working great mischief in the community, they opposed the practice and agitated for reform. Through this public agitation the people became sufficiently enlightened on the subject to protest, and thousands refused to submit, or suffer their children to be vaccinated. Prosecutions, fines, and imprisonment followed.

The public clamor became widespread, and Parliament was repeatedly petitioned to repeal the law, which it refused to do. It was then asked to appoint a commission to investigate and report on their grievances. This also was repeatedly refused. Finally, after repeated refusals by the government, a Royal Commission of Inquiry on Vaccination was at length granted—in April, 1889. This was granted in consequence of popular pressure. It was professedly to be constituted a fair and impartial tribunal; but its real object was to "expose the distortions and misconceptions of the enemies of vaccination." It was really to become a "white-washing" commission to silence the public clamor and to intrench place-hunting officials and an army of vaccinators more strongly under the protection of the state. Not one of the fourteen members appointed was opposed to vaccination, though some of them did not favor compulsory legislation. Indeed, this commission of experts was a pretty good paralllel to that appointed in our own United States in 1898—also in obedience to popular clamor—ostensibly to investigate official abuses, but really to "white-wash" the "embalmed beef frauds" perpetrated on our soldiers in the field by corrupt agents who had pushed their way to the front and secured federal appointments. The commission found that our soldiers had "no occasion to complain (?)." The agents did the best they could under the circumstances. The system of

army contracts is a good one; it pays, and therefore the people
should submit without complaint. The "taffy" offered them by
this body of trained experts ought to taste good and quiet their
murmurings. Well, this Royal Commission spread its labors
over a period of seven years, on big government salaries, before
it made its final report. It is this report which Prof. Wallace
so unmercifully scores.

What I have said in the preceding paragraph may likewise
be applied in large part to the National Vaccine Establishment
in England, which was founded in 1806 and endowed by government with £3,000 per year. During the eight years succeeding
the Jenner discovery, cases of failure continued to multiply
which occasioned a deal of trouble to Jenner and his party to
explain away. So the doctors sought the co-operation of government to extend and perpetuate their schemes. Dr. Scott
Tebb, after detailing these early failures, continues:—

"The reports of failure at length became so numerous, that
it was found necessary to take action. In a letter to Mr. Dun-
ning in reference to Dr. Benjamin Moseley's publication of failures, Jenner expresses the opinion that nothing would crush
the hissing heads of such serpents at once but a general mani-
festo with the signatures of men of eminence in the profession,
unless Parliament had a mind to take the matter up again."

So Jenner had a conference with Lord Henry Petty (chan-
cellor of the exchequer) who gave assurances that he would
bring the matter forward in the ensuing session, which, when
convened (1806) was readily persuaded to vote the Crown an
address, praying "that His Majesty will be graciously pleased to
direct his College of Physicians to inquire into the state of vaccine inoculation in the United Kingdom, and to report their
opinion and observations upon that practice, the evidence which
has been adduced in its support, and the causes which have
hitherto retarded its general adoption; and that His Majesty

will be graciously pleased to direct that the said report, when made, may be laid before this House.

"The College reported favorably, and the National Vaccine Establishment was founded with a vaccine board of eight, each having a salary of £100 a year. Although the profession and Parliament had been practically committed to vaccination at the time of Jenner's petition (1802), this was the first instance of the establishment and endowment of the practice, and the natural tendency was to stifle opposition; indeed, it may be said that one of the principal functions of the National Vaccine Establishment was to explain away the failures of cow-pox to protect from small-pox. * * * * * * In some towns failures were such as to lead to a discontinuance of the practice. * * * * * * * The practice afterwards became more general, until the small-pox raged epidemically. It was then observed that many of the children who had been previously vaccinated, and were supposed to be secure, caught the complaint; some of them died and others recovered with difficulty."

—" A Century of Vaccination," pages 122-23.

In the "Medical Observer" for November, 1809, the details of fourteen fatal cases are given :—

"1· A child was vaccinated by Mr. Robinson, surgeon and apothecary, at Rotherham, towards the end of the year 1799. A month later it was inoculated with small-pox matter without effect, and a few months subsequently took confluent small-pox, and died.

"2· A woman-servant to Mr. Gamble, of Bungay, in Suffolk, had cow-pox in the casual way from milking. Seven years afterwards she became nurse to the Yarmouth Hospital, where she caught small-pox, and died.

"3 and 4. Elizabeth and John Nicholson, three years of age, were vaccinated at Battersea in the summer of 1804. Both contracted small-pox in May, 1805, and died. They were attended by Dr. Moseley and Mr. Roberts.

"5· Mr. J. Adams, of Nine Elms, contracted casual cowpox, and afterwards died of confluent small-pox.

"6· The child of Mr. Carrier, Crown Street, Soho, was vaccinated at the institution in Golden Square, and had small-pox three months afterwards, and died.

"7. Mary Pinney's child, aged one year, died of small-pox in July, 1805, five months after vaccination.

"8. The child of Mr. Blake's coachman, living at No. 5 Baker Street, died of small-pox after vaccination.

"9. Mr. Colson's grandson, at the 'White Swan,' White-~·~ss Street, aged two years, was vaccinated by a surgeon at Bishopsgate Street, in September, 1803. He died of confluent small-pox in July, 1805.

"10. Mr. Brailey's child, aged two years and eight months, was vaccinated at the Small-pox Hospital, and forty weeks after-wards died of confluent small-pox.

"11. Mr. Hoddinot's child, No. 17 Charlotte Street, Rathbone Place, was vaccinated in 1804 and the cicatrix remained. In 1805 it caught small-pox and died.

"12. C. Mazoyer's child, No. 31 Grafton Street, Soho, was vaccinated at the Small-pox Hospital. Died of small-pox October, 1805.

"13. The child of Mr. R—— died of small-pox in October, 1805. The patient had been vaccinated, and the parents were assured of its security. The vaccinator's name was concealed.

"14. The child of Mr. Hindsley at Mr. Adams' office, Pedler's Acre, Lambeth, died of small-pox a year after vaccination."

Such entire failures of vaccination, as a remedy or protection, multiplying on every hand, had no effect either on Parliament or the College of Physicians. The failures were concealed, glossed over or explained away. Once committed to the vaccine superstition there was no backing down to be thought of or tolerated. No confession of error must be allowed to cast reproach upon so learned a body as the College of Physicians. And then, it was a good thing—an establishment endowed by the crown; a goodly number of government offices with fair salaries; an army of vaccinators in government and municipal employ; these are not to be lightly surrendered. Christ—if he were here—might plead for the little ones, for the rising generation. But why should the rising generation stand in the way of business? "Business is business." "We must live." These

are corporation and class ethics, without soul, without conscience, cruel as fate, knowing no other object or goal than
what self interest dictates. This is the code by which oppressive
laws become recorded on our statute books, and are kept there;
the code by which otherwise good men will enter into compacts
which, in their composite character, become merciless tyran-
nies—a veritable car of Juggernaut—bearing down its victims
without pity and without remorse!

Again, the "Medical Observer" for August, 1810, states
that the poor of the parish of Witford, in Hertfordshire, were
vaccinated by Mr. Farrow, apothecary at Hadham, with matter
procured from London Cow-pox Institute. During the small-
pox epidemic that followed, of 69 vaccinated, 29 took small-pox,
nine of whom died. The editor gives a list of the fatal cases :—

Name.	Age.
William Barton	5 years
Mary Catmore	13 years
Ann Catmore	13 years
Emma Prior	6 months
Martha Wrenn	6 years
William Catmore	3 years
Charles Wybrow	6 months
John Fitstead	1 year
James Thoroughgood	2 years

—Tebb, page 129.

The "Medical and Physiological Journal," Vol. XXXII,
page 478, said the cases of failure at Creighton were so numerous
and decisive that they could not fail to excite alarm. Twenty-five
cases were given where the vaccinations were considered perfeet. In these cases the fever was violent; the heat was excessive,
the pulse very quick, universal languor, pain in the head and
loins, frequent vomiting; occasional delirium, and sometimes
convulsions.

In the same journal, Vol. XXXVII, pages 2 to 12, the following cases were reported:—

No.	Name.	Age when vaccinated.	By whom.	Age when infected with small-pox.	Nature of the Small-pox.
1	Robert Jones' two children..	Infants	Mr. Redhead	10–8	Small horny pox, which continned out only five or six days; were not seen by a medical man. One child had considerable fever during four days previous to the eruption
2	Elizabeth James	Infant	Mr. Harrison	12	Very feverish. Pustules distinct. A well-marked case of small-pox.
3	Jos. James.....	Infant	Mr. Redhead	15	Very feverish, and thought dangerously ill for a few days. Eruption not so full as with Elizabeth.
4	Wm. James....	Infant	Mr. Carter	8	Had them (eruptions) milder than the two former. Continued out a few days.
5	Wm. Parker .	4	Mr. Close, Dalton	18	Delirious two days before the eruption appeared. Pustules numerous, and continued out seven or eight days.
6	Elizabeth Fell	3	Mr. Briggs	12	Considerable fever previous to the eruption, which was of the distinct kind.
7	Maria Stable..	10	Mr. Carter	1)	Feverish before the eruption, which was of a small horny kind, and soon disappeared.
8	Betty Turner..	Infant	Mr. Redhead	6	Feverish three days, with delirium. Face full of pustules, and many on her body; small horny kind, which disappeared in five or six days.
9	Alice Turner.	Infant	Mr. Redhead	12	Feverish. Not so much indisposed as Betty; had fewer pustules, but larger.
10	Robert Braithwaite's daugh.	Infant	Mr. Carter	14	Very feverish. Had a full crop of small horny pox. Face swelled. Blind three days.
11	Mr. Rawlinson's son....	—	Mr Briggs	—	Much fever. Very full of pustules, and much marked.
12	Ellen Physaclea..........	Infant	Mr. Redhead	13	Very feverish. Had large distinct pox. Has marks on the face.
13	Wm. and Benjamin Kirby	5–3	Mr. T. Carter	—	The eruption on William was larger, and continued longer than the rest These two children were infected four weeks after vaccination. Pustules of the horny kind.
14	Joseph Kirby..	Infant	Mr Redhead	5	Got easily through the complaint.
15	Sarah Bond..	Infant	At Liverpool	12	Much fever, with delirium. Had many pustules of the horny kind, which soon disappeared.
16	Jane Ellis....	Infant	Mr Lodge, Ingleton	11	Had a remarkably full crop; in fact, was one complete cake of incrustation. Recovered pretty well, but is much marked. Was about a month confined.
17	Isabella Dixon	Infant	Mr. Harrison	10	Had a full crop. Is marked, but recovered well.
18	Marg'r't Dixon	Infant	Mr Redhead	12	Not very full. Pustules perfectly distinct. Recovered well.
19	Betty Garnet..	Infant	Mr. Carter	14	Distinct pustules. Was at the height in eight days, and recovered well.

Dr. Macleod—as quoted by Dr. Scott Tebb,—says:—
"I have seen too many instances of small-pox in children

vaccinated in London, where that process was carried on in the way which the National Vaccine Establishment has recommended as the most efficacious, to retain much faith in its preventive powers, in whatever manner conducted.' Again he remarks (pages 8-9):—'The history of vaccination altogether forms a severe satire upon the mutability of medical doctrines. In the first ardor of discovery, not contented with its blessings to mankind, its benefits were also extended to the brute creation. It was to annihilate small-pox, prove an antidote to the plague, to cure the rot in sheep, and preserve dogs from the mange. These good-natured speculations, however, were soon abandoned; and more recently all had agreed in acknowledging its anti-variolous powers, which, we were told, were as well-established as anything human could be.'

"But the present epidemic shows too clearly the mortifying fallibility of medical opinions, though founded on the experience of twenty years, and guaranteed by the concurring testimony of all the first physicians and surgeons in the world."

Sir Henry Holland—a high authority—indulges in expressions of disappointment in view of the general failure of vaccination as a protective against small-pox, and particularly its failure during seasons of epidemic, the only time such protection is really needed. In his "Medical Notes and Reflections," he writes:—

"Not only in Great Britain, but throughout every part of the globe from which we have records, we find that small-pox has been gradually increasing again in frequency as an epidemic; affecting a larger proportion of the vaccinated; and inflicting greater mortality in its results." Again he says (page 414):—"It is no longer expedient, in any sense, to argue for the present practice of vaccination as a certain or permanent preventive of small-pox. The truth must be told, as it is, that the earlier anticipations on this point have not been realized."

Dr. Gregory well observes:—"It is often noticed that persons—vaccinated or not—who resist small-pox in common years, though fully exposed to the contagion, are attacked by it in years of epidemic prevalence." This is well worth remembering. It has been illustrated scores of times in all civilized countries. It is indeed during seasons of small-pox epidemic that we most fully realize the utter worthlessness of vaccination—if we but use our eyes rationally. Yet with all these facts before them, boards of health in a great number of cities and towns in our own country, dogged on by a motley crew of second-rate doctors, drag forth a mouldy Compulsory Vaccination Act from its pigeon hole, and then order all school children vaccinated, on pain of expulsion from the public school, if their parents refuse. Why should not those who really think vaccination a protection be content when they get their own children vaccinated? If that is really their protection certainly they would receive no harm by contact with the unvaccinated.

But people are prone to compel their neighbors to adopt their own modes of thinking and practice. And then, this vaccination practice has become a business and source of revenue to a privileged class, which neither professional or politician will ever consent that it shall grow less. I say "professionals" with a qualification, since I have reference only to the mercenary class within the ranks of the medical profession. If this class do not constitute a majority, they have "cheek" sufficient to accomplish a vast amount of mischief. A mercenary doctor, lawyer, or priest is a curse in any community; but when they form cabals and compacts to perpetuate a monstrous practice they augment the curse into a public scourge!

The following items are from Dr. A. M. Ross' pamphlet, "Vaccination a Medical Delusion." Dr. Ross is a physician of high standing in Toronto, and is a prominent leader in the vaccination controversy in this country:—

"Whoever closely watched the course of the epidemic in Montreal must conclude that vaccination is utterly useless as a protection from small-pox. Much of what transpired in our small-pox hospitals was suppressed, especially whatever was likely to operate against the progress of vaccination, which proves a golden harvest to the vaccinators. But notwithstanding the conspiracy of silence a few official reports pregnant with proof against vaccination, and proving beyond question that a large proportion of the patients admitted into our small-pox hospitals had been vaccinated, and that many of them died, some with two and others with three, vaccine marks upon their bodies.

"I refer to the official report from the Civic Hospital, dated August 17, 1885: 'Up to this date, 133 patients suffering from small-pox have been admitted to the Civic Hospital; of these 73 were vaccinated, 56 had one mark, 13 two marks and 4 three marks.'

'I refer to the official report from St. Roch's Hospital, dated October 22, 1885: 'Number of vaccinated patients admitted since April ... 197.'

"I refer to the official report from St. Camille's Hospital, dated November 1 to 7, 1885: 'There are now in this hospital, 188 small-pox·patients; of these 94 are vaccinated. Among the dead are 12 who were vaccinated.'

"I refer to the first official report from St. Saviour's Hospital, November 1 to 7, 1885: 'Thirteen small-pox patients admitted; of these 9 were vaccinated and 4 (only) unvaccinated.'

"I refer to the official report from Crystal Palace Hospital, November 28 up to and including December 5, 1885: 'Number of patients admitted, 36; of these 19 were vaccinated.'

"I refer to the second official report from St. Saviour's Hospital, covering a period of 15 days, that is, from October 15 to 31, it was stated there had been in all 67 patients admitted, of whom 60 had been successfully vaccinated, 36 having two vaccination marks, 2 having three, and 3 having four.'

"I refer to the third official report from St. Saviour's Hospital, November 28 up to and including December 6, 1885:

'Number of patients admitted, 6: of these 4 bear evidence of vaccination, and 2 were not vaccinated.'

LATEST OFFICIAL TESTIMONY FROM ENGLAND.

"Read the following summary of the last report of the Registrar General of England, which proves conclusively that vaccination does not diminish or protect from small-pox:—

In the first 15 years after the passing of the Compulsory Vaccination Act, 1854 to 1868, there died of small-pox in England and Wales...............	54,700
In the second 15 years, 1869 to 1883, under a more stringent law, ensuring the vaccination of ninety-five per cent. of all children born, the deaths rose to	66,447

Total for 30 years.........................	121,147
Of these, there died under 5 years of age.............	51,472
From 5 to 10 years of age.........................	16,000

Total under 10 years.....................	67,472

Sir Thomas Chambers. Q. C., M. P., recorder of the city of London, says: "I find that of the 155 persons admitted to the small-pox hospital, in the parish of St. James, Piccadilly, 145 were vaccinated. At Hampsted Hospital, up to May 13, 1884, out of 2,965 admissions, 2,347 were vaccinated. In Marylebone, 92 per cent. of those attacked by small-pox were vaccinated."

"Of the 950 cases of small-pox, 1,870, or 91.5 per cent. of the whole cases, have been vaccinated."—Marson's "Report of Highgate Hospital for 1871."

"There were 43 cases treated in the Bromley Hospital between April 25 and June 29, 1881. Of confluent small-pox there were 16 cases; of discrete, 13; of modified, 13. All the cases had been vaccinated—three re-vaccinated."—F. Nicholson, L. R. C. P., "Lancet," Aug. 27, 1881.

But I must bring this chapter to a close, having already exceeded the limits I had assigned to prove that vaccination has failed to fulfill the flattering promises of its advocates and promoters. A volume could easily be filled with a record of these failures; but it is only a small part of my purpose to point out what vaccination has failed to do; I shall likewise hold up to view a portion of the detestable record of what it has done and is now doing in the world, as also some items of legislation which has made large portions of the general population involuntary and compulsory victims of this unholy covenant with disease, death, and hell.

The widespread mischief which inoculation—the forerunner of vaccination—accomplished in the eighteenth century, is less a matter of surprise when we compare that period of general intellectual enlightenment with the nineteenth century; but that vaccination should be so generally submitted to, or even tolerated as it has been the last fifty years, is one of those marvels which prove the desperate persistence of a practice when once it has become intrenched in the self interest of a privileged class, and when a powerful profession discover an adequate motive to invoke legislation to establish its permanence. It is incredible to believe—after the disclosure of such a multitude of facts, and after the amount of discussion already expended on the subject —that the majority of physicians who still continue to vaccinate have the slightest faith in the operation. Must we then conclude that the fee takes precedence in their minds over any public benefit they confer? Aye, must they not be conscious not only that they do not confer a benefit, but that they are corrupting the blood and undermining the health of a large percentage of the community, sowing seeds and planting upas trees which must eventuate in a terrible harvest of disease and death in the near future? If they do not realize the wrong they are perpetuating on the rising generation God pity their professional acumen; and may He with the good angels of heaven especially pity the little children who are turned over to the lance and putrid pus of this modern molock! Dion Casius, the Roman historian, writing of the plague which scourged Rome in the second century, relates: "many died in another way, not only at Rome but over nearly the whole empire, through the practice of miscreants, who, by means of small, poisoned needles, communicated, on being paid for it, the horrible infection so extensively that no computation could be made of the number that perished."

Unhappily, the "miscreants" are not all dead. They still walk the streets with their "poisoned needles" armed with a "permit" from the legislature to puncture and poison at so much per head, in the name of that public protection and benefit which they ruthlessly insult and over-ride. Look out for this public enemy reader, and bar your door against his approach!

Fifty years ago it was a serious thing to fall sick with fever and have a doctor—I mean the doctor was the serious part of the business—for in those old-time days the doctor said: "Cold water is death," and so fathers and mothers were solemnly forbidden to give a drop of cold water to the child, tossing with a raging fever, and vainly pleading like Dives for "just a drop" to quench the fire that was fast consuming the life. But the parent must refuse this agonizing appeal for the doctor had forbidden the cooling draught. Instead of water—the remedy which nature prescribed—it was mercury and blood-letting in those days which made the weary hours of sickness a crucifixion, and which left hundreds of thousands of human wrecks by the wayside. But we can forgive the average doctor of those days, since his sin was the sin of ignorance. Not so the vaccinator of today; he is sinning against the light, and his motives can plead no such excuse as we readily grant to members of the medical profession of fifty years ago.

CHAPTER IV

VACCINATION LEGISLATION.

"I can sympathize with, and even applaud, a father who, with the presumed dread in his mind, is willing to submit to judicial penalties rather than expose his child to the risk of an infection so ghastly as vaccination."—Sir Thomas Watson, M. D.

The Anglo Saxon peoples have always proved to be refractory soil in which to plant authoritative dogmas—medical or ecclesiastical—and then attempt to put them in force by legislative enactments. True, they will tolerate encroachments to a certain limit; for a time they will endure stripes and fines and persecution; but at last the spirit of liberty is sure to flame up in emphatic protest, when noble reformers enter the arena, a season of intense agitation ensues, and when the people are made fully aware whether legislative encroachments—in the interest and at the behest of a privileged class—are conducting them, they invariably rise and strike down the marauder, even though it involves a political revolution.

This insistence of the Saxon that his personal liberty shall be respected and held inviolate, has been illustrated in three notable instances in the last four hundred years in those world-famed movements headed by Luther, Cromwell, and Washington. The first was a successful protest against the divine right of the church to rule over both soul and body of the subject; the second was a revolt against the divine right of kings to rule over the citizen instead of guarding and protecting him in his rights; the third transferred sovereignty from the king to the people, and made the powers of government derivative from the people—made sovereignty to inhere in the people; but this chiefly in theory, since the people have not yet learned how to either protect or exercise that sovereignty in their associate capacity.

The people's sovereignty is continually being menaced by class interests which, through legislation, seek to acquire special privileges by which they may be able to compel them to pay a perpetual tribute. Last but not least among these class interests, is the vaccination syndicate, which is continually lobbying our legislatures for an extension of privileges on the pretense that the public welfare will thereby be enhanced. How exceedingly grateful the public ought to feel towards these gentlemen for their continued good health and welfare! But dear gentlemen, let me remind you—you who pose as government vaccination surgeons, members of departments of health, boards of health, municipal vaccinators, and small-pox scare promoters; let me remind you, your time is nearly up! The people—when a trifle better informed about what you are really doing—are going to get rid of this vile vaccination nuisance and turn you out of the office you have usurped, disgraced, and run for all the "traffic would bear." You will then be relegated to your proper station, put upon your good behavior, and compelled to wait until you are asked, before you will be permitted to enter our households with lance and putrid pus and run up a fee from one to three dollars per victim!

The government has no more constitutional right to compel the people to submit to vaccination in the nineteenth century, than it had in the eighteenth to enforce inoculation which is now made a penal offence, or of legalizing the mercury practice and blood-letting of the last generation. All these were once regarded as cure-alls and preventives, and would now be occasions for little harm so long as the people are left free to adopt or reject them. It is when physic and the state become united—when the state legalizes and enforces the creed of a particular sect in medicine—that the serious and fatal mischief begins to be manifest. No class or creed or practice was ever granted special recognition and support by the state that did not forthwith begin to abuse those powers and make of them an occasion for human oppression.

The people desire health and safety quite as much as the doctors desire it for them. And their common sense moreover demands the "open door" and a free struggle for the final survival of the "fittest" among the remedial agents brought forward. When these are found and tested —as cleanliness and wholesome living, for example—common sense people will adopt them without a resort to such coercive measures as repeated fines and imprisonments. Those who think vaccination is the absolute safeguard, by all means leave them free to erect this wall of protection, and then if vaccination is the thing they claim it is, at least they will not take the smallpox though every unvaccinated gentile falls a victim to the disease. Excuse us, gentlemen of the lancet, we do not propose to jump out of the "frying-pan into the fire" by substituting the doctor for the priest. You are all right in your proper place; but when we found the claws of the priest were growing too long for the safety of the innocents, we clipped them; and we warn you—gentlemen doctors—if you continue to press legislation to assist you in your vaccination scheme, we shall pretty soon clip your claws also. We don't mind having our bodies dragged through the mud now and then—good clean mud—but when you lobby the state to assist you in consigning our bodies, or our children's bodies, to the filthy pool of your vaccine putridity, we object; our Saxon patience has then gone beyond its limit, and unless you quit this business something serious is going to happen! Mark it well!

Happily, though compulsory vaccination laws are on the statute books of nearly every state in our commonwealth, they remain for the most part a dead letter on account of the extreme difficulty experienced in enforcing them. They are a flagrant violation of our constitution, and opposed to the genius and common sense of our average Anglo Saxon intelligence. And if the people adequately realized what consequences are involved by submitting themselves or their children to the vaccine poison, they would very soon sweep every vaccination act from our statute books, and relegate this vile superstition to the same obscure retreat to which the inoculation practice of the preceding century has been consigned. In the meantime, I should still leave the ordinary "scrub" doctor free to ventilate his fads, for so long as he would be unable to invoke compulsory legislation in behalf of his practice, the common sense of the citizen, left free to make his own choice, would in the long run choose what best conduces to his own health and welfare. Mrs. Eddy's unique medical creed may, or may not, benefit the world; at any rate, while left in free competition with the multiplicity of forms constantly arising for treating disease, it is quite powerless for harm. But if it were to receive state support and made compulsory, it would then become a glaring wrong and outrage which the people would be justified in overthrowing without much ceremony.

We should bear in mind that physic is in a state of transition. Harsh and drastic modes of treatment were common a century ago. These have been dropped by the profession, one after another, until now the instinctive calls of nature are more or less heeded by the practitioner, and the profession as a whole is daily approximating nearer and nearer a constructive art of healing, which takes more account of sanitation and hygienic living, and far less account of drugs and poisons—

whether taken into the stomach, or introduced directly into the blood through the skin, as in the accursed practice of vaccination. Inoculation has come and gone, taking with it its hundreds of thousands of victims. Calomel and bleeding have had their day as well as the good will of the profession, and during that terrible day the sick chamber was a torture chamber—a gloomy and dreadful place; the doctor's visit the most dreadful part of the composite calamity. The light of heaven and the free air were excluded; pure cold water was "sure death!" The life-blood was drained off through the puncture of the lancet; the mouth and throat and stomach were corroded with mineral poisons—and all this was part and parcel of the "healing art" of those days. From the time of Jesus Christ to the present it has been the same. The "woman' which had the issue of blood for twelve years, and had suffered many things of many physicians, and had spent all that she had, and was nothing bettered but rather grew worse," it seems had much the same experience with the doctors which each generation from that time to the present has repeated. Now we have the greater curse of vaccination, backed up by the state, and an effort by its promoters to make it compulsory and universal. But with the growing good sense of the medical profession, I apprehend this superstition would have been short-lived, but for the fact that the practice became allied with the modern commercial spirit and an unscrupulous class of medical men, who forecasted material advantages in an alleged discovery which they warranted as a sure safeguard against a disease in regard to which the public stand in constant dread.

The appointment of municipal boards of sanitation for the enforcement of cleanliness in crowded and filthy quarters is often urged by vaccinators as identical in principle with compulsory vaccination. I insist that it is nothing of the kind. Vaccination is the medical creed of the class, the relative value and the relative peril of which a diversity of opinion exists, both in the

community and among medical men; while no class or profession believe that any peril is threatened by thorough sanitation.
The public are in practical agreement touching its propriety and
necessity. Nobody has conscientious scruples against it. No
popular revolt ever rose up to fight against it as a common
enemy. The liberty of the citizen is not infringed by the most
thorough sanitary measures. Nor do we object to isolation and
quarantine during the prevalence of small-pox, yellow fever, or
cholera. To insist on the identity of these two procedures is another instance of "borrowing the robes of an angel to serve the
devil in." No, filth and vaccination are boon companions; they
both belong to the devil's order. Sanitation, like the golden
rule, belongs to the divine order, which nobody but the devil or
the devil's servants will oppose, or otherwise attempt to identify
with their own abominable practices.

COMPULSORY VACCINATION IN ENGLAND AND EXTENT OF REPEALS EFFECTED.

Before the repeal of the compulsory clause in the English
vaccination acts in England, there was annually paid out of the
public funds on account of vaccination, over half a million dollars, while the aggregate receipts of private practitioners must
have been largely in excess of this; and well do these gentry understand how to multiply their fees. A few cases of small-pox
are reported, and immediately a rumor is started which is taken
up by the press, and a small-pox scare is soon spreading terror
among the populace. Then the vaccination harvest follows.

As in all reforms, so in this, the laity are the first to abandon vaccination; for the medical profession has an interest in
addition to the pecuniary one. Having once committed itself—
save an honorable minority—to vaccination as a beneficent discovery and great boon to humanity, and having adhered to this

medical creed for the space of a century, it will not do now to show the "white feather;" not do to "back water," to surrender prestige by a confession that the profession framed a monstrous fallacy into its medical creed, which would be an imputation of fallibility. No, it is the air and attitude of infallibility that must be uniformly maintained. Keep the purple robe on the medical oracle and insist that he shall stick to a lie when once told. This is better than the modest truth coupled with a confession that the College of Physicians made a great mistake when they took Jenner to their bosom and asked Parliament to vote him £30,000.

When compulsory vaccination was urged upon the attention of Parliament (1853) for adoption, the lords and commons were assured that the medical profession were practically unanimous on two fundamental points in the vaccination controversy:—

(1) That vaccination is an absolute protection against small-pox, and therefore that the vaccination of the entire population would prevent small-pox epidemic.

(2) That universal vaccination involves no risk to life or health; that the operation is of a benign character and free from peril.

This protection was promised by Lord Lyttleton, the promoter of the Vaccination Bill of 1853, upon the unanimous assurance of the entire medical profession. And when still more stringent legislation was demanded and secured by the doctors in 1867, Lord Robert Montagu, who introduced the bill, re-affirmed the original promise, and declared it to be absolutely certain that no person after vaccination could thereafter be in danger of an attack from small-pox. Today there is not a director of a small-pox hospital in the civilized world who holds to that extraordinary view of vaccination.

The worst epidemic of the century (1871-72), which ravaged thoroughly vaccinated communities, causing the death of

50,000 persons, in England and Wales, gave a most emphatic negative to the assurances of Lord Lyttleton in 1853, and by Lord Montagu in 1867 in behalf of the doctors.

In regard to the second claim, namely, that the operation is "benign and free from peril," we have already seen how absolutely untrue it is; and I promise that I shall in later chapters summon a "cloud of witnesses" to prove the terrible consequences which have resulted from the perpetration of this crime, in the name of the law, on the bodies of millions of defenceless victims. There is now on record in the London archives hundreds of pages of evidence brought before the Royal Commission, which declares that loathsome and incurable diseases—syphilis, leprosy, cancer, etc.—have been inoculated into healthy persons at the point of the vaccinator's lancet; and these facts were fully known to the profession when they lobbied to secure more stringent acts for the most complete enforcement of compulsory vaccination. The Borgia, in the sixteenth century, were distinguished for their cunning, cruelty, and perfidy. They plotted and poisoned to remove people who were in their way—if it were a pope, it didn't matter—they resorted to cruelty and perfidy to secure the places and livings they coveted. How much better than these will the vaccination plotters stand in the day of judgment?

Compulsory vaccination laws were passed in England in 1853, 1861, 1867, 1871, 1874, and 1878. In 1840 a vaccination act was passed, making inoculation a penal offence, and providing facilities for public vaccination, but the compulsory vaccination was not enforced until 1853, which made neglect of vaccination punishable by fine and imprisonment. The most important act of the whole series, however, was that of 1867, which imposed upon guardians the duty of seeing that all children were vaccinated; and empowering them to appoint and pay officers to prosecute, fine and imprison all recalcitrant parents. True, no person in England has ever been vaccinated by main force;

but the repeated fines and imprisonment of the poor for refusal to comply, is equivalent to force, since the punishment inflicted exhausts their entire resources and wears them out. In Germany compulsion is applied literally, as any person who objects is held down by four men and vaccinated by force.

Until 1867 no great amount of pressure was brought to bear to compel obedience to compulsory legislation; but after that date, the doctors having secured a more vigorous law, began to push the vaccinating business with enterprising zeal and persistence. About 25,000 prosecutions were made in the interval of five years before 1873. During the six years following, the total number of persons proceeded against under the vaccination acts, was 34,286. Of these 136 were committed to prison, 19,482 were fined, 14 were bound over, and 7,354 suffered various kinds of punishments. The number of prosecutions reached their maximum in 1888, when vaccinations and prosecutions both began to rapidly decline, because boards of guardians were now being confronted with a thoroughly aroused public sentiment and protest against these outrageous and oft repeated insults against personal liberty. A house to house census, taken about this time in a hundred towns and districts by sturdy members of the opposition—which had now become organized—revealed 87 per cent. of the people opposed to compulsory vaccination, and 68 per cent. opposed to both state interference and to the vaccine practice.

Among the British colonies, Canada, Queensland, and New South Wales, there has never been any compulsory legislation on vaccination. In New Zealand they have a compulsory law, but public sentiment is decidedly against its enforcement, and therefore it remains practicallly a dead letter. In Tasmania a law was on the statute books for some years, but it has finally been repealed. In Switzerland vaccination was rejected at the referendum by a large majority in 1882. It has also been abandoned by Holland. In state-ridden Germany the doctors are

backed up by the government on this question; yet it is signif-
ieant that the emperor will not permit his own children to be
vaccinated. (See Vac. Inq. July, 1892.) At last in England, by
the recent vaccination Act (1898), the compulsory feature in the
vaccination laws was repealed. So Switzerland and grand old
England, after discussing the matter in parliaments for ten or a
dozen years, hearing the reports and sub-reports from men
having small-pox hospitals in charge, have rescinded the compulsory features in their vaccination laws, and have thereby
lifted a degrading and oppressive yoke which had fettered and
galled the people to the utmost limit of endurance. Don't forget
that in republican Switzerland and conservative old England,
vaccination is now optional with parents and the people. And
yet, be it said to the shame of America, that we still permit this
foul blot from the filth pens of barbarism to smear and blacken
the uages of our statute books. Shame on the state that legalizes prize fights, "embalmed beef," cow-pox virus, discourages
woman's suffrage, and persecutes the Mormons. Shame on the
state that shuts the door of the school room against the child
whose parent has sufficient enlightened common sense not to
submit that child to the abominable pollution which, like a
fanged serpent, strikes the victim from the point of the vaccinator's lance! Indeed, the Garrison's and Philipp's and Parker's
have only entered the American vaccination arena to sound the
clarion of reform. Not long—not long will the parents of the
land permit this brazen marauder to flaunt his legal credentials
as a badge of privilege to continue in his merciless slaughter of
the innocents!

ORGANIZED ASSAULT AGAINST VACCINATION IN GREAT BRITAIN.

Previous to 1880 the numerous reformers that entered the
field to battle against this common enemy, fought single-handed.

and though they did much in the way of enlightening the general public on the real dangers of the vaccine practice, they accomplished little or nothing toward mitigating the oppressive laws that were in force throughout the kingdom. The effect of the vigorous measures adopted after the great small-pox epidemic of 1871-72, called for an organized and more skillfully conducted movement against compulsory legislation. Hence the formation of the "London Society for the Abolition of Compulsory Vaccination." Notices were sent to every known anti-vaccinator in the kingdom, requesting their attendance at a meeting called in London, Feb. 12, 1881. Only eight persons responded to this call. These met in an upper room at 76 Chancery Lane. In our Revolutionary war for American Independence, the ball opened with the banding together of seven famous leaders. In this later movement the forces mobilized with one better,—there were eight, but these were scarred veterans who had seen service on many a battle-field. One—Mr. William Tebb—fought by the side of Garrison in our own anti-slavery struggle. This little organization included a chairman, secretary, treasurer, and a provisional executive committee. Everybody told them their enterprise was the most insane project that pestilent agitators and lunatics ever attempted to devise. But they were neither daunted nor discouraged, for the spirit of martyrs and the sublime devotion of Apostles was in their hearts and heads. The London journals ridiculed and abused; the doctors warned; the proprietors of public halls closed their doors "for fear of the Scribes and Pharisees." Bill stickers refused to post their bills lest they should lose their jobs. The thorny path of the reformer was indeed theirs to traverse; but the field of their operations gradually widened; adherents multiplied; new centers for propaganda were established; literature was circulated; the "Vaccination Inquirer" was launched, and writers of ability rallied around their standard. The following year (1881), a new and powerful impulse was given to the movement, by the access of P. A. Taylor, S. P., for Leicester, who was made president and became a powerful advocate of the abolition cause. Within two years 300,000 pamphlets had been published and circulated.

Perhaps the most notable event in the history of this organized crusade, was the "Leicester Demonstration." In that city the doctors had overdone the business of coercive vaccination and public prosecutions, until the people rose en masse in open revolt. Upright, well-to-do and patriotic citizens of Leicester had been imprisoned, dragged through the streets hand-cuffed, and subjected to the most degrading punishments, because they stood for the defense of their children against the detested vaccinator's poison. This public demonstration and popular protest included a procession two miles long. Hundreds of flags and banners with pictorial displays and a comic setting forth of the Jenner imposture, were carried, of which I will here append a sample :—

Entire Repeal and no Compromise.

Sanitation not Vaccination.

From Horse Grease, Cow-pox, Calf Lymph, and the Local Government Board "Good Lord Deliver Us."

Better a felon's cell than a poisoned babe.

Who would be free themselves must strike the blow.

It is not small-pox you are stamping out, but human creatures' lives.

Revolt against bad laws is a christian virtue and a national duty.— Wm. Tebb, "Fourteen Years Struggle ," page 8.

The vaccination acts were publicly burned in the market place, in presence of the mayor and other public officials. In the evening there was a large mass meeting and energetic speeches. I have in previous chapters made prominent mention of Leicester, as the foremost city in England which has come to the front, not only in the complete over-throw of the vaccination practice, but with the most rational method for stamping out small-pox which any crowded population has yet devised; namely, in a thorough system of sanitation, which, though diminishing doctor's fees to an alarming extent, gives a most satisfactory result in an enormous reduction of zymotic diseases over other cities in England. This was one of the practical fruits springing out of the labors of the society which only the year before organized with eight members.

In 1888 and 1889 the labors of the London society were powerfully accelerated by the appearance of two able works against vaccination, by the highest authorities in England—Dr. Creighton and Prof. Crookshank. The former is a distinguished graduate of Cambridge, and at the top of his profession as a pathologist; while Dr. Crookshank is professor of comparative pathology and bacteriology in Kings College, London. Dr. Sir Benjamin Ward Richardson, in a critical review of Prof. Crookshank's work, concludes :—

"The work as a whole is one of reference to which the people, as well as the profession, will often turn. Already, indeed, the people have turned to it, and the so-called anti-vaccinators with a relish of revenge which is quite dramatic to see, have literally grabbed it. To many of them the work, without doubt, affords a vindication of much that has been said against vaccination, especially on the point of the evidence adduced by the too earnest advocates of vaccination and the method of enforcing it by compulsory law on free and yet sceptical members of the community. Some will feel that this disqualifies the book in a professional point of view. It should not do so. If it be true that we of physic have really, for well-nigh a century past, been worshipping an idol of the market-place, or even of the theatre, why, the sooner we cease our worship and take down our idol, the better for us altogether. We have set up the idol, and the world has lent itself to the idolatry, because we, whom the world has trusted, have set the example. But the world nowadays discovers idolatries on its own account; and if we continue the idolatry it will simply take its own course, and, leaving us on our knees will march on whilst we petrify."
—Wm. Tebb's Pamphlet, page 10.

Previous to the public appearance of Doctors Creighton and Crookshank in the vaccination controversy, the reformers chiefly depended upon laymen for their literary authority on the vaccination practice; and these, medical men affected to wholly despise and discredit. In Doctors Creighton and Crookshank however, they found foemen worthy of their steel.

Soon after the appearance of Dr. Creighton's work, Mr. William White, an accomplished literary champion of the anti-vaccination cause, and author of "The Story of a Great Delusion," wrote:—

"Lord Wolseley says the first axiom of war is to know everything about your enemy. It is an axiom we ought to realize about vaccination. If we are to prevail, it is not sufficient to dislike the practice; we must dislike it intelligently. On the political side we have some powerful allies; our weakness has hitherto lain on the medical side. We are told that medical authority is against us overwhelmingly, which is true, although we might dispute the grounds of that assertion. There is scarcely an affirmation by any authority relative to vaccination that is not contradicted by some other authority equally authoritative. Such is our position, and the trouble has hitherto been that we could not obtain a hearing for the facts against authority. The inconsistencies of the practice and its multiform irrationality have been persistently disregarded. A front of brass has been maintained towards the public by the medical profession.

"This situation has been completely changed by Dr. Creighton's exposition and criticism. Upwards of twelve months have elapsed since his 'Natural History of Cow-pox' was published. It has been widely read and indifferently reviewed, but, so far, not a single statement made in its pages has been impugned. Next, in the 'Encyclopaedia Britannica,' the article 'Vaccination' has been written by Dr. Creighton, wherein he re-states his position as to the origin and character of cow-pox, its irrelevance to small-pox, its consequent impotence as a preventive of that disease, and its close analogy to syphilis.

"Now another work has been published by Dr. Creighton, the title and contents of which are given above, in which he reviews the history of vaccination, and describes the various arts and manoeuvres whereby it was conjured into popularity in England and the Continent. It is an extraordinary history, full of interest and instruction; and no attentive reader who takes up Dr. Creighton's volume will lay it down a believer in the Jennerian craft."

The following letter by Mr. William Tebb, which appeared in the "Manchester Guardian," shows the general situation in 1892:—

"Sir.—The importance of the unanimous recommendations of the Royal Commission in their recent interim report, the promise of the government to consider the weight of evidence upon which this recommendation was made, and the notice given by Lord Herschell to call attention to the subject at an early day, prompt me to ask permission to present certain considerations which, in view of the present state of the question, can hardly be disregarded at this juncture. When Lord Lyttleton introduced the first Vaccination Bill, in 1853, he stated that the absolute protection from small-pox by Jenner's prescription was a point upon which the entire profession were agreed. Nothing was said about a temporary benefit which needed renewing by re-vaccination or was effective only when conjoined with improved sanitation. Nor was there any allusion to the risk of disease and death now admittedly attendant upon the operation. The evidence disclosed before the Royal Commission shows that vaccination has been a failure from its commencement, and this failure, coupled with the mischievous results of the practice in spreading serious diseases, has caused a widespread and constantly augmenting opposition to the law. The feeling is so acute in places like Keighley, Gloucester, Eastbourne, Leicester, Oldham, and other towns, that thousands of intelligent people declare they would suffer any punishment rather than expose their children to the perils of vaccination. A large majority of the people of England (including nearly all the working classes), are opposed to compulsory vaccination, as I have found by personal inquiries in every part of the United Kingdom. Household censuses made in about 100 towns and districts show that 87 per cent. are opposed to compulsion and that 68 per cent. have no faith in vaccination whatever.

"It is unfortunate that the evidence laid before the Royal Commission on vaccination should have been given with closed doors, no newspaper reporter being allowed to be present, so that the public are still uninformed of the extent to which vaccination has been discredited. On numerous occasions when the houses of vaccine recalcitrants have been stripped of furniture, or when anti-vaccinators have been handcuffed and sent to prison, large bodies of exasperated citizens have assembled and the public peace has been endangered. I have been told again and again by the more ardent spirits of this prolonged struggle, especially by those who have suffered numerous prosecutions or had their children injured by vaccination, that unless they resorted to violence they would never get the law repealed. I have unfailingly counselled the use only of active but legitimate means of agitation, and begged them not to disgrace the cause by overt acts, inasmuch as by the exercise of patience and devotion we should be sure to win, the best forces of society being with us. There is a limit to this forbearance, which will not, like Tennyson's brook, 'go on forever,' and the patience of the long-suffering people is already well-nigh exhausted. If new legislation is enacted, as recommended by the Royal Commission, and compulsion is continued even to the extent of one penalty, and that a nominal one, the government will be subjected to daily defeat and defiance. In the interests of public order, a modus vivendi should be established, as with the Quakers, Nonconformists, Catholics, Jews, and infidels.—Yours, etc.,
WILLIAM TEBB.
Devonshire Club, St. James's, London, June 9, 1892.

Four years before the object of the London Society was consummated, in the midst of the heat and struggle for emancipation from the vaccination tyranny, Wm. Tebb penned the following temperate but earnest words:—

"I would specially take this opportunity to call upon all boards of guardians, in the exercise of that discretion which the law gives them, to abstain from prosecution which inflames popular passions and creates an acute sense of injustice. I would also urgently appeal to our fellow countrymen and country women who cherish liberty, to countenance and aid us in this righteous struggle for parental emancipation. I would respectfully invite the press throughout the land to give wide publicity to the resolution of the London Society, exposing the unfair treatment we have received at the hands of the Royal Commission."

It is generally conceded to the meanest and most wicked criminal, that he has some redeeming feature; that he is not wholly and hopelessly depraved. This much too, we may concede to the Royal Commission, which though appointed and instructed to ascertain and report the facts upon the whole vaccination controversy, was nevertheless privately acting in the interest of a vaccination clique—a combination of vaccine promoters—apparently determined that the vaccination interests should "pass muster." It was not the people of England, but the vaccine syndicate whom the commission evidently regarded as their real clients, and whom they were bound in honor to vindicate at all hazards.

In their interim report the commission recommended the exemption from compulsion of the "conscientious objector." They did this, however, because the popular clamor had reached the danger point, and because the House of Commons had come to recognize the practical impossibility of forcing English people to obey a law which they practically regarded as committing them to a species of self-destruction. After forty-six years of compulsory vaccination over one-half of the 270 boards of guardians were declining to put the Act in operation on account of the vigorous nature of the popular revolt. Not only this, but boards of guardians were being elected all over the kingdom on the express ground that they pledged themselves not to enforce the act. Every effort has been made to force the boards to make the vaccination laws operative, but to little purpose. The board in Keighley, in Yorkshire, was sent to prison, but they had to be let out, and the local government board found that as long as representative government was left the people, they could not be ruthlessly trodden upon until hopelessly deprived of personal liberty.

But why this stubborn persistence on the part of the government, in cramming vaccination down the throats of a long-suffering and unwilling people? Answer: A corrupt ring of medical gentlemen had lobbied a measure through Parliament, and by false promises secured a compulsory law, which their pecuniary and professional interests required should be vigorously enforced; and the government was constantly reminded that it was expected to faithfully perform its part of the agreement with the doctors; which it did until it found it had a thoroughly aroused and indignant public sentiment to reckon with. This is certainly the most rational explanation which the case will admit of.

The main feature of the Vaccination Act of 1898 is the "conscience clause"—properly the common sense clause:—

"(Sec. 6). No parent or other person shall be liable to any penalty under section twenty-nine or section thirty-one of the Vaccination Act of 1867, if within four months of the birth of the child he satisfies two justices or a stipendiary or metropolitan police magistrate, in petty sessions, that he conscientiously believes that vaccination would be prejudicial to the health of the child, and within seven days thereafter, delivers to the vaccination officer for the district, a certificate by such justices or magistrate of such conscientious objection."

In all other regards vaccination is still compulsory in England. The dissentient can avoid arrest, fines and imprisonment only by working the "conscience racket," which he will probably not be slow in doing since only vaccination promoters and the uninformed portion of the community have any interest to continne their connection with the business firm at the "old stand."

REVOLT AGAINST COMPULSORY VACCINATION IN INDIA.

The report of the working of the vaccination department in Bengal for 1872, the commissioner says the compulsory law in the rural districts is practically a dead letter. Vaccination is rejected by all high class Hindoos—the Brahmins, Burmahs, Rajputs, and Marwaries; while among the Mohammedans, the Ferazis hold the rite in the utmost contempt. Nearly every village—according to the commissioner's report—many families persistently refuse vaccination, and secrete their children to escape the vaccinators.

In order to overcome these prejudices, advantage was taken of the Hindoo's known reverence for their ancient sages and philosophers, by palming off upon them deliberate literary frauds. A Mr. Ellis, of Madras, well versed in Sanscrit literature, composed a short poem in the native's language on vaccination, tracing the origin of vaccine pus to their sacred cow. This he professed to have deciphered from very ancient parchments. In Bengal, similar attempts were made to deceive the inhabitants. Some very ancient leaves were purported to have been found, containing a chapter on "Masurica," or chickenpox. The doctors quoted the following words, which they alleged were contained in the ancient Sanscrit, on these musty parchments :—

"Taking the matter of pustules, which are naturally produced on the teats of cows, carefully preserve it, and, before the breaking out of small-pox, make with a fine instrument a small puncture (like that made by a gnat) in a child's limb, and introduce into the blood as much of the matter as is measured by a quarter of a ratti. Thus the wise physician renders the child secure from the eruption of the small-pox."

—See "Life of Jenner," by Bazon, Vol. I, page 557.

Think of it—forgery—the actual forgery of manuscripts to keep the Hindoo mind chained to the blood-poisoning Moloch, vaccination. What could be more infamous?

It is much like the practice imputed to the church in generations long gone by; namely, that it is right and proper to lie and deceive when the interests of the church could thereby be enhanced. At any rate, the vaccination-business syndicate is up to that sort of thing, not seeming to recognize even a remote connection between corporation-conscience and Sunday service. In India, it can be shown that this species of deception has been practiced on a large scale. Not only this, and notwithstanding the multiplied proofs that vaccination in that country, is not only a complete failure as a prophylactic against smallpox, but a cruel injustice to the native population. Yet there are plenty of English doctors continually plotting to extend coercive legislation and increase the penalties for non-compliance with the law. When the Vaccination Bill of 1892 was before the Bombay legislative council, to make vaccination compulsory in certain additional districts, a native Brahmin asked for an amendment, and pointed out the danger of transmitting leprosy and syphilis by means of arm-to-arm vaccination, and then read before that body a letter from a Brahmin physician—Dr. Bahadurjee—in which he writes:—

"In answer to your letter in which you ask me my personal opinion on the arm-to-arm vaccination method, which it is intended to be enforced by the new Vaccination Bill, I have no hesitation in saying that, besides it being not suited to the peculiar conditions which obtain in this country, on professional grounds the method is objectionable, and for these reasons:—

1. Arm-to-arm vaccination obviously acts as a channel for the transference of some skin diseases, and affords a ready means for propagating such inherited constitutional taints as those of syphilis and leprosy. No doubt, special rules, with full details, will be framed for the guidance of the operators in their selection of proper subjects, with a view to avoid those mishaps; but

having regard to the class of men from whom the supply of district vaccinators is to be obtained, the detailed rules will be of as much use to them as the paper on which they were printed

II. Syphilitic taint does not necessarily show itself in ill-health at the early age at which vaccination is practiced and demanded by law. A child may be in fair health, and yet have inherited syphilis. Moreover, syphilis does not stamp itself on the face and arms, so much as on the back and legs—parts not generally examined by the vaccinator, and thus apt to be overlooked. Only yesterday I was asked to see a case of skin disease in a child. On stripping the child bare, I found him fairly healthy to look at, and could see no skin blemish on his person. But closer examination of the hidden parts revealed the presence of unmistakable condylomata (syphilitic). These condylomata unnoticed, I should have passed the child as a very fair specimen of average health, and a fit subject to take the lymph from. Syphilis, as betrayed in obtrusive signs, is not difficult to recognize, but when concealed, as is more often the case, it is by no means easy to detect it.

III. In the case of leprosy it is still worse. There is no such thing as a leper child or infant. The leper heir does not put on its inherited exterior till youth is reached. And it is by no means possible by any close observation or examination of a child to say that it is free from the leprous taint. Surely arm-to-arm vaccination will not help to stamp out leprosy. On the contrary, it has been asserted, and not without good reasons, that it has favored the propagation of the hideous disease.

IV. It is acknowledged that extreme care is required in taking out lymph from the vesicles to avoid drawing any blood, for blood contains the germs of disease. Extreme care means great delicacy of manipulation, and delicacy of manipulation with children is not an easy task, and requires some experience and training. Is this to be expected from the class of men who are going to act as public vaccinators in the districts? Supposing a district vaccinator to acquire it to some extent after considerable practice, what about the delicacy of manipulation of one newly put on?

V. Puncturing a vesicle with such delicacy as not to wound its floor and draw blood is one great difficulty. But the selection of a 'proper' vesicle is another as great if not a greater difficulty. Products of inflammation are charged with the germs of disease, the contagion of contamination media, as much as the blood itself is. And the contents of an inflamed vesicle are quite as contaminating as the blood itself of a subject who, though charged with the poison of (inherited) syphilis or leprosy, has ,none of the obtrusive signs of the taint for identification. And as here inflamed, i. e., angry-looking vesicles are not the exception but the rule, as can be easily told by personal observation and experience and equally easily surmised if the habits of our poor be duly considered. Thus, even if no blood is drawn, the danger of transferring constitutional taints by the arm-to-arm method is by no means small; remembering that leprosy that claims India, and not England, for one of its homes, does not admit of any detection on the person of a subject from whose arm lymph may be taken, and that syphilis is more often difficult to detect than otherwise, and remembering, also, that both these are often met with largely in some districts."

—"Leprosy and Vaccination," Wm. Tebb, page 355.

In nearly every village in India arrests and imprisonments for evading vaccination are of daily occurrence. Of this I speak from personal knowledge having witnessed the fact during my several visits to India and Ceylon. There are numerous families who if they fail to keep their offspring out of reach of the detested vacinator, after his departure they employ every means to wash and rub out the vaccine poison; suck it out, cauterize the wound, and treat it much as we should a rattlesnake bite, or the bite of a mad dog. In a future chapter I shall return to the case of India again.

VACCINATION IN THE WEST INDIES.

On the Island Barbados, with a population of 1,096 to the square mile, there is no compulsory vaccination. The popular feeling in the island is so vigorously emphatic against vaccination, that its advocates are afraid to move in the matter, and any attempt to enforce it would undoubtedly create a riot. William Tebb, who made the tour of the island in 1888, interrogated all classes upon this question and he writes :—

"From the chief justice, Sir Conrad Reeves, to the poorest boatman or sugar plantation laborer, from one end of the island to the other, I failed to discover a single advocate of compulsion. Let those have it who want it, but don't force it upon me and mine, was the general straightforward reply."

Yet epidemics are less frequent in this island than in the well vaccinated islands of Jamaica, Martinique, Guadeloupe, and Hayti. Another reason why they have kept compulsory vaccination at bay, is that they have representation in the government of the island.

In Grenada, another island under English rule, the people being less proud and independent, compulsion is enforced with a rigor which amounts to cruelty, and as might be expected, small-pox frequently occurrs.

The following is from a local paper, "The Grenada People," June 9, 1892 :—

"During this week, upwards of thirty or forty of the peasants have been hauled before the police magistrate of the southern district for alleged violation of the vaccination act. In nearly every case fines of half-a-crown have been imposed, representing almost half of the week's wages which these unfortunates, if they are employed, can hope to earn. In face of the Royal Commission on Vaccination, we do not see why the old law, making vaccination compulsory should be still enforced. At most, it is of doubtful benefit; and doctors differ as to the positive good or injury which it does. The advocates of Jenner's specific can quote very few cases, if any, in its support; whilst its opponents point with force and truth to the positive injury it has inflicted. Here, in Grenada, pure lymph is seldom employed. As a consequence, many of the children submitted to the process of vaccination contract therefrom fatal diseases. The lymph, in many cases, is collected from children inheriting a taint of the scrofulous disease which prevails amongst the peasantry; and many an otherwise healthy child, after the process

of vaccination, presents the appearance of a disgustingly yaw-
sey patient. As eminent medical men differ as to the value and
utility of vaccination, we think it ought not to be made an offence punishable by fine or imprisonment if parents refuse to
vaccinate their children; but that the law should be amended
in the direction suggested by the Royal Commission in their recent report, i. e., it should be optional with the parent whether
the child should be vaccinated or not."

ON THE CONTINENT.

Among the Latin populations—France, Austria, Italy, and
Spain—where personal liberty is taken far less account of than
among Anglo-Saxon peoples, the government has far less
trouble in carrying out compulsory legislation. In France it
has not generally been as rigorously enforced as in England.
The higher thinking classes generally opposed it; but new regulations are coming into force which makes vaccination a necessary preliminary for admission into the public schools and into
the army. In Italy the vaccination laws are extremely stringent
and yet they are yearly meeting with stronger opposition. The
authorities are disposed to attribute the spread of small-pox in
all cases to the existence of a small percentage of vaccinated
persons; and this in face of the fact that large sections of the
Italian population live in the midst of notoriously filthy conditions. There are many eminent medical men in Italy, however,
who view this whole subject from the most enlightened stand-
point; and if once the commercial element could be eliminated
from the vaccination practice, it would take but a short time to
consign the superstition—so far as legislation is concerned—to
the under-world where eighteenth century inoculation has gone.

In Holland, Switzerland, Belgium, Norway and Sweden, no
soldier is now compelled to be vaccinated. In Switzerland, the
terrible effects which followed many cases of vaccination caused

"Vaccination is the Curse of Childhood."

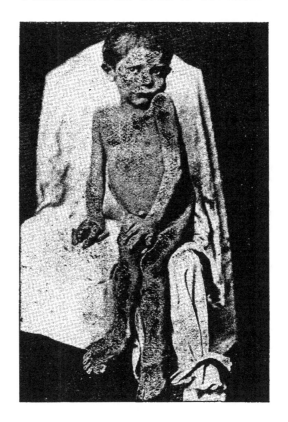

JOHN PFAENDER.

(See Page 113)

the people to rise in their majesty and overthrow the compulsory vaccination system. Here is one from a large number of Swiss cases where vaccination published its own repulsive characteristics. I subjoin a reprint from a monthly journal of health —Terre Haute, Indiana.

VACCINATION IS THE CURSE OF CHILDHOOD.

"John Pfaender, child of healthy Swiss parents, born September 23, 1875, was sturdy, beautiful, and healthy until vaccinated, June 16, 1876, by the official vaccinator. Eight days later his feet began to swell, abscesses formed, his teeth began to rot, his glands to swell and fistulous sores appeared on his hands and feet. The foregoing photograph was taken in May, 1882. He could neither walk, nor stand. Several of the bones of his hands had rotted out.

"It was such cases as this that led the Swiss people to overthrow the infamous system of blood poisoning, yclepted vaccination, which a medical clique was seeking longer to impose upon them. Since its rejection, not only has there been less small-pox, but the general death rate is the lowest in Europe. There are thousands of such cases in this doctor-ridden land. It is time the American people should know the truth in all its hideousness. Surely the spirit of freedom, the good sense and parental affection will soon arise and banish forever this murderous outrage and insiduous cause of so much disease and death."

AUSTRALIA.

New South Wales has but a very small per cent. of vaccinated persons. This fact I fully established during my several visits to this country—and yet small-pox has been literally stamped out by adopting a vigorous policy of isolating small-pox patients and by thorough sanitation in urban districts. Sir Richard Thorne, in his testimony before the Royal Commission, said: "The evidence is so abundant that I could keep you for hours in telling of cases in which epidemics have evidently been prevented by cleanliness and the isolation of the first cases." Sir Richard speaks of twelve different occasions where the disease did not spread beyond the house originally attacked.

COMPULSORY VACCINATION IN UNITED STATES.

In nearly all, if not in every state of our American union, compulsory vaccination laws have been enacted, but in nine-tenths of these states the law is a dead letter on account of the extreme difficulty of enforcing it. The thinking, reasoning masses are strongly opposed to it and this opposition is becoming an army. Occasionally boards of health in municipalities are instructed to enforce the law. Then for a time the schools are closed against all children whose parents positively refuse to expose them to this public enemy—this serpent that stings and scars. A hot contest immediately succeeds; mass meetings of indignant citizens are held and anti-vaccination leagues are organized; a test case is carried to the higher courts, and in the long run, when the fight is maintained with vigor and unyielding persistence the law is decided to be unconstitutional—as in the celebrated case from Geneseo, Ill.,—and the doors of the school-room are again opened to children who have been cruelly deprived of at least one entire term of school privileges. And for what? That a hungry hoard of second-class, scrub doctors may compel every householder in the land to pay tribute for a public commodity upon which the devil (personified meanness of the vaccine syndicate) has put his stamp. How much longer—oh, how much longer, I ask will the American voter tolerate this infamous travesty of justice, this flagrant outrage upon his personal rights. The American's house is his castle and no doctor with poisoned lancet has a right to cross the threshold of his door and poison and scar his children.

Usually from one to two new-school doctors, or psychic physicians, in a municipality, head the agitation for reform. The balance go with the Scribes and Pharisees and affect to sneer at and despise the dissentients as a crazy lot of agitators, "who make a great ado about a perfectly harmless operation which injures nobody, but is a wholesome precaution against a common danger." Bourbons learn nothing. They are stupidly conservative. While the rank and file, go the easy way; and not until the danger becomes painfully apparent with swollen arms, ulcerous sores and perhaps death in their own households, do they consider the question of vaccination of sufficient importance to engage their serious attention. True, no one is vaccinated by physical force in this country as they are in some parts of Germany, but exclusion of children from public schools and of grown persons from government employ are unjust and illegal, constituting an oppressive meanness which American citizens will not continue to tolerate when they come to fully realize the true danger and degradation of the situation.

A decision of the supreme court of the state of New York in June, 1874, deprived the health commissioners of the powers which they had previously claimed to enforce vaccination and revaccination of adults. The attempt to compel free-born citizens of a representative commonwealth to submit to vaccination on the pretence that it is the "greatest good to the greatest number," when their common sense and higher intelligence not only rejects its prophylactic value, but when their souls likewise abhor the vile intruder as a hundred times more to be dreaded than small-pox—the attempt to coerce, I repeat— will ere long meet with such an angry, if not violent, protest that every compulsory act will be swept from statute books, else I fail to interpret rightly the quality and rigid energy of our Americanized, Anglo Saxon genius.

Humanity constitutes a brotherhood and what affects one sympathetically affects the whole. Two classes in the United States particularly suffer in consequence of our outrageously unjust vaccination legislation—namely, the poor man and child, and the emigrant who lands at Castle Garden to make his home in this widely proclaimed, the land of the free. "Be vaccinated or be returned in the next census as among the illiterate," we say to every poor man's child. And the public vaccinator— who has become nothing less than a scourge in the land—would have the state keep those innocent children in illiteracy until the parents consent to hand them over to them to be punctured and poisoned at $1.00 a head. "Be re-vacinated or stay out," we say to every emigrant who proposes to adopt an American citizenship. Here are a few instances of the practical working of our vaccination laws as they relate to emigrants :—

A German physician left Bremen on the steamer Nekar— Lloyd line—in November, 1882. Besides 110 cabin passengers there were nearly eight hundred in the steerage. This physieian writes :—

"The United States law provides that every emigrant without regard to age or physical condition, shall be vaccinated within twenty-four hours after leaving the foreign port. Many of those on board were exceedingly ill, and to anyone who has ever suffered the pains and pangs of "seasickness" it will be apparent that that was not a favorable nor a proper time for vaccination, but it must be done, for the law is clear and peremptory; there is no evading it, for on our arrival in New York, all those who cannot show a certificate from the ship's surgeon are consigned to Blackwell's Island.

"During the three days following our departure from Bremen, vaccination was the order of the day in the steerage. I was enticed thither by curiosity, and what I there saw was suggestive, to say the least, to me, and may be of interest to you. The surgeon sat on a box in the storeroom, lancet in hand, and around him were huddled as many as could be crowded into the confined space, old and young, children screaming, women crying; each with an arm bare and a woe-begone face, and all lamenting the day they turned their steps toward 'land of the free.' The lymph used was of unknown origin, kept in capillary glass tubes, from whence it was blown into a cup into which the lancet was dipped. No pretence of cleaning the lancet was made; it drew blood in very many instances, and it was used upon as many as 276 during the first day. I inquired of the surgeon if he had no fear of inoculating disease, or whether he examined as to health or disease before vaccinating. He replied that he could not stop for that, besides, no choice in the matter was left with him. The law demanded the vaccination of each and every one, and he must comply with it or be subjected to a fine. I thought it a pitiful sight, and am persuaded that could the gentlemen through whose instrumentality the law was enacted, see what I saw of the manner in which it was carried into effect, they would be as zealous in seeking its repeal. As conducted, the law is an outrage, and no one can estimate the number of helpless, innocent children, as well as adults, who are inoculated with syphilis or other foul disease, on every ship bringing steerage passengers to our shores."—G. H. Merkel, M. D., in the "Massachusetts Medical Journal," November, 1882.

The following extracts from a graphic letter by a scholarly layman, describes the painful treatment to which emigrants are subjected:—

Brooklyn, New York, May 7, 1883.

Dear Sir:—I found the vaccination tyranny much more than sentiment on board the Adriatic. Aboardship, as everywhere, it has attained terrible proportions, which makes it probable that in the near future it will become the Great Terror that shall 'cause that as many as will not worship the image of the beast shall be killed,' and that 'no man may buy or sell save he that has the mark of the beast.' * * * * * * * * *

"One morning it was rumored that the doctor was coming to examine the passengers, and I went with two friends to the surgeon to state our objections. I told him that as we had been vaccinated, if that fact would let us pass without further trouble, we could satisfy him; but if not, vaccinated we would never be.

Like most doctors, he was without capacity to understand our conscientious objections, and the degradation involved in submission to the rite. He curtly told us the law was not his; it was United States law. He should come forward at two o'clock and if we showed him that we had been vaccinated he would give us a certificate, and if not, he would vaccinate us if we chose; if not, we must take the risk of passing the doctor at the port. It mattered nothing to him. * * * * * * * *

"By and by came the doctor in his gold-laced cap, with his bottle of 'lymph,' pure from the sores of children or heifer's buttock, and commenced operations. First a rope was stretched from a post, and held by two stewards in a horseshoe form, and into this enclosure passed, one by one, the victims of an insane medical legislation, and bared their arms to the Medical Ignoramus, who stood on the other side. If he there saw the orthodox scars, he forthwith bestowed a ticket like this:—

White Star Line.
                          S. S. 'Adriatic.'
            VACCINATED.
                       C. S. Murray,
                             Surgeon.
14th April, 1883.
Which further had this exhortation on the back:—
             PASS.
      Keep this card to avoid detention
      at quarantine, and on railroad in the
      United States.

"There was nothing in common among them save their degradation, and. as I thought, the most degraded of the lot was the vaccinator. How a man with any sense of decency and the congruity of things, could for mere pay consent to the folly that the individuals of such a heterogeneous crowd were all alike liable to small-pox, and were all alike saved by his performance, passes my understanding. It is hard to believe in a man's sincerity in view of such absurdity; and yet he may be sincere. When a lie is taught, and still more when a lie is praeticed, it confounds the intellect, and is ultimately taken for the truth of truth.   Yours truly,

F. SCRIMSHAW.

In the issue of the New York Tribune, March 18, 1884, is a significant editorial of the "Cow and Hog Doctor" trying to work up a panic among the farmers when some sickness appears among their live stock. These editorial comments apply so exactly to the vaccination doctors that a paragraph will be appropriate here.

"Whence, then, all this noisy affirmation? It emanates from a few persons already in government employ and naturally anxious to enlarge and perpetuate their easy places. Every slight local sickness is magnified and telegraphed over the whole land, as was the case the other day in Columbia county, N. Y. The alarmists are thoroughly organized; they have been working toward this one end half a dozen years, and it is proverbial that Plea is much more active than Protest."

Certain doctors in San Diego, Cal., headed by one pretentious Jones endeavored to get up a small-pox scare by starting the report: "Small-pox is spreading with alarming rapidity in Los Angeles and we shall have hundreds of cases here in a few weeks unless the city is thoroughly vaccinated." The cry spread, lancets were unsheathed, and doctors' pockets were filled. I repeat, if it were possible to eliminate the commercial feature from the vaccination enterprise, this pathetic solicitude, on the part of the dear doctor to guard the public against the alleged danger of small-pox epidemic, would soon be found drooping.

"A SMALL-POX SCARE PROBABLE."

"Compulsory vaccination has been knocked out for the time being in Duluth, and we know that most of the really progressive and up-to-date physicians hope that it is knocked out for all time, but not so with the vaccination doctors, who made all the way from five to fifteen dollars a day in the way of vaccination fees during the last three weeks. It is estimated that the recent bulldozing scheme only brought about one-fourth of the children for vaccination after all, and the professional vaccinators wish as many of the other three-fourths scared into camp at no distant day, as possible. So, look out for another small-pox scare during the coming winter."—Duluth (Minn.) Tribunal.

A judge of the circuit court of Milwaukee recently decided that compulsory vaccination of children by order of the board of education as a preliminary to their admission to the public schools of Wisconsin, was unconstitutional. The circuit courts in several other states have rendered similar decisions.

But the noble state of Illinois has given the hardest blow to compulsory legislation which has yet come under my observation. Thanks to the pluck and persistent fighting qualities on moral grounds of a single man. A test case was brought from Geneseo in which George Lawbraugh was the plaintiff. Five years ago the board of education of that town issued their mandate, that all unvaccinated children after a certain period would be excluded from the public schools. Mr. Lawbraugh had a little girl whom he proposed should remain in school, which as a citizen owning real estate, he had paid his lawful tax to support. He also proposed that his daughter should not be polluted with the vaccinator's lance and poison pus. He had already lost a little boy from the effects of vaccination and he declared in terms most positive that his remaining child should not take a similar risk; and yet, she was peremptorily excluded from the school. Upon Mr. Lawbraugh's representation the state superintendent of schools advised the board of Geneseo not to enforce their mandate against this little innocent girl; but the doctors standing shoulder to shoulder behind the board, the board stood by their mandate. Then Mr. Lawbraugh brought an action in the circuit court on two grounds:

(1). That compulsory vaccination was unconstitutional.

(2). That it was dangerous to the health of the rising generations.

That court decided against Mr. Lawbraugh. He then carried the case up to the appellate court and again lost it. Brave, honest, cultured, and true to principle, he then carried his case to the state supreme court, where, after a patient hearing, that august body rendered a sweeping decision for the plaintiff—a decision which declared the vaccination act unconstitutional.

This moral contest upon the part of Mr. Lawbraugh was not only noble and commendable, but it has likewise established a precedent in this country by which hundreds and thousands of children will escape the wicked work of the detestable enemies of our rising generation. It is indeed a sad commentary on the form of society under which we live, that human interests instead of being mentally helpful, morally up-lifting, and productive of brotherhood, are largely destructive and antagonistic to health and happiness. Each class thrives, or strives to thrive, at the expense of every other class, warring not only against its rivals in the same field of activity but likewise against the common social integrity.

The corner-stone of modern society is self-interest and in its service we do not identify our brother's interests with our own, but rather sacrifice that brother that our own selfish self-interest may the better thrive. It has been too often and too truly said, that the interest of the lawyer is prompted by quarrels; that of the priest by ignorance, superstition, and creeds; the dividends of corporations by the helpless dependence and impoverishment of the masses; and finally that the self-interest of the doctor depends upon a sort of composite degeneration and degradation, ignorance, dirt, disease, dependence, and transmitted superstition. Thus we have a "brotherhood of thieves," for each of the four cardinal points of the compass. How is it possible then for the masses to rise and throw off this and that incubus when all institutions are framed with a special reference to plunder and despoilation manipulated by politicians?

Nevertheless, it must needs be in this preliminary state of unfoldment, "that offences will come;" but great and good men—men full of faith, the meantime, will hail the faintest token of the approach of the normal order in which there will be no bitter war among the members, but each will contribute to the up-building and moral integrity of the whole, while the whole will exercise more than a mother's care for the nourishment and protection of each member. Good men will hail the approach of that order in which the lawyer, unless peradventure their breed will have become extinct—will have no quarrels to promote or prolong; wherein the priest will give love for love and service for service, instead of preaching the obsolete dogmas of a petrified

Calvinist creed for five thousand dollars a year; an order in which corporate interests will include the whole people and where commerce will bestow its unstinted blessings upon every member of the commonwealth; aye, an order in which the physician, a physician, indeed, from whose ranks the blood-poisoning vaccinator shall have disappeared; an order in which the doctor will become the chief educator, a welcome guest in every household; a friend whom the youth and maiden can counsel with and confidingly trust, who will rejoice in the public health and the private health of both soul and body, and from whose abundant personality will radiate and flow forth the same quality of health and life and joy which made the Christ dear to his disciples. Jesus healed both soul and body. This is the work of the true physician.

SUMMARY OF VACCINATION ACTS, OF ENGLAND, CONSIDERED.

1840. To extend the practice of vaccination.
1841. To amend the vaccination act.
1853. Vaccination made compulsory.
1861. To facilitate prosecutions.
1867. To consolidate and amend the acts.
1871. To amend and more vigorously enforce the act.
1874. To explain the act of 1871.
1898. To insert the "Conscience Clause."

CHAPTER V.

LOCAL CONTESTS ON THE VACCINATION QUESTION.

"I can sympathize with, and even applaud a father who, with the presumed dread in his mind, is willing to submit to judicial penalties rather than expose his child to the risk of an infection so ghastly as vaccination."—Sir Thomas Watson, M. D., London.

Although the courts in many states have decided that boards of health or education cannot compel school children to be vaccinated, there is nevertheless a general and a vigorous move of late by these same boards to enforce compulsory legislation on the subject. These "boards" pretend to be acting in the interests of humanity and of the public health. Similar public interests were near and dear to the hearts of the Spanish Inquisitors, who drove the Huguenots out of France and burned scores of thousands at the stake on account of their "mischievous" opinions. No, the intelligent portion of the American people have at last taken the true measure of such physicians as wield the lancet and the poisoning, putrifying calf pus. As doctors they are behind the age in their profession; as business men they will pocket fees, though their professional edicts turn every poor man's child out of the public school. I ask, how much longer are intelligent Americans going to submit to this

infamy? How much longer will they permit an unscrupulous
class to victimize their children and defraud them of their birth-
right for the sake of putting shekels in their pockets? These
health boards and examining boards be it remembered, have
only in rare instances been asked for by the people. They are
part and parcel of the vaccinating business firm, who instead of
teaching sanitation and cleaning up centers of pollution where
zymotics originate, enforce upon a long suffering populace a
vile and discredited commercial commodity. As we always
have the "poor" with us, so likewise the body politic is weighted
down with a surplus of doctors turned loose from the medical
colleges every year to prey upon society, not one-half of whom
have the slightest genius for physic, and ought by all means to
have kept their place in the ranks of the "Man with the hoe."
Not able to get a living in the field of legitimate medical practice, they become "shysters" of the noble profession, secure appointments on boards of health, corrupt legislatures, get up
small-pox panics, and saddle the public with fees for services
which are curses and nothing else.

Doctors must be supported, aye, right royally supported.
Vaccination and compulsory laws are what they have found to
be a superb thing. The public welfare—it is a hypocritical pretence! Some of them would consign every child in the community to an incurable disease, or slam the door of the school
room in their faces, for the sake of the profit their lymph-poi-
soning practice affords them. The public health is the least
and last thing that concerns many of them. The compulsory
law was not gotten up to make people more healthy, nor to prevent disease. If it had been, its promoters would manifest some
solicitude regarding the real causes which every well informed
person knows are the principal sources of all the zymotic diseases in this country, in the poor and crowded quarters of all
large cities. These the vaccinators, like the Levite, pass by.

Read the fearful arraignment of the distinguished Dr. A. M. Ross, of Toronto:—

"In March, 1885, my attention was aroused by a report that several cases of small-pox existed in the east end of Montreal. Knowing something of the filthy condition of certain localities, I made a careful sanitary survey of all that part of the city east of St. Lawrence street, and southwest of McGill and St. Antoine streets. What I saw I will attempt to describe—what I smelt cannot be described! I found ten thousand seven hundred cesspits reeking with rottenness and unmentionable filth; many of these pest-holes had not been emptied for years; the accumulated filth was left to poison the air of the city and make it the seed-bed of the germs of zymotic diseases. Further, I found the courts, alleys, and lanes in as bad a condition as they possibly could be—decaying animal and vegetable matter abounded on all sides. Everywhere unsightly and offensive objects met the eye, and abominable smells proved the existence of disease-engendering matter, which supplied the very condition necessary for the incubation, nourishment and growth of small-pox.

"Knowing well the fearful consequences that would result from the presence of such a mass of filth in such a densely populated part of the city, I gave the widest publicity to the subject, hoping thereby to rouse the municipal authorities to a proper appreciation of the danger that menaced the health of the city. But I was an alarmist; my advice went unheeded and the filth remained as a nest for the nourishment of small-pox, which grew in strength and virulence rapidly, until it swept into untimely graves, from the very localities I have mentioned, thirty-four hundred persons!—victims of municipal neglect. Instead of removing the filth and putting the city in a thoroughly clean, defensive condition by the enforcement of wise sanitary regulations and the adoption of a rigid system of isolation of small-pox patients, the authorities were led by the medical profession to set up the fetish of vaccination and proclaim its protective virtues, through the columns of an ignorant, tyrannical and time-serving press. Day after day the glaring, snaring headlines of 'Vaccinate! vaccinate!' 'Alarm! alarm!' appeared in the morning and evening papers. A panic of cowardice and madness followed, and tens of thousands of people were driven (like sheep to the shambles of the butcher), to the vaccinators, who reaped a rich but unholy harvest. Not less than 100,000 people were vaccinated while the panic lasted, yielding an unrighteous revenue to the vaccinators of at least $50,000.

"Cleanliness, sanitation, and hygiene were 'nonsense,' unworthy of notice or consideration by the board of health! Tens of thousands of beastly vaccine points were imported and distributed among the vaccinators, who were sent forth to poison the life blood of their victims and kindle the flame of small-pox.

"I did all in my power to convince the authorities and the people of the sad mistake they were making; but ignorance, vaccination, and love of money gained the ascendancy, and three thousand four hundred innocents were sent to untimely graves.

"The truth of my prophetic warnings in March, 1885, was amply and sadly verified by the sickening and mournful fact that thirty-four hundred persons, mostly children under twelve years of age, died from small-pox in the very localities I pointed out as abounding in filth; while in the west end, west of Bleury and north of Dorchester streets, where cleanliness prevailed, there were only a few cases and these sporadics. I do not hesitate to declare it as my solemn opinion, founded upon experience acquired during the epidemic, that there would have been no small-pox epidemic in Montreal if the authorities had discarded vaccination and placed the city in a thoroughly clean and defensive condition when I called upon them to do their duty in March, 1885. The greatest incompetency, cowardice, indifference and fickleness prevailed among the health officials. When at last the dread disease carried off sixteen hundred victims in October (although 100,000 people had been vaccinated), they began to enforce a system of isolation, which I had repeatedly but vainly recommended during March, April and May. When vaccination ceased and isolation was enforced, the epidemic rapidly subsided.

"The causes, then, which gives rise to and propagate small-pox are within our control and are preventable. They may be summed up briefly as follows:—

"Overcrowding in unhealthy dwellings or workshops, where there is insufficient ventilation, and where animal or vegetable matter, in a state of decomposition, is allowed to accumulate; improper and insufficient diet, habits of intemperance, excess in eating, idleness, immorality, and unsanitary habits of life, such as the neglect of ablution and the free use of pure water, want of proper exercise, and other irregularities of a like nature."

No money in that sort of thing for the third rate vaccinating doctor! It may be conceded that the average physician is an honorable man personally, the same as the average priest or lawyer or merchant; but vaccination with him is not philanthropy, but business; it is one of his modes of making a living and getting on in the world.

Dr. Ross, above quoted, and most of the truly great physicians whom I have quoted in these pages, belong to the real nobility of the profession. These are physicians who place the public health and welfare above merely commercial motives. These are physicians of the normal order, the true friends of the race, whom future generations will delight to honor. These not only see where the trouble is located, but do what they can to remove the active causes of disease. It is this class who are laboring to secure better sanitation, and who are trying to teach the people that the real preventives of sickness lie in the observance of the natural law. But it is small headway that a few noble reformers can make in the direction of thorough sanitation when they have to deal with corrupt and unscrupulous politicians and municipal boards who are continually plotting selfish schemes for place, pelf, and privileges for themselves.

Now, if the citizens of each municipality will exhibit a little firmness and more conscientious enthusiasm they can make a dead letter of the "edicts" of local boards of health and education. In the highest courts these edicts are invariably set aside. To each parent I declare: if you submit to have your children vaccinated; if you allow this public enemy to enter your households with his lancet and putrid pus to imperil the future of your children, you are morally responsible before high heaven!

The legal authority by which the vaccinator assumes the right
to perpetuate this outrage upon the innocent little ones committed to your charge, is a base, infamous, and un-American usurpation which your state constitution and your highest court
do not sanction. You need not submit your children to this accursed rite, nor need you submit to have them defrauded of
school privileges which you have been taxed to provide. In
many towns local boards have been chosen in accordance with
an enlightened public sentiment; and these, knowing their constitutional rights, pay no attention to the Philipics and edicts
of any state board. In other towns the sentiment is aroused,
but the health and educational boards, being creatures of the
political "ring," issue their mandates and then a hot contest is
at once precipitated.

A HOT CONTEST IN SAN DIEGO, CALIFORNIA.

I spent the winter and early spring of 1898 in my sunny
home in San Diego. Early in February—if I remember—the
local board of health directed the school board to issue a peremptory order that every child attending the public schools
should be required to present a certificate of vaccination to their
teacher, and on failing to do so should be excluded from further
attendance. The battle was on. Among the papers in the city,
the Union was conservative, rather siding with the vaccination
doctors; but the Sun and Vidette freely opened their columns
to my pen sketches of the situation. Only one doctor—P. J.
Parker, M. D.—saw fit to publicly notice my arraignment of the
vaccination practice, and he was extremely reserved and
guarded. I opened the ball with the following letter to the
Daily Sun:—

"Editor Sun: At the close of my lecture Sunday evening
in the hall, literally packed, the subject came up relative to vac-

cinating our school children. The consensus of opinion was decidedly against it—a majority of certainly nineteen-twentieths of those present. Further, it was a general expression that the doctors, lawyers, druggists, and merchants be vaccinated or revaccinated, and that the school children—our dear school children—be spared.

"When I began the practice of medicine over 50 years ago, bleeding was far more popular with doctors than vaccination is today. Times change. Vaccination 'wearing out,' as the theory is, in from about three to seven years, I was induced to be revaccinated in San Francisco just after the commencement of our late civil war, and came near losing my arm from the dire effects of the deadly poison. It put me in bed three weeks and impaired my health for several years. Personally, I should infinitely prefer the small-pox, treating myself, than to undergo another such life-endangering siege of suffering from vaccination.

"While there is no epidemic of small-pox in our city, nor the likelihood of there being any, it seems not only presumptuous but absolutely appalling that health officers should order vaccination. It certainly cannot be for the picayune finances that will accrue to a few physicians. They surely are not so grasping and heartlessly greedy as that. Can it be from a lack of information?

"It is well-known by the most eminent and erudite physicians of today that while vaccination is not even a common safeguard against small-pox, it often conduces to blood-poisoning, erysipelas, eczema, and consumption.

"Am I told, referring to 'tubes and points,' that calf-lymph-glycerinated vaccine, 'the pure,' will be used? Pure poison! Think of it, parents! Pure pus-rottenness—think of it! Pure calf-lymph from calves' filthy sores put into the arms of innocent babes and school children. 'Pure!' Why it is virtually beastly calf-brutality thrust into our children's budding humanity!

"The battle for compulsory vaccination was waged by spells most vigorously in the British house of parliament for nearly a dozen years, and finally a parliamentary commission, after a long and most rigid investigation, virtually reported that vaccination should be 'optional,' rather than compulsory.

" A personal friend of mine, William Tebb, of London, one of God's noblemen, was arrested, if I rightly remember, fourteen times for refusing to have his children vaccinated. He paid his fines—and now wears a victor's wreath. And I, too, would be arrested—aye, I would rot in jail before I would again have that damnable vaccine poison thrust into my arm or into my children's arms.

"Prof. Kranichfield, of Berlin, said in an elaborate report: 'I, too, vaccinated my children at a time when I did not know how injurious it was. Today I would resist if necessary the authorities and the police law.'

"Dr. Gregory in the Medical Times, June 1, 1852, (and then medical director of the London Small-pox hospital) said: 'The idea of extinguishing the small-pox by vaccination is as absurd as it is chimerical, and is as irrational as it is presumptuous.'

"Dr. Stowell, after twenty years' experience as a vaccine physician in England, said: 'The general declaration of my patients enables me to proclaim that the vaccine notion is not only an illusion, but a curse to humanity.'

"In a house to house census of a number of cities, towns, and villages in the north of England to furnish an average test of the dangers of vaccination, there were reported '3,135 cases of injury and 750 deaths, alleged to be due to vaccination.' This report was sent to the members of Parliament and to the prime minister.

"P. A. Taylor, a member of Parliament, said in a Commons' speech: 'I have seen scores of parents who tell me that they honestly believe that their children had died from vaccination. I am opposed to making it compulsory.'

"Alfred Russell Wallace, LL. D., F. R. S., the compeer of the great Charles Darwin, says: 'that vaccination is the probable cause of about 10,000 deaths annually, by five inoculable diseases of the most terrible and disgusting character.'

"William Tebb on July 2, 1892, gave evidence before the Parliamentary Royal Commission as to 2,138 cases of injury, and 540 deaths alleged by the proper medical signatures to be due to vaccination up to the end of 1889. * * * In the third report, (page 172), the number of injuries is increased to 10,309—think of it—and this in solid, conservative old England. '

"If necessary I can furnish the testimony of many eminent American physicians, college professors, in confirmation of the danger, and of the deaths resulting from compulsory vacination.

"Upon the grounds, therefore, of continuous good health to our children; upon the grounds of absolute right; upon the grounds of personal liberty vouchsafed by the constitution of the United States, and upon the grounds of regard to the mature judgment and cultured consciences of many educated parents and prominent San Diego citizens, I hope—earnestly hope—that this vaccination order will not be pressed.

J. M. PEEBLES, M. D."

The moral indignation of the community was aroused, and the local press teemed daily with articles from indignant citizens and with spirited editorials on the all-absorbing controversy— the two papers named siding with the people; but the Union editorials abounded in expressions of "good Lord and good Devil," yet leaning perceptibly toward the latter. Among the protests from citizens, the following is a sample:—

"Editor Sun: I consider that I have a grievance that it is my duty to put before the people of this city.

"My son tells that he is excluded from the schools because he can not show a certificate of vaccination. I sent a note by him this morning to Professor Freeman in which I desired the following information: If Jamie, my son, is not allowed to continue in the school, please, in justice to me, give me a written notice of his expulsion. I added also: I have been a taxpayer for many years, and if I am not to have any of its benefits, unless I bow down before one of the most un-American laws that was ever lobbied through a legislative body, I should have notice of it.

"He wrote on the back of the note with a pencil, as follows:—

"'Mr. Nulton: You appear to be aware of the law. We simply do our duty under it when we forcibly exclude children who have not been vaccinated.'

"What conclusion can I arrive at from his answer? I have

never brought his devotion to duty in question, neither do I doubt that he may have excluded pupils from his school during his past life. But I would like to know whether the boy is playing 'hookey,' or whether it is the professor himself?

"Is there anything in his answer that would show to a court of justice that the boy has been excluded from the schools?

"I have been required several times to write notes to teachers why the boy was absent from school on certain days, and when I want information they seem to be as silent as a graveyard.

"In regard to vaccination, I have this to say. I have heard of many that have died from vaccination and a great deal of suffering resulting from it. Now, the question is, shall I offer up my child to this vaccine god with the hope that a ram will be caught in the bushes and his life spared? or shall I stand on my feet like a true American and say to this Moloch, whose taste for children is proverbial, 'Stand out of the way and let the car of progress move on.'

"If a parent forces his child to be vaccinated and he die from its effect, who murders him? Is it the parent, the vaccinator, or the law, or should we wag our long ears and exclaim: 'Mysterious Providence.'

"A good thing can never be over-multiplied; inflate it as much as you please, there will be no bad results. If vaccination is a good thing you cannot overdraw at this bank either. Commence with the doctors, then the old men and women, and some of us have nothing but an old shell left, and it would not take much vaccine matter to fix us; then the middle-aged, then the youth, babes, cats, and dogs.   S. D. NULTON."

It is but justice to say, that Dr. Remendido, the leading physician and surgeon of the city, came out through the press and definitely condemned compulsory vaccination. The other physicians, with one exception, were as dumb as the dens of frozen adders.

About this time—early in February, 1899—258 children had been sent home by the teachers for not presenting certificates of vaccination, and many more were kept home by their parents who wished to spare their feelings, knowing what the result would be if they appeared without the official vaccinator's "tag." Parents were calling at my residence every day for advice about what they could do; so accordingly I published the following letter in the Daily Vidette: —

"Editor Vidette: Honoring your moral bravery and admiring the breadth of thought and freedom of expression that characterize your daily columns, allow me to say that the heads of twenty-three families have called upon me at my residence during the past week, saying, 'What shall we do, doctor, about having our children vaccinated? We think vaccination dangerous. We do not believe in it, and yet we want our children to attend school and be educated. What shall we do?'

"My invariable reply has been, I am not 'my brother's keeper.' You must exercise your own judgment. I am frank, however, to tell you what I should do.

"First: I should send my children to school unvaccinated, unpoisoned with pox-lymph virus, and put the responsibility upon the official authorities for refusing to educate them in the schools, for the support of which I had been taxed. I should then, as they have in Philadelphia, commence legal proceedings. It should not be forgotten that before the adjournment of our recent legislature, Senator Simmons introduced a bill providing that if any injury or detriment to health was produced by vaccination, both the school authorities and the vaccinators might be sued for damages. This was right. The bill did not come to a vote. How could it, in a legislature charged and counter-charged with bribery—a legislature neither intellectually nor morally competent to elect a United States senator?

"Second: Or, I should teach my children in my own home, inviting some of my neighbors' more advanced scholars to come in and teach them the higher branches.

"Third: Or, I should unite with the citizens of my ward and organize a private school, employing competent and cultured teachers. For such a purpose I will contribute liberally in the eighth ward.

"Fourth: Or, I should emigrate from slow, lag-behind San Diego, to some one of the states east where compulsory vaccination is not enforced; or, perhaps what would be more preferable still, bidding adieu to the American flag (the presumed symbol of freedom and personal liberty), I would settle in some country, decent enough, civilized enough not to enact a monstrous compulsory vaccination law, and enlightened enough not to enforce if there was such a law.

"Queensland, Australia, has no compulsory vaccination law; and grand, conservative old England, after a dozen years' fight of the people, assisted by the ablest members of Parliament, against a majority of the doctors (who evidently had an eye to business), passed what has been termed the 'conscience clause,' as an addendum to the vaccination bill. This was signed by the queen, August 12, last year. Therefore, any person, now going before the registrar of the district, and making declaration before the justice of the peace that he conscientiously believes vaccination to be detrimental to the health of the child, is exempt from arrest or penalty. All honor to England!

"Accordingly, in the single city of Oldham, Lancashire, England, 43,000 certificates of exemption under the 'conscience clause' had been issued up to the first of March. Other cities and towns are doing nearly as well. Shame, shame, to San Diego to thus snail-like drag—drag along in great reforms behind England, Australia, and some of the isles of the ocean.

"There are not only thousands of our citizens, but there are members of the health and school board, just as strenuously opposed to compulsory vaccination as I am. I speak by the book. 'But it is the law.' Granted. 'It has been sustained by the supreme court.' Then, in the name of law and oredr, why was it not entorced by the previous health and school board authorities? Did they not know their duty? Why were they not dismissed from office or fined $500? Who was responsible for that gross, official neglect? and why has this vaccination law been virtually a dead letter throughout California these past ten years? and what has caused this present health-spasm? There is no small-pox in our city—and it is the general opinion that there has been none. Why do not doctors post themselves? Why are they such consummate cowards?

"Finally, this so-called compulsory law, now the terror of so many parents, is not law. That only is law which is based upon the principle of justice, of right and of personal liberty. Enactments are not necessarily laws. Enactments made by one legislature are very often repealed by the next. The 'fugitive slave law' was once pronounced 'law' by politicians influencing even the supreme court; and yet a band of Quakers, with myself and many others deliberately violated that law—defied it, in fact, as often as possible, by helping such frightened, fleeing negroes as Fred Douglas, on their way toward the freedom of the British flag in Canada. The framers of that law are now remembered only in pity, or deserved infamy. And so history will brand the mark of Cain upon the legislature that ten years ago passed that infamous, unconstitutional, compulsory vaccination enactment. I would not—will not, obey it! I defy it! Arrest me, jail me, imprison me behind iron bars. I would stay there and rot in prison before I would obey it. And further, in the future I will vote for no member of the legislature till I know—positively know, how he stands upon this vaccination question. We must organize for the battle as they did for years in England; we must call meetings and distribute literature.

"Only recently a judge of the circuit court in Milwaukee, Wis., decided that 'the compulsory vaccination of children by order of the board of education as a prerequisite to their admission to the public schools of that state, was unconstitutional.' Another compulsory vaccination tumble! And yet, San Diego, sitting under the shadow of Old Mexico, and brooded by the skeleton of a dead-letter legislative enactment, forbids her children to enter the public schools—compels them to remain in ignorance because, forsooth, their intelligent parents refuse to have brutality—cow-pox virus, calf-lymph cussedness, or anything of this nature thrust into their system, believing it to be unconstitutional, a violation of personal freedom, and dangerous to health. Is this America—proud, progressive America, or old sixteenth century Spain? J. M. PEEBLES, M. D."

Next came what may be designated the Peebles-Parker discussion which appeared in the columns of the Daily Sun. The following is Dr. Parker's first letter:—

"Editor Sun: In a recent issue of your paper you say you are opposed to vaccination of school children, as required by law, and you give as your reasons that physicians are divided among themselves as to the utility and advisability of vaccination, and also that you do not like the idea of sticking scabs onto people. Permit me to reply that we do not use scabs for such a purpose. We use lymph taken from healthy young cattle sterilized, put up in glass tubes and hermetically sealed up until used. The greatest care is used in vaccination. The arm or leg where the little wounds are made is thoroughly disinfected and cleansed before the work is begun, and the instrument used is boiled before using, and then a light dressing of sterilized gause placed over the wound to prevent the entrance of any poisonous germs. Done in this way there is no danger. Some years ago when scabs were used at times as well as lymphs, and no great care used to sterilize or keep the vaccine pure, and surgeons were careless in breaking of the skin without sterilizing or boiling instruments, we had trouble with infection and blood poisoning. Also sometimes diseases were conveyed by using humanized virus. But with the old methods vaccination was a God-send to the human race. Before the days of vaccination the annual death rate from small-pox was about 3,000 per million of the population in England. At that rate, the death rate in the United States per annum would be over 200,000. Deprive the people of this country of the privileges of vaccination for twenty-five years and we would have about the same result. Modern treatment and care would lessen mortality some, but modern facilities of travel would spread it more than in former times.

"One great danger in the spread of small-pox is the long incubation period, for it is about twelve days after exposure before a person becomes sick. Anyone could be exposed to smallpox in Cuba or Porta Rica and travel to San Diego before he would get sick.

"In reference to the division of opinion among physicians, there is in reality very few who oppose it. It is about as near unanimous as it is possible for any question to be. Only about one physician in this city speaks against it, and he says pus is used for vaccinating. I would expose vaccination if we had to use pus for such a purpose. This Dr. Peebles also stated in a public address before the Mother's Club that he had treated hundreds of cases of small-pox without losing a case. Any comment on such statements are unnecessary.

"In the year 1889, Queen Victoria appointed a commission composed of eight of the most noted medical men of England and quite a number of eminent men in other professions, to investigate the question of the effect of vaccination. The commission spent seven or more years in their investigations, held one hundred and thirty-six meetings, examined about two hundred witnesses and investigated six epidemics, which has occurred in recent years at Gloucester, Sheffield, Warrington, Devosberry, Leicester, and London. In Gloucester the praetice of vaccination had been greatly neglected for some years prior to the outbreak of small-pox. At Gloucester 26 vaccinated children under ten years of age were attacked, of whom one died; of unvaccinated children of like age 680 were attacked, of whom 279 died. The report of the commission was unanimous in favor of vaccination as the only effective means for the protection against the ravages of small-pox. In Germany where vaccination has been compulsory for years, small-pox is almost unknown in recent years. Hoping I have not made this too long, I am, Yours very truly,

P. J. PARKER, M. D."

Peebles replies:—

"Editor Sun: In-as-much as Dr. P. J. Parker, of our city, brought my name before the public in your issue of the 11th, touching the question of compulsory vaccination, you will certainly grant me equal space in your ably conducted journal.

"In expressing an opinion adverse to compulsory vaccination, you doubtless reflected the convictions of a large majority of the parents of San Diego. That the eighty-nine doctors, or the most of them, favor it, counts but little. Doctors without an exception once favored bleeding in fevers. Both Washington and Byron, it is believed, died from blood-letting. Doctors do not bleed men now-a-days; nor will they vaccinate in the near future. Much less will they dare, however ignorant they may be of Jennerism and the dangers attendant upon calf-poison, to compel vaccination. I recommend medical incompetents to weigh well these candid words (published Sunday) by the leading physician and surgeon of our city:

" 'I am not in favor of anything that interferes in any way with the personal liberty or action of any individual. If a person seriously objects to being vaccinated or to having any member of his family vaccinated, the feelings of such a party are entitled to respect, etc.'—Dr. Remendido.

"Certainly every man's 'feelings,' every man's conscientious convictions, are entitled to 'respect.' Every man's house is his castle, and upon the constitutional grounds of personal liberty, no vaccination doctor, lancet in one hand and calf-pox poison in the other, has a legal or moral right to enter the sacred precincts of a healthy home and scar a child's body for life.

" 'This' Dr. Parker informs the public that 'scabs' from cow and calf-pox sores are not used now. That is true—doctors have advanced from arm-to-arm 'scabs' to a more refined filth—a more delicate form of the poison pox-lymph. It is taken from 'healthy young cattle,' we are told. How is it known that these cattle were 'healthy?' They were dumb. That they were 'healthy' could only be proven by vivisection and dissection. Physicians know that tuberculosis is common among cows in some parts of the country. To say that these cattle are 'healthy' is an assertion—nothing more! All technical terms and pedantic jargon aside—would a man be considered healthy if any portion of his body was spotted and dotted with pustules, with inflamed bases—'running sores?' 'Only about one' doctor, we are gravely told (there are some eighty-five or ninety in San Diego) speaks against vaccination—so much the worse for the doctors! 'Only about one.' Well, I am proud to be that one! for in fact one with the right, is a majority. Truth is never in minority—and laggards often find it out to their sore disadvantage.

"Yes, 'Dr. Peebles stated in a public address that he had treated many cases of small-pox and never lost a case.' How many did 'this' Dr. Parker ever treat? and how many of them lived? I shall be pleased to hear the doctor's 'comments.' I pledge you my word he will be dumb.

"On my journey around the world, while in the Godavari district, India, with a population of between two and three millions, not a day passed after the first week there that I did not treat or assist in treating from twelve to twenty small-pox patients lying in bungalows, outside tents, and bamboo huts.

"In July, 1869, appointed by General Grant, the United States consul to Trebizonde, Asiatic Turkey, I was in this old city, crowded with Turks, Circassians, Georgians, Armenians, and other races—a city of filth—during its small-pox epidemic

—and here again I treated or assisted other physicians in treating for weeks and months small-pox patients. Small-pox is closely allied to filth, and sanitation, hygiene, pure air, healthy diet, sunshine, and bathing are much more efficacious preventatives than vaccine virus, in whatever way manipulated, and whether called scabs, pus, lymph, serum, or calf-virus—words do not render poisons any the less malignant.

"Speaking of 'humanized virus,' Dr. Parker says: 'The old method of vaccination was a God-send to the human race.' On the contrary I pronounce it emphatically a death-send, a scourge, and a most damnable curse. Here are a few of my authorities proving it:

"In the English 'Digest of Parliamentary Returns,' No. 488, session of 1878, entitled, 'Vaccination Mortality,' we find the startling statement that: 'Twenty-five thousand children are annually slaughtered by disease inoculated into the system by vaccination, and a far greater number are injured and maimed for life by the same unwholesome rite.'

"Prof. Trousseau, of Paris, France, wrote in the 'Clinique Medicale,' 1874, a medical journal published in France: 'The transmission of syphilis by vaccination appears now to be an estalished fact.'

"Prof. German, in 1878, in an address to the Diet of the German empire, said: 'Above all, the direful fatality which lately occurred at Lebus, would alone warrant the abolition of the vaccination laws. Eighteen school girls, averaging 12 years of age, were re-vaccinated and thereby syphilized, and some of them died.'

"The report of the German vaccination commission of 1884, contains the following: 'Up to 1880, fifty cases have become known in which syphilis, inoculated with vacine virus, caused severe illness to about seven hundred and fifty persons.' A strange 'God-send!'

"The report of the British commission, appointed by the queen in 1889. was not unanimous in favor of compulsory vaccination which fact ought to know it. By this report, anti-vaccinationists 'obtained a great measure of parental freedom,' writes Dr. Winthrop from London to the New York Sun.

Dr. Parker's statement concerning Gloucester and its vaccination, is not only misleading but false. If figures do not lie those that make them can, and often do. The Gloucester Official Reports are decidedly against the benefit of vaccination. I have them at my command. Dr. Parker is no authority. His Ipse Dixit neither counts nor carries weight with either students of science or medicine. The report of the British commission so influenced Parliament that it pronounced against compulsory vaccination—and made the matter optional with the people. And so the matter still stands.

"In Rhode Island, after a committee of the senate had heard evidence on both sides of the question, it repealed the vaccination law by a majority of 16 to 9. Petitions should be hurried on to Sacramento demanding that this disease-breeding law be promptly repealed.

"A late press dispatch informs us that Wm. Nagengast, of Cleveland, O., aged 11 years, was vaccinated in the free dispensary on January 4th. His arm soon became terribly swollen. The same night he exhibited symptoms of lockjaw, and the next evening he died, suffering intense agonies. In London, from 1859 to 1896, there were one thousand and two hundred and seventeen admitted deaths from vaccination. There were doubtless five times this number, say the minority reports, but they were 'hushed up to prevent vaccination from further reproach.'

"Engaged wholly in literary pursuits and depending upon a livelihood from neither the vaccination business nor local medical practice of any kind, I can find leisure to ventilate the viciousness and villainous consequences of compulsory vaccination, and I shall do it with ungloved hands, and will therefore say that if Dr. Parker desires a journalistic controversy with me upon the merits and demerits of compulsory vaccination he will find me girded for the conflict; and I promise him a "foeman worthy his steel."   J. M. PEEBLES, M. D.
San Diego, Cal., Feb. 13."

I will now extend my above reply and notice the following statements contained in Dr. Parker's letter:

(1). "The instrument used is boiled before using."

(2). "England before the days of vacination had a death rate from small-pox of 3,000 per million of the population."

(3). "Deprive the people of this country of the privilege of vaccination for twenty-five years * * * and we should have the same result."

(4). "At Gloucester 26 vacinated children under ten years were attacked with small-pox—one died. Of un-vaccinated children of like age 680 were attacked, of whom 279 died."

(1). This statement by Dr. Parker is very careless, for in many noted instances it is conspicuously untrue, in fact. I will give one instance where a United States official vaccinator uses the lance on scores of immigrants without once cleansing it. Our laws require that every immigrant arriving at Castle Garden shall be vaccinated before they land, unless they can show a vaccine mark or a certificate. "The surgeon sat on a box in the storeroom, lancet in hand, and around him huddled as many as could be crowded into the confined space, old and young, children screaming, women crying; each with an arm bare and a woe-begone face. * * * No pretense of cleaning the lancet was made; it drew blood in very many instances. and it was used upon as many as 276 during the first day. I inquired of the surgeon if he had no fear of inoculating disease, or whether he examined as to health or disease before vaccinating He replied that he could not stop for that, besides no choice in the matter was left with him. The law demanded the vaccination of each and every one, and he must comply with it or be subjected to a fine."—G. H. Merkel, M. D., in Mass. Ec. Med. Jour. November, 1882.

Here is a fact which I offset against Dr. Parker's statement —"the instrument used is boiled before using." When we consider that the point of a cambric needle, dipped in the blood of a leprous or syphilitic patient is sufficient to communicate the disease. if this is punctured through the skin, what a fearful indictment we have against the practice of vaccination! Two hundred and seventy-six victims vaccinated without the lancet once being cleaned! In this way it is possible for the "calf-lymph" to pick up on its way about all the curses which human flesh is heir to.

(2). "Small-pox deaths in England before vaccination were 3,000 per million of the population." In the connection in which it is used this statement as before said is entirely misleading. There is no hint here that other zymotic diseases in England have declined in a similar ratio with small-pox during the century just closing; and we are entitled to claim that the same causes that diminished scarlet fever also diminished small-pox.

But the decline in small-pox has really been far less than in other zymotics, from which it may be fairly claimed that vaccination instead of mitigating it has kept it alive notwithstanding the presence of other really mitigating causes. By implication Dr. Parker assumes that such investigation of the disease as we have been able to secure, is to be set down to the credit of vaccination. No other mitigating factor is hinted at. In discussing the causes of small-pox vaccinators stick to vaccination as Mr. Gladstone stuck to "Mitcheltown." They never pollute their lips by speaking aloud the word filth—having plenty of that article in their antidote. They are silent about sanitation. They do not tell us that small-pox is a filth-disease; that it thrives on filth; that it is chiefly confined to the dirty and crowded quarters in our cities. Had the doctors vaccinated for the plague, black-death, and the sweating sickness, they would now be claiming the credit for vaccination as the sole agent that was efficient in practically stamping these three zymotics out of Europe. Since they cannot set up that claim, pray what has been the cause of their decline? I answer, sanitation and improved habits of living. Prof. Wallace, taking the Reports of the Registrar General from 1838 to 1896, makes a thorough statistical analysis and presents the result in diagramatic form—"Wonderful Century," page 305. Then he writes:—

"The main teaching of this diagram—a teaching which the commissioners have altogether missed by never referring to diagrams showing comparative mortalities—is the striking correspondence in average rise and fall of the death-rates of small-pox, of zymotics, and of all diseases together. This correspondence is maintained throughout the whole of the first part, as well as through the whole of the second part, of the diagram; and it proves that small-pox obeys, and always has obeyed, the same law of subservience to general sanitary conditions as the other great groups of allied diseases and the general mortality. Looking at this most instructive diagram, we see at once the absurdity of the claim that the diminution of small-pox in the first quarter of our century was due to the partial and imperfect vaccination of that period. Equally absurd is the allegation that its stationary character from 1842 to 1872, culminating in a huge epidemic, was due to the vaccination then prevailing, though much larger than ever before, not being quite universal

—an allegation completely disproved by the fact that the other zymotics as a whole, as well as the general mortality, exhibited strikingly similar decreases followed by equally marked periods of average uniformity or slight increase, to be again followed by a marked decrease. There is here no indication whatever of vaccination having produced the sligtest effect on small-pox mortality."

How utterly misleading and untrue therefore is the statement of Dr. Parker which I am here commenting upon. Nothing but his vaccination hobby is permitted to come in sight when he would explain the causes which effect the periodical acceleration and decline of small-pox mortality. Vaccination is paraded as the sole cause of small-pox decline; neglect of vaccination the sole cause when small-pox waxes strong and rages like a conflagration.

Dr. Parker must be aware that during the period he refers to, before Jenner's discovery (?) when he says small-pox waxed stronger; that the doctors then had a "sure thing," congener of vaccination, inoculation,—which they had "boomed," as they now boom vaccination. Inoculation was just as rational as vaccination; yet by the same act in 1840 England made inoculation a penal offence and vaccination compulsory.

But finally, I utterly deny Dr. Parker's allegation that small-pox deaths in England before vaccination was "3,000 per million of the population." This monstrous statement was taken from Dr. Lettsom's evidence before the Parliamentary Committee in 1802. How did Mr. Lettsom arrive at this figure? He first assumed that the small-pox mortality of London before vaccination was 3,000 per million of population—which, in a future chapter I shall prove was only 2,000 per million— and then takes that as basis for the entire population of the kingdom, town, village, and country, making not the slightest allowance for the cleanliness and general wholesomness of the country in comparison with over-crowded, filth-accumulated and poverty-stricken districts in the city of London. The popula-

tion of the kingdom was estimated to be twelve times as large
as that of London, so London population was multiplied by
twelve to yield the 36,000 annual small-pox fatality for the kingdom. Difference in sanitary conditions never was taken the
slightest account of by advocates of vaccination. It is such
glaringly false statistics as these that Dr. Parker, and vaccinators generally, are in the habit of quoting.

(3). "Deprive the people of the country of the privileges,
etc." Here again has Dr. Parker by implication raised an ir-
revelant issue. Who has said anything about depriving the
people of this country of the privilege of vaccination? I would
not deprive one American citizen of the "privilege" of taking
a half gill of calf-pus daily—either through the skin or into the
stomach if he is inclined that way. That is not the present issue. What I am contending for, doctor, is that you have taken
the state in with you in this vaccination disgrace; and that you
two have agreed between you, that I shall be compelled—or my
children shall be compelled—to take your medicine! Hence I
say—and I speak it in stentorian tones—take your unholy hands
off from me and mine! Leave me to my liberty regarding the
practice of superstitions and degrading calf-lymph-poisoning
rites, and be assured , I shall leave you to yours.

(4). The statements of Doctor Parker relative to small-
pox fatalities in Gloucester are still more misleading and untrue than any of the above. He is silent regarding the quarter
of the town in which nine-tenths of the small-pox cases occurred; silent too, regarding the unmistakable causes that made
the epidemic so fatal. I have space here to merely summarize
results; and I shall state nothing but what I stand ready to support by the annual reports of the medical officers of health.
Those for the years 1875 to 1888 are the work of Mr. John P.
Wilton; those for 1889 to 1895 of Dr. John Campbell. At the
time of the Gloucester epidemic—1895-6—the urban population
was 40,000; the rural population 11,000. In the southeast
quarter—the poor, filthy and crowded quarter—the drainage
was the worst possible. The new system of drains was connected with the old, crooked and much dilapidated brick culverts. The water supplied for domestic use was totally unfit to
drink, charged as it was with sewage pollution. Into an exten-

sive bed of gravel—from which this portion of the city was supplied with water, the drainage from cesspools and sewers had
free access. In the language of the medical officer: "The
drainage of houses either empties into cesspools constructed
close to them, and leaking into the bed of gravel, or is carried
away in brick culverts, which, whenever they are uncovered,
are found to be faulty, thus allowing their contents to ooze into
the gravel. It is thus absolutely impossible that there can be
any pure water in the district."

In 1889 a flood choked these sewers and caused a back flow,
mixing vast quantities of sewage with the water on the surface.
The medical officer reports: "This water became so charged
with sewage that I feared serious consequences in the houses
that became flooded."

In this pestilence-breeding and foul quarter the epidemic
started late in 1895. At the end of the year 25 cases had been
reported, 24 of which we confined to this southeast end. Here,
my dear doctor, was the breeding ground and source of the
Gloucester epidemic of 1896. You did not think these facts
worthy of mention! Just so, that is a common fault with vaccinating doctors. You should have also stated, that out of the
2.036 cases of small-pox reported during the epidemic, 1,822
were confined to this same God-forsaken South Hamlet while
only 214 cases were reported north of St. Michael's Square,
where the city possessed a tolerable sanitary aspect.

Another fact: The great scarlet fever epidemic of 1892
was likewise practically confined to this South Hamlet. Everybody with a grain of common sense knows that this epidemic
was caused by the wretched unsanitary condition at the southeast end of Gloucester. They know, too, that the small-pox
epidemic originated in the same causes and was fed from the
same source. Yet we are assured that the "un-vaccinated"
were the occasion of the whole trouble. Get vaccinated and re-
vaccinated, and then if the sewage comes up to your window-
sills and you have no other fluid to drink, still you need not
fear the small-pox! These little matters are unworthy of men-

tion when a vaccinator is handling small-pox statistics. "Vaccination had been greatly neglected in Gloucester before the epidemic," from which the reader is supposed to infer that this species of neglect was the real occasion of the fearful outbreak. What was neglected before the other epidemic broke out—the scourge of scarlet fever? Vaccination cannot be made to do duty here. Now I place these facts by the side of Dr. Parker's statements, and leave the decision to the common sense of my readers as to what occasioned the small-pox epidemic in Gloucester.

Dr. Parker also refers to Leicester as one of the stricken cities, due to vaccinal neglect. He had better have remained silent regarding Leicester, for it has a thunderbolt in reserve for the vaccinators. After their small-pox epidemic of 1892-4, the citizens rose to the dignity of the occasion and turned the vaccinators out of office; then elected boards of guardians who were pledged not to enforce the compulsory law. At present the vaccinations are only one per cent. of the births. Did they stop there? No, but they set about real prevention by putting the city under more thorough sanitary regulations. Now Leicester is not only the freest city in England from the small-pox scourge, but the freest from scarlet fever and other zymotics as well.

It is just as silly and illogical to refer small-pox fatality to neglect of vaccination, as it would be to refer fatalities from cyclones in the middle west to this same neglect.

I will now resume account of the struggle in San Diego. The next step in the program was the organization of the Anti-Vaccination League—Dr. J. M. Peebles, president; E. P. Brooks and Col. J. L. Dryden, vice presidents, and F. M. Gregg, secretary. A little later—some time in April—a rousing mass meeting was held in the M. E. church. The following are extracts from my address on that occasion, published in the Daily Sun:—

"We have assembled tonight from the different city wards to take into consideration the compulsory vaccination law of California—a law that has thrown nearly four hundred of our children out of the public schools, that we have been taxed to support.

This compulsory cow-pox enactment, so at variance with the higher medical science and personal liberty; so repulsive to cultured manhood, the finer instincts of womanhood, and the God-implanted intuitions of childhood has remained like other unconstitutional laws passed by politicians and lobbied legislatures for the past ten years, a dead letter. Why—why, if this law was just and right, has it not been executed? Why is it now raised? Who rolled the stone away from its mouldy and moss-shingled tomb? Who were the instigators? There is no small-pox in the city, and in the opinion of Mr. Hedges and the general public, there has been none. Who was responsible then, for the "scare," and who have been the financial gainers by it?

Why are children with certificates in their hands from Dr. Stockton, the health officer, stating that, owing to their physical condition, they were not fit subjects for vaccination, turned away from the schools? Why this merciless blow to education and personal freedom? Why are the conscientious convictions of hundreds of intelligent San Diego parents violated or ridiculed by vacincating officials? Why are the public school doors slammed in the faces of innocent children—children who, turned into the streets, wend their way home weeping for a lack of the privilege of gaining an education? Do these health and school boards feel justified in making and enforcing a compulsory ignorance law? Need I say that not only thousands of San Diego students, thinkers, and tax-paying parents, but thousands upon thousands are indignant at this state of things. It is currently reported that one of our city doctors said that nobody but 'Mexicans, niggers, and ignoramuses' were opposed to compulsory vaccination. This is the compliment that superstition, bigotry, and infamy pays to the intelligence of San Diego's cultured citizens. It is as certain as the stars are abiding, that thousands in this city will never—NEVER submit to thrusting a blood-poisoning virus into their children's systems. They will do as two families have done today, move over to Coronado, or they will move into the country townships to educate their children, or they will establish private schools—and I honor them for their decisions. Some families have already left the city to educate their children.

"This meeting has been called to consider—to devise ways and means concerning this very serious subject, and I counsel calmness and dignity of deportment. No matter how intense the indignation that may thrill you to your soul's depths, control the temper and be guided by the dictates of moderation and reason. You are in the right. And in the end you are sure, each to wear a victor's wreath. This meeting is but the prelude to a series of similar gatherings. These will be educational, and thrillingly interesting, and, further, they will probably continue here and in other portions of the state until the assembling of the next legislature, when our votes will count. There is nothing that a wiley, unprincipled politician so much fears as an honest vote.

"The battle touching this compulsory vaccination law is fully on. The people are aroused. They are organizing. They are thoroughly in earnest. There is no lack of finances to conduct the campaign. And like the immortal Wm. Lloyd Garrison, these anti-vaccinationists 'will not equivocate, will not excuse, and they will be heard.' And I may add, they will politically 'mark' every man at future elections who favors compulsory blood-poisoning.

"Anti-vaccinationists, anti-compulsionists, you are a power. You have culture, finance, influence, conscience, energy, and I charge you to mark such doctors as seek to enforce this dead-letter compulsory vaccination law; mark such doctors as tell you privately that they are opposed to compulsory vaccination, yet are too sneakingly cowardly to openly express their honest convictions; mark such school officials and members of health and school boards as make themselves unnecessarily offensive to those who conscientiously differ from them on the vaccination question; mark such public men, especially politicians as hunt with the hounds and run with the hares, and all to catch votes to get into offices; mark such daily newspapers (NEWS-papers), as are owned, or edited by hunting poltroons, shaped like men, rather than by brave, fair-minded, royal-souled men, the worthy sons of this magnificent century!

"This cow-pox poison put into innocent children's arms is often from diseased calves or heifers, and can resultant disease prevent disease or produce health? Do men gather grapes of thorns? I say diseased heifers. You take supposed healthy heifers from the fields, confine them in 'sterilized stables' (a phrase used by a San Diego doctor), rope them, throw them, shave their abdomens, puncture this portion of the hairless body with 'small-pox pustular poison;' and then watch the irritation, watch the animal's thirst, the increasing inflammation up to the point of pus-rottening—and now call this brute healthy do you? Would you consider your own body healthy if half-covered with inflamed pustules and discharging sores? Then watch the applied clamps as they squeeze out the putrid mucus-like pus mingled with a little of the animal's inflamed blood, to be manipulated into 'pus-lymph' for your children's arms! Is not the thought, the sight disgustingly infamous? *

"How would it do to take catarrh mucus from the nose of some otherwise healthy young lady and manipulating up to the point of pure catarrh lymph, introduce it compulsorily into the school children's arms as a preventive say, against the grippe, erysipelas, or some kind of eczema? Some doctors advanced the theory awhile since, that traced back through the complex laws of heredity far enough, it might be shown that there is a close genetic relation existing between pure catarrh lymph, pure syphilitic lymph and pure cow-pox lymph. Be the relation near or afar, I would stoutly resist any compulsory vaccination law that insisted upon introducing any such lymphs— 'PURE LYMPHS'—into the human system.

"During this conflict we shall demonstrate beyond any possible question that:

*NOTE—In gathering the materials for this volume I failed to secure one of Dr. Parker's letters in defense of compulsory vaccination, appearing in the "Daily Sun." Writing him for his full correspondence and forwarding the same by special messenger, he informed me later that he did not wish his correspondence to appear in the volume. Considering its diluted contents in connection with that bad cause, calf-lymph poisoning, none can seriously blame him. Nevertheless his published letters in the "Daily Sun" became public property. And as such I am justified in using them. Only one however appears. His last letter was an indirect plea to be let down off from his "compulsory" stilts, gently as possible. This I did with my accustomed grace and gentleness.

"I. Vaccination does not prevent small pox. This every well-read, intelligent physician already admits.

"II. Vaccination, by reducing the vitality through transmitting poisonous pus-brutality into the human system, not only tends to, but actually invites the epidemic termed small-pox.

"III. That our soldiers vaccinated in the San Francisco camps previous to sailing for the Philippines, and told that they were immune from small-pox, a number of them had the small-pox over there and several died from the disease.

"IV. That, as vaccination weakens the constitution, affects deleteriously the red blood corpuscles, it necessarily deteriorates the public health and is a danger, a menace, to the same. The death rate was greatly diminished both in Switzerland and in Leicester, England, after compulsion was abandoned.

"V. That vaccination lays the foundation for erysipelas, eczema, carbuncles, abscesses, nervousness, pimpled faces, consumption, and cancers.

"VI. We shall show that there is no such thing as pure calf lymph. To talk of pure lymph is equivalent to talking of pure poison originating from a putrified pustular sore, which, according to the distinguished Dr. Creighton, bears a striking resemblance symptomatically to syphilitic poison. The Hon. J. A. Bright, M. P., and member of the London Royal Vaccination commission, testified that 'there are no means of determining the purity of lymph or limiting the certainty of its inflammatory effects.' (The Lancet, Oct. 20, 1892.)

"VII. We shall show that compulsory vaccination, while it does not prevent small-pox, has maimed thousands for life and caused the death of hundreds upon hundreds. In the third report of the minutes of the vaccination evidence commission, 1890, testimony was given before the Royal Commission of six thousand two hundred and thirty-three cases of serious injury and eight hundred and forty-two deaths from vaccination. Can parents afford to run the fearful risks of vaccination poisoning?

"VIII. Finally, as a registered physician in the state of California, as a professor for several years in a medical college, as a United States consul in Asiatic Turkey, during a portion of General Grant's administration, counseling with an English physician, or personally treating small-pox, which, by the way,

I should prefer to have, under proper sanitary conditions to Jenner's cow-pox, I protest against the compulsory vaccination law of this state that turns many of our children out of the public schools. I denounce it as a menace to good health, as a violation of personal freedom, and opposed to all those fraternal interests that constitute us the parts of one great brotherhood, clearly conscious that what affects one affects all through the laws of thought, of sympathy, of heredity, and the amenities of social life."

Previous to sending the manuscripts for this volume to the press, I forwarded a communication to Dr. Parker by a special messenger, asking him for all his letters appearing in the daily press in defence of vaccination, for publication in this volume. He but briefly noticed my request. Evidently he was not very anxious to be booked and read in public libraries. This, on his part, was a shrewd stroke of discretion.

Compulsory vaccinationists dare not meet in open manly debate anti-vaccinationists. They lack the courage of their convictions. Statistics and yawning graves face them. During this struggle in San Diego with the doctors, the health and school boards, with my didactic energies, saying nothing of an innate Scotch grit, I challenged the vaccinating-believing doctors to meet me in open discussion upon this subject in the opera house, the proceeds above the expenses to go to some benevolent institution. These were to be the questions or propositions for consideration.

1. Resolved, That the Jenner inoculation and the later calf-lymph-virus vaccination, while not a preventative of small-pox, endangers health, by poisoning the blood and promoting various zymotic diseases.

2. Resolved, That compulsory vaccination laws are unconstitutional, un-American in genius, a barrier to education, and a menace to personal liberty.

And believe me, readers,—not a doctor entered the arena. Such dastardly cowardice required no comment! * * * * Now, in the face of California's compulsory vaccination laws, the un-vaccinated children of the city attend the public schools side by side with their cow-pox scarred playmates.. Such results can be secured in any town or city of the commonwealth if the people will arouse themselves, distribute literature, get up public meetings and air this terrible delusion—calf-lymph vaccination.

In the midst of this local controversy I sent the following communication to the R. P. Journal, San Francisco, which was published in its issue of Feb. 16, 1899:—

CALIFORNIA VACCINATION LAW.

For over fifty years I have been battling in such movements as anti-slavery, temperance, prohibition, the reform health-dress, woman suffrage, class legislation, "doctors' trusts," and now I am fighting on the vaccination battlefield. And the mad battle is fully on, here in San Diego.

A vaccination law, passed some ten years ago by the California legislature, has remained nearly a dead letter; but now, without a case of small-pox in our midst, the board of health, afflicted with a sort of health-spasm, has proposed that all the school children of this city, whose population is 22,000, be vaccinated. And the threat is thrown out that unless parents comply and have that putrid calf-lymph put into their children's arms, their children will be denied the privilege of attending the schools. I repeat, the battle is on. My whole nature is aroused and I have written articles in every San Diego newspaper except one against the enforcement of this unjust law. Of the eighty-five resident doctors in San Diego, only three or four are opposed to vaccination, and these, with one exception, are too cowardly to stand up and say so, or to even sign a legislative petition to repeal the law or so amend as to make it optional with the parents. The school board has not yet issued the order, though the health board is urging them to do so.

The public is thoroughly awake. At the Mothers' Club meeting in our city lately the lower room in the school house was literally. packed to hear the vaccination question discussed. Though many doctors were invited to come and defend vaccination, only two made their appearance. These spoke in its defense. I was present, clad in medical war paint, with my left hand full of anti-vaccination documents, sent me by Wm. Tebb, of London, Prof. Alexander Wilder, of Newark, and others. The discussion was keenly, critically hot. Thank the gods, a large portion of the mothers present were opposed to vaccinating the children. My opposition was vehement, if not violent. I defied the law. I pronounced it unconstitutional; and, treasonable or not, I advised the mothers present to positively refuse to have that diabolical poison put into their children's arms —a poison that upon the highest medical authority does not prevent small-pox—but does kill thousands every years. Foolishly vaccinated a second time myself when in San Francisco in 1861, I was in bed three weeks from the poison. I came near losing my arm, and I felt the effects of the villainous virus for several years.

What the doctors call pure virus—"tubes and points"—I publicly pronounced filthy, vile, impure, calf-lymph "cussedness." During the discussion I advised that instead of vaccinating and poisoning the blood of our clean, sweet-faced children, that the doctors, druggists, lawyers, and preachers of San Diego—*all* be vaccinated and the dear, innocent children be spared. This was not a popular presentation to the vaccinationists present, and yet, two-thirds of the ladies cheered me roundly. Oh, that our mothers, wives, sisters, and daughters could vote, as they do in New Zealand, Wyoming, and some other states! Heaven hasten woman-suffrage.

IS THIS VACCINATION LAW CONSTITUTIONAL?

Assuredly not. The law of God, written in the moral nature, is above any law enacted by political legislatures. Many of their pronounced laws, though having the signatures of governors, are not laws. They are often repealed during the very next session of the legislature. Law to be law, must be based upon the eternal principle of right—the absolute principle of right and justice. I will not obey an unconstitutional law—a law that entails disease and death—a law that infringes upon my personal liberty. And be it treason or not,—I will urge in the faces of popes, priests, and politicians, others not to do it. This vaccination law is undoubtedly unconstitutional—and is in perfect keeping with "medical trusts" and these nefarious "doctors' laws" that seek to compel patients to employ only physicians of their own school.

This vaccination law is so odious, so dangerous to health, that it has never been enforced to any considerable extent in our noble state, California. It never will be. The people are too progressive. Petitions are now being circulated in this city for its speedy repeal. The English Parliament has recently, be it said to the glory of England, made vaccination optional with the parents.

The old fugitive-slave law was once the law of this country, North and South. And this law was compulsory; Northern men were required to hunt, catch, hold, and return the negro (nine-tenths white perhaps) back into slavery, who were running for the freedom of Canada, and for safety under the British flag. I would not, did not obey this law. Though comparatively much younger then than now, I defied it, and I am proud to say that with a family of good Quakers in Cayuga county, New York, I helped several runaway negroes to make their way by the "underground railroad," as it was called, into the Canadian dominion. Wendell Phillips, William Lloyd Garrison, the Quakers, and thousands of reformers, were charged with treason for criticising a government that enacted such a congressional law (the Fugitive Slave Law), in the interests of perpetual slavery. They refused to obey it. Garrison was mobbed in Boston, Foster was egged in Worcester, Foss was stoned, others were vindictively persecuted by unprincipled politicians and conservative bigots. But the law was finally repealed—and slavery itself abolished. Now Phillips, Garrison, Foss, Abbie Kelley, Parker Pillsbury, Henry C. Wright, and many of those brave old soldiers of freedom,—scarred soldiers, fighting for personal liberty and equality before the law,—are honored, and their very tomb-stones are wreathed in unfading laurel; while the congressional and political manufacturers of that old fugitive-slave law, are either forgotten, or their names have half-rotted-away into the silence of merited infamy. Such will be the fate of this California vaccination law, and its doctor-inspired makers. Let the eighty-five doctors of San Diego. and the board of health—one or more of which are doctors—take due notice. Justice is sure to come!

J. M. PEEBLES, M. D.

A SMALL-POX SCARE!

During February (1899), as the controversy was waxing warmer, the doctors of San Diego made a sortie to get up a small-pox scare! The wife of J. Q. Hedges came to San Diego from Los Angeles, and died Feb. 19th. Before leaving Los Angeles she received a severe strain from lifting a heavy box. This caused back-ache, headache, vomiting and hemorrhage. The doctors pronounced it a case of small-pox and further reported the woman knew she had been exposed to small-pox, and confessed to this. But the husband denied that she had been exposed or that she had made any such confession; as he was in the room during the consultation and heard all that was said. Nine different persons had been in the sick-room before the woman died, and everyone of these was quarantined for twenty-one days, not one of whom took small-pox. One doctor admitted the woman died from hemorrhage—so the husband stated —and not from small-pox. But the doctors succeeded just the same in working up a panic, in moving the local board to enforce the compulsory law on vaccination—and withal, in enriching their purses. There was not the shadow of a small-pox case in the city.

The sequelae as the doctors would say, or after effects of this scare, may be in part gleaned from a Sun editorial, March 17:—

"The finance committee of the common council will meet tonight at 7:30 o'clock and some interesting bills will come up for approval or rejection. Among the number will be one from Dr. Jones, who was quarantined for 21 days by order of the board of health. Dr. Jones wants $210 for the twenty-one days' service." How modest the fee!

"Then there are claims of $2.50 per day each for three extra policemen for twenty-one days necessitated by this same suspected small-pox case. The pest house, too, has been repaired at an expense of some $350 to date and small claims for medicine, disinfectants, etc., amounting to $50 will also be presented, making a total of $767, chargeable to the small-pox scare to date. The bill of Nurse Lowe, who escaped quarantine has not yet been settled nor that of the undertakers, who buried Mrs. Hedges, but both bills will doubtless bring the amount up to over $1,000.

" 'A few more small-pox cases and we're a busted community, rain or no rain,' said a city official this morning, and really it does seem expensive to have these little luxuries.

"By virtue of sec. 17 of article 13, of the city charter, the board of health has power to appoint additional health inspectors and at a conference held yesterday it was decided to appoint a committee to inspect all passengers coming on trains from Los Angeles. This will cost a few hundred dollars, but the health board feels the precaution is necessary."

This small-pox scare—when there was no small-pox—made San Diego's doctors the laughing stock of all the regions 'round about. Only one, Dr. Jones, however, was quarantined! * * * It can now be stated that the labors of our Anti-Vaccination league have been largely crowned with success. True, we have not as yet secured a repeal of the detestable compulsory law, but we have compelled a truce on the part of the local boards and opened wide once more the doors of the public schools. Complete victory is in sight.

The municipal boards of Los Angeles are still enforcing the compulsory law, and so in my October "Temple of Health," I thus warned northern tourists who were expecting to spend the winter in Southern California to shun Los Angeles:—

"Persons with families, proposing to spend the winter in Southern California, sending their children to the public schools, should avoid Los Angeles as they would a den of vipers, and go on down to San Diego, where parents are not (now) compelled by school boards to have their children's blood poisoned with cow-pox virus, before they can enter the public schools."

This, the editor of a Los Angeles paper, Dr. A. P. Miller of the East Side News, copied, and then added:—

"Let us add, that it was Dr. Peebles' efficient work which rescued the children of San Diego from the tyrant's clutch. Live another hundred years, doctor, and sweep all such monstrous usurpation of power from off the earth."

The Boston Daily Globe—Nov. 24, 1899,—says: "Four children of one family at Highland Falls, N. Y., are dangerously ill as the result of vaccination. All are badly poisoned, and the results will probably prove fatal. The school trustees ordered the vaccination. The father of the little ones is an inmate of the Soldiers' Home, and the mother is a poor washer-woman." A "poor washer-woman!" No redress for that stricken family, for that disrupted and ruined home; and the next time the conservative M. D. comes down from his professional stilts to notice an anti-vaccinator, he will repeat the stale declaration: "We use lymph taken from healthy young cattle, sterilized, put up in glass tubes and hermetically sealed up until used." Hence, how could the lymph be to blame? It must have been an "act of Providence." The school trustees ordered it. Who takes the risk in this business? Why, the American people of course, among whom there is only a small per cent. of such characters as Wm. Tebb and Dr. Ross. The rank and file of our American citizens are today tamely and supinely submitting to this form of legal criminality, contented with a passing record of facts as a matter of daily news, and only rarely proving themselves equal to the supreme occasion, as Mr. Lawbraugh did in Geneseo, Ill., fighting the vaccinators until he reached the steps of the state supreme court, where he got his rights.

Here is another case reported in a Boston paper. I clip the following from "The Banner of Light," of Dec. 9, 1899:—

"The supporters of that divinely-inspired barbarism known as vaccination are no doubt rejoicing with exceeding great joy over the beneficent effects of its application in Malden, Mass. Percy Tanner, a boy of thirteen years, is the latest victim to this wicked practice. He was vaccinated on Friday, Dec. 1, and his arm began to swell shortly afterward. On Saturday he went into convulsions, and passed away on Sunday. Medical aid was summoned, but the doctor could do nothing to save the boy. If the boy had been stabbed, or killed by a blow, his assailant would have been arrested for murder. As it is, the vaccinating doctor is still at large, ready and even anxious to treat other healthy patients by similar methods. Wherein does murder by assault differ from murder by vaccination? Only in one respect —the latter is enforced by law, and those who commit it are protected from punishment. Other kinds of homicide are deemed crimes, but this one seems to be a special privilege of a few men called doctors, to whom the state gives a license to kill ad libitum. Young Tanner's death is the third caused by vaccination in Malden alone.

"N. B.—There are no cases of small-pox in Malden, nor is there any special danger from that disease. When will the people assert themselves and secure the repeal of this most odious law?"

This winter (1900) there is a movement all along the line to enforce the compulsory law. In almost every state school boards have issued peremptory orders to vaccinate, or otherwise to exclude the children from the public schools. The taxes paid by the parents for public school service are not considered. The law, the boards and the vaccinators have the power of life and death, the same as was arrogated by the ancient kings. Lobbies and corrupt politicians make the laws. "Damn the people," say these impious usurpers; "their province is to obey the laws and pay taxes." And half the people seem willing to pay this price for the privilege to live. The millionaire classes near rule in America today. The idea of the sovereignty of the citizen, has come to be regarded by the privileged classes as a form of silly twaddle which orators may affirm and re-affirm on the Fourth of July; but it has become obsolete as a working principle for business men. Aye, business men, including the vaccinating syndicate, who "stand in" with the politicians and get the kind of legislation they want, and then proceed to dictate terms to the protesting citizen with impunity.

I admit that the coined phrase—"damn the people"—stands for a certain fact, since only a minority in the mass are sturdy and self-sacrificing defenders of both general and personal liberty. A very considerable contingent among our voting population do not appreciate or care for any stake they may have in the government, and therefore hold their vote as a commercial commodity which they are ready to sell in the market and which political parties are just as ready to buy. This class of people, too, will generally turn their children over to the vaccinator rather than be subject to any expense or inconvenience in protecting them.

Civilization breeds curses unknown to barbarism. A primitive and childlike people are sure to fade and die out by contact with a civilization like the mercenary Anglo-Saxon. Our sectarists and schools do not compensate for the evil effects of our vaccination-virus syphilis and "rotgut" whiskey. In a later chapter I shall show that vaccination imposed by the countries of Europe and the United States upon the West Indies, Sandwich Islands, South Africa and Hindustan, outweigh all the other curses we have imposed upon those unfortunate peoples. Japan, though civilized, is departing from her ancient traditions and borrowing her models from the West. She is now being taken in hand by the commercial sharks and has recently adopted our vaccination practice and issued a decree making it compulsory. In the Philippines, too, the irrepressible vaccinator is plying his unholy calling. There, as here, it is financially profitable.

Down in Georgia the vaccinators are likewise busy. I clip the following from the New York World, Nov. 17, 1899:—

"Americus, Ga., Nov. 16.—Two cases of small-pox exist here and the local authorities have passed an ordinance making vaccination compulsory. Half a hundred members of the First Church of Christ (Scientists) oppose vaccination as against the doctrines of Christian Science, and the affair will be settled in the courts.

"Where citizens have refused to obey the new ordinance charges of disorderly conduct have been made against them in the Mayor's court.

"Yesterday Mrs. C. B. Rames, wife of a prominent physieian, was summoned to court for refusing to be vaccinated. She is a Christian Scientist. Upon her refusal to be vaccinated or leave the city, Mrs. Raines was sentenced to thirty days in the police barracks. At the request of friends sentence was suspended until today, when the entire Christian Science church congregation was summoned to court upon the same charge. Among the number were many young girls, business men, matrons, and mothers with their babies.

"Attorneys for the Christian Scientists secured a continuance until tomorrow. The Christian Science church is an incorporated body and holds a charter from the state of Georgia guaranteeing religious liberty. The members will steadfastly refuse to be vaccinated contrary to their religious creed, and the entire membership will doubtless be sent to prison tomorrow for contempt of court.'"

This appears in the daily press merely as an item of news; no comments; no protest against this flagrant injustice and violation of individual rights. Here is a religious body who have normal and conscientious scruples as well as rational and seientific objections, against vaccination. The vaccinated are safe anyhow—according to the oft-repeated assertion of the vaccinators—from all danger of taking small-pox from the unvaccinated. Then why not leave the unvaccinated to their own liberty? Answer: because the aggregate fees from the whole population being vaccinated would be greater than those accruing from only a part being vaccinated. As long as the state has guaranteed this business, why not run it on "business principles?" In the tithing days of the compulsory priest-tax, if we didn't pay up promptly, we were threatened with future damnation. Now, having transferred the privilege of compulsion from the priest to the doctor, he brings calf-lymph-virus-hell right into our households, here and now;—brings it to stay and blossom out into eczema, sores, tumors, and various skin diseases.

I clip the following editorial from the Los Angeles "Medium," Sept. 21 :—

"The foulest blow that could possibly be struck at liberty of conscience has been dealt out this morning, (Monday, Sept. 18,) when the doors of the public schools (by decree of school directors backed by the board of health and an infamous state law,) closed against our children because we cannot consent to have their young bodies poisoned and enfeebled by the injection of vaccine rottenness into their healthy veins.

"This invasion by the doctors of the most sacred right of home, (the protection of our children's welfare,) is the most humiliating subjugation to another's will in a matter where intelligent conviction of duty points in the opposite direction, which parents can endure. Humiliating as it is for the fathers to bare their backs to the lash of these diplomatized tyrants, these rascally whippers-in, it is ten thousand times more so for the mothers. Fathers have the one noble and unquestioned right remaining, viz. legislative protest and appeal. Woman has no such able weapon as the ballot with which to defend the objects of her supremest love from desecration by these M. D.'s in their unholy work. Is it possible that woman needed this last and most audacious heart-thrust to goad her on to demand and secure the noblest right of citizenship,—a voice in making the

laws by which she shall be governed in the fulfilment of her duty
to her children?

"Mother love is the highest expression of the human soul,
and must yet command every resource for the carrying out its
sacred impulses.

"We especially ask our brother voters, to meet with us and
tell us whether they intend to pay their school taxes while their
children are robbed of the benefits so precious to every American heart;—to consider what steps to take toward the repeal of
the infamous law;—to take counsel with the mothers as to the
surest and most speedy way to secure an honorable representation in the legislative halls of the state.

"Since our children cannot be allowed to run in the streets
deprived of the advantages of school, while we carry forward
measures for the repeal of this unrighteous law, we must devise
means for assuming the unjustly imposed burden, of private
schools for them.   Come one, come all, to the meeting an-
nounced on opposite page.   MRS. O. F. SHEPARD."

I clip another protest from the Chicago "Times-Herald,"
Nov. 20, 1899:—

"Chicago, Nov. 20.--To the Editor: The article bearing
the title 'Vaccination for Chidren' should be read by the parents
of all school pupils.   I had just such a case of vicious vaccinating and my little boy died from the poison introduced into his
system by the vaccination.   When the entire city becomes
aroused against the crime of vaccination then will every attempt
to carry out the outrage of vaccinating healthy children be suppressed.   There is no law to compel pupils to suffer any person
to tamper with the health of school children, and the doctors
know it, yet they threaten the parents with keeping out of school
the children who are told to leave the school if vaccination is attempted to be enforced.   Let no rest be given the agitation of
anti-vaccination.   It is a crime, and no mistake, to infect a
healthy babe with poison of any kind.

HENRY C. STRONG,
778 North Rockwell Street."

I will now go a little outside the local province and insert a
letter from an able Italian physician—Charles Ruata, M. D.,

Professor of Hygiene and of Materia Medica in the University of Perugia, Italy. It was published in the New York Med. Jour., July 22, 1899:—

VACCINATION IN ITALY.

PERUGIA, Italy, June 21, 1899.

To the Editor of the New York Medical Journal:

"Sir: In his presidential address to the American Medical Association Dr. Joseph M. Mathews had the goodness to call mad people, misguided people those who have not the good luck to be among the believers in the preventive power of vaccination against small-pox. It is not surprising to hear such language from fanatics; in fact it is most common to see ignorant men make use of similar vulgar expressions; but it seems to me almost incredible that the president of such a powerful association as the American Medical Association in his address showed himself so enthusiastic in his belief as to forget that respect which is due to his colleagues who do not have the same blind faith.

"It may be that we anti-vaccinationists are "mad" and "misguided," as Dr. Joseph M. Mathews affirms in his late address, but I feel that we are far more correct in our expressions, although we do not believe, but are quite sure, that vaccination is one of the most wonderful and most harmful mistakes into which the medical profession has ever fallen. I can assure you that if I am a madman, my madness is very contagious, because all my pupils for several years have become as mad as I am, so that several thousands of the foremost medical men in Italy are suffering now with the same kind of madness.

"One of the most prominent characteristics of madness is shown in illusions and hallucinations which are accepted as fundamental truths. Now, let us see what are the main facts about vaccination and small-pox in Italy:

"Italy is one of the best vaccinated countries in the world, if not the best of all. This we can prove mathematically.

"All our young men, with few exceptions, at the age of twenty years must spend three years in the army, where a regulation prescribes that they must be directly vaccinated. The official statistics of our army, published yearly, say that from 1885 to 1897 the recruits who were found never to have been vacci-

nated before were less than 1.5 per cent., the largest number being 2.1 per cent. in 1893, and the smallest 0.9 per cent. in 1892.
This means, in the clearest way, that our nation twenty years
before 1885 was yet vaccinated in the proportion of 98.5 per cent.
Notwithstanding, the epidemics that we have had of small-pox,
have been something so frightful that nothing could equal them
before the invention of vaccination. To say that during the
year 1887 we had 16,249 deaths from small-pox, 18,110 in the
year 1888, and 13,413 in 1889 (our population is 30,000,000) is
too little to give a faint idea of the ravages produced by small-
pox, as these 18,110 deaths in 1888, etc., did not happen in the
best educated regions of our country, but only in the most ignorant parts, where our population live just as they lived a century
ago—that is, the mountainous parts of Sardinia, Sicily, Calabria, etc. Among the great number of little epidemics which
produced the 18,110 deaths mentioned, I will only note the following: Badolato, with a population of 3,800, had 1,200 cases
of small-pox; Guardavalle had 2,300 cases with a population of
3,500; St. Caterina del Jonio had 1,200 cases (population,
2,700); Capistrano had 450 cases (population, 1,120); Mayerato
had 1,500 cases (population, 2,500). All these villages are in
Calabria. In Sardinia the little village of Laerru had 150 cases
of small-pox in one month (population, 800); Perfugas, too, in
one month had 541 cases (population, 1,400); Ottana had 79
deaths from small-pox (population, 1,000), and the deaths were
51 at Lei (population, 414). In Sicily 440 deaths were registered
at Noto (population, 18,000), 200 at Ferla (population, 4,500),
570 at Sortino (population, 9,000), 135 at San Cono (population,
1,600), and 2,100 deaths at Vittoria (population, 2,600)! Can
you cite anything worse before the invention of vaccination?
And the population of these villages is perfectly vaccinated, as
I have proved already, not only, but I obtained from the local
authorities a declaration that vaccination has been performed
twice a year in the most satisfactory manner for many years
past.

"Vaccinationists were not a little puzzled by these facts,
and yet with the greatest certainty they asserted that this enormous number of deaths was due to want of revaccination. Happily, in Italy we are able to prove that revaccination has not the

least preventive power. I only give a few figures: During the sixteen years 1882-'97, our army had 1,273 cases of small-pox, with 31 deaths; 692 cases, with 17 deaths, happened in soldiers vaccinated with good result, and 581 cases, with 14 deaths, happened in soldiers vaccinated with bad result. This means that of a hundred cases of small-pox, fifty-four were in persons vaccinated with good result, and only forty-six in those vaccinated with bad result, and that the death rate among those vaccinated with good result was 2.45 per cent. and only 2.40 per cent. in those vaccinated with bad result.

"Vaccinationists say that when vaccination does not 'take' the operation must be repeated, because no result means no protection given. Now, we see that soldiers not protected because vaccination did not 'take' were less attacked by small-pox than those duly protected by the good result of their revaccination; and that the death rate in those vaccinated with good result was greater than among those in whom vaccination did not 'take.'

"Our vaccinationists did not lose their extraordinary courage before these facts, and they objected that they might be accounted for by considering that during the years before 1890 vaccination was not well performed. I can not understand this objection, but accepted it, and have limited my analysis to the last six years, during which the only lymph used in all our army has been animal lymph, exclusively furnished by the government institute for the production of animal lymph. The results are the following: The total number of our soldiers during these five years was 1,234,025, of which 783,605 were vaccinated with good result, and 450,420 with no result. In the first the cases of small-pox were 153—that is, 1.95 to every 10,000 soldiers, while in the others the number of cases was only 45—that is, 0.99 cases to every 10,000 soldiers. The 'duly protected' soldiers were attacked by small-pox in a proportion double that among the 'unprotected' soldiers.

As you see, these are official statements, extremely trustworthy, because the official statistics were made in a country where and at a time when no one thought that it was possible to raise a doubt against the dogma of vaccination. In our country, we have no league against vacination, and every father

thinks that vaccination is one of the first duties; for these reasons no bias could exist against vaccination in making these statistics. I could continue for a long while to quote similar facts,
but I wish to call your attention only to the two following ones:
During the three most terrible years of epidemics that we have
had in Italy lately (1887, 1888 and 1889) the death rate from
small-pox among our people of the same age as the soldiers
(twenty, twenty-one, and twenty-two years) has been 21 per
100,000, and it was 27.7 during the worst year (1888). In our
army the same death rate during nine years (1867-75) has been
20 per 100,000, and it was 61.3 during the worst year (1871).

"In consequence of our young men being obliged to spend
three years in the army, it happens that after the age of twenty
years, men are by far better vaccinated than women, and, if vaccination did prevent, after the age of twenty small-pox should
kill fewer men than women. But in fact just the reverse has
happened. I give here the statistics of the three years 1887,
1888 and 1889 as the ones of greatest epidemics, but all the other
years give the same results:

Deaths before	Man.	Woman.	Man.	Woman.	Man.	Woman.	Man.	Woman.
the age of 20....	5.997	5.983	7.349	7.353	5.625	5.631	18.972	18.968
After the age of 20	2.459	1.810	1.990	1.418	1.296	863	5.749	4.091

"After these facts I would most respectfully ask Dr. Joseph
M. Mathews if he can show that in considering them I have lost
my mind. At any rate, I do not consider it correct for a medical
man to make use of such language against other medical men,
who have the only fault of considering facts as they are, and
not as one wishes they should be.

"The progress of knowledge has for its principle base, truth
and freedom, and I hope that in the name of truth and freedom
you will publish these observations, badly expressed in a language that is not my own, in your most esteemed journal.

                          CHARLES RUATA, M. D."

CHAPTER VI.

VACCINAL INJURIES AND FATALITIES.

"Small-pox, typhus, and other fevers, occur on common conditions of foul air, stagnant putrefaction, bad house drainage, sewers of deposit, excrement-sodden sites, filthy street surfaces, impure water, and over-crowding. The entire removal of such conditions is the effectual preventive of diseases of these species, whether in ordinary or extraordinary visitations."—SIR EDWIN CHADWICK, C. B.

In the last century it was the intelligent poor who, with an unerring instinct in such matters, were the first to rise in open revolt against the practice of inoculation, a practice which the doctors assured the general public would modify and mitigate the severity of small-pox to the extent that would render it harmless. The inoculators had a pecuniary interest in the practice then, the same as vaccinators have in the practice they are now, through legislation, pushing to the front for its compulsory enforcement. It was thoughts and votes—it was the popular dread and the persistent opposition of laymen which finally overthrew the old inoculation practice. So in this more modern practice, if the doctors were not supported by political legislation, there would be little to complain of. The vaccinator would be but rarely consulted, and it would not be long before the general verdict would be pronounced against it.

There are very many painful facts associated with the praetice of vaccination which point toward a distinct vaccinal diathesis as having been engendered in the general population from
the presence in the blood of the vaccinal virus as an active morbid agent. But few families in this country have escaped its
baleful effects. This deadly virus works its way slowly, perhaps,
into the weakest organs of each child, and there industriously
sets up its inversive kingdom to wage an unrelenting war against
the physiological integrity of the organism. The vaccine virus
once introduced into the blood it extends its poisonous influence, and later usurps permanent possession. It has come to
stay, and henceforth make a hades of trouble for the possessor.
This malignant spirit, intrenched in the very center of the life
forces, will defy all the arts we may employ to exercise it. Some
poisons are swift, instantaneous; they speedily accomplish their
destructive work and then depart; but the vaccine-poison is a
composite fiend into which has entered the subtle germs or
sporules of eczema, leprosy, consumption, cancer, erysipelas,
scrofula, syphilis, and tetanus together with other diseases
known and unknown, picked up on the way from Jenner to the
present time. Once installed beneath the skin, they take their
time to "develop their claim"—one year, ten years, this generation or the next; no matter, death has a mortgage on the prem-
ises and will claim his own and receive it on demand. If vaccination were made a penal offence today, yet would the crop of diseases which the vaccinator has sowed continue to yield its terrible harvest of disease and death for generation to come. And the
major portion of all this—like a bastard bundle of live flesh—is
set down at the door of compulsory legislation—legislation
which has been urged and manipulated and lobbied through by
politic-members of the medical profession.

In the present chapter I shall reproduce a small per cent. of
the reports of vaccinal injuries and fatalities, as furnished by hospital surgeons, medical practitioners, and official reports of

boards of health. And I may here premise that vaccinal injuries among the upper classes are far less frequent than those reported from the lower walks of life. The children of the upper class, particularly in England, have good resisting powers, the result of good feeding, plenty of exhilerating exercise, comfortable clothing, abundant bathing, and a clean neighborhood where filth and infection do not abound. Nor is vaccination enforced among the upper class as with the poor.

Vaccinators are never troubled about filthy quarters in a crowded city. They never call a mass meeting of citizens to discuss the menacing danger of cess-pools. Cess-pools have no terrors for them; but an unvaccinated person is a "focus of contagion" that threatens the very foundations of the public health. Even the vaccinated are not safe while a town is menaced by the presence of an unvaccinated person! How fortunate that we have among us a class of skilled experts (?) who thrill with disinterested solicitude for our citizens of every class, lest they catch the small-pox!

A small-pox epidemic is feared; the doctors fan the flames of public anxiety until a panic is on. The order then goes forth to vaccinate—to vaccinate everybody. A motley crowd of mothers with their children from among the poor gather at the vaccination station. No mother is asked by the doctor in charge: "Have you any one at home down with a fever, or suffering from any disease, the virus of which floating about in the air may taint the blood of anyone who may have an abrased skin?" No, the business on hand is to vaccinate. The consequences may be considered later. The prospect of the fee is not to be lightly considered. The thing has to be done. It is law, and it is—it is—business. Bring forward the children.

The first case I shall here present is a marked one; a most pathetic and distressing one. I reproduce it from Dr. John

Pickering's large work, "Which, Sanitation or Vaccination," page 159. Dr. Pickering is a prominent physician of Leeds, England:—

"I proceeded to Colne to investigate the circumstances surrounding this impotent lad early in March, 1890. My visit attracted some attention, and on its reaching the ears of the editor of the 'Burnley Gazette,' one of the staff was sent to Colne to furnish a full report. I take the following particulars from the above-named periodical, dated March 26, 1890, and as it is from the pen of a strictly impartial observer it will have more weight with some people than one written by myself.

FEARFUL CONDITION OF A CHILD AT COLNE.

"The victim of the disease which is attributed by the parents and various medical men, including Dr. Miller, medical officer of health for Nelson, to the effect of vaccination, is a young lad ˜residing with his parents in Sutcliffe's Place, Colne. Thither our representative proceeded for the purpose of investigating the matter. The mother of the lad, a cleanly and intelligent woman received myself and guide, and conducted us to the spacious kitchen. Here we found the lad seated listlessly in a large, comfortable rocking-chair by the side of a glowing fire. He was clothed in a shirt, vest, and knickerbockers, his arms and legs being left uncovered, and presented an appearance painful in the extreme. Dwarfed and deformed, with a small pale face, large eyes which instead of beaming with intelligence, showed a hopeless indifference to everything which passed around him, the lad's condition looked pitiable indeed. His mother informed us that he was nearly twelve years old, but the unfortunate boy looked no more than five at the outside. The right arm, which had been vaccinated, was much the worse deformed of the two. It was scarcely as thick as three fingers of an ordinary man's hand, and was drawn up across the narrow chest, as if in a sling, the hand being turned away at an unnatural angle, giving a dislocated and claw-like appearance. Only two thin, skeleton-like fingers were extended, the others being clutched together in one close clasp. The whole limb was paralyzed and totally useless. On the back of the hand, the elbow, and shoulder, were sores too hideous to be described in detail, which exuded, almost continually, a foul yellow matter. The elbow joint was swollen and contrasted strongly with the slenderness of the arms above and below, which were merely skin-covered bones. Two other sores existed, one on the body under the arm, and another under the chin. This latter wound had closed up, but the mother of the lad said that some time ago, a hole under the chin, where the sore now existed, went so far down that 'you could see the roots of the tongue.' On the left cheek was another large sore which disfigured the little face sadly. The left arm, although not so deformed as the right, was of very little use to its owner, being thin as a lath, except at the joints. The back of the left hand too was covered with a foul, festering mass, and the fingers were slender and elongated until they also resembled the claw of a bird. Sores, little better than those on the hands, almost covered the lad's knees; and both feet, which were naturally small, bore similar corrupt excrescences. The mother informed us that all the sores exuded filthy matter which made perfect cleanliness among the lad's clothing and bedding impossible, although she made every effort within her power to effect this end.

"Another young lad of about nine years old was in the room, and he presented an appearance the exact opposite of that of his elder brother. He was a sturdy strong little fellow with ruddy cheeks and bright eyes, and looked as if he had never known a day's illness. 'This child,' said the woman, 'has been vaccinated too, but I plucked the stuff off the minute it had been put on, and I wouldn't have another child vaccinated like the other one if I was to go to Court every day.'

' Several doctors, it appeared, had attended the eldest lad at different times, but all had been equally unsuccessful Dr. Brodiibb, Medical Officer of Health for Colne, had lanced one of the sores on the lad's right hand, but this treatment only made the hand appear worse, and the mother would not permit him to use the lancet on the other hand. Dr. Miller, Medical Officer of Health for Nelson, had attended the lad and had told

the mother that neither he nor any other doctor could cure
him. 'The child's blood,' he said, 'is poisoned from head to
foot.'

"Questioned as to how long the child had been in that condition the mother said that from the time the child was vaccinated it had never been healthy, but not until two years after
the operation had been performed did the sores break out in
the manner described. The child then had endured nearly ten
years of this 'living death,' as his condition has been described.
Many people had done their best to relieve him, the woman told
us. 'I had him at one doctor and he said that if he did not cure
him he would not charge anything. He gave him fifteen bottles.
at 2s. a bottle, and he was just as far off when he had got it as he
was before he began, and he said, 'I'll give him up.'

"The mother of the boy said she had had twelve children,
and had always been a hearty woman. Her husband was also
a healthy man, and she could not think that the lad had taken
any disease from them. They had always lived in Colne, in
Chapel Fold 15 years, and in Colne Lane 20 years. After describing the various treatments to which the child had been subjected, the woman went on to speak of the manner in which his
life was spent. He had never learnt to read. He had been sent
to school when he was able to get about, but he had been ordered back. as it would not do for him to sit with the other
children. When he was better than usual he was able to run
about a little and on fine days he would wander about the street
on which they lived; and on one occasion he was even able to
walk as far as the station. The other children in the street
would not play with him, and directly he went into the thoroughfare their parents called them into the house until the boy
had gone. Thus the poor lad was shunned like a leper and at
that early age, experienced one of the greatest trials to which
he could possibly be subjected."

Dr. Pickering continues:—"The subject of my illustration
has been described by medical men as a case of 'vaccinal syphilis.' Not that I think much of their opinion. It may be that or
it may be that and something more. I lean to the latter opinion. * * * My illustration shows what an ugly blot and
what a ghastly risk vaccination is when it can change a healthy

ECZEMA FROM VACCINATION.

child into an object the mother can never look at without a shudder. No consideration in the wide world, save that of its money value, would lead a body of men, claiming some knowledge of pathology, physiology, and chemistry, to retain an observance where such accidents are possible."

This poor boy died while Dr. Pickering's book was going through the press. His agonies were so terrible a few days before his death, that he said to his mother, "Mother, give me some poison to send me home." That had already been done by the vaccinator, who probably felt as little concern over the result as the saloonkeeper does over the wrecked and wretched home whose husband and father he prepared the pit-falls for which precipitated his destruction.

Many children die of diseases after vaccination, previously unknown to physicians—diseases so malignant as to suggest a connection with a distinct order which requires new rules of classification in order to refer them to their proper categories; an order in which the last and highest potency of both humanized and animalized virus have formed a conjunction and evolved a new species, from which a new and distinct diathesis has been established in the human organism. Those who wish to experiment with these poisons on their own person, by all means leave them to their liberty; but to subsidize this practice by state grants and enforce it by means of state penalties, is a usurpation of personal liberty which the American people would not tolerate a single day if they could once realize the really dangerous situation.

As early as 1808 Dr. Richard Reece wrote—Prac. Dict. of Domestic Medicine, London:—

"Even if the cow-pox did afford a certain security against small-pox infection, as Dr. Jenner has represented it, it would still remain a question whether the human race would really be benefited by its universal adoption, since the cutaneous eruptions that have followed have in many instances proved more fulsome than even small-pox itself. That those eruptions do occur after cow-pox infection must be allowed by its most stren-

uous advocates, being perfectly novel, of a nature unknown before the introduction of vaccination, and peculiar to those who
have been vaccinated, and often so inveterate as more than
to counterbalance the trivial advantages that we were first led to
expect from its introduction." Again, he says:—"It must be
allowed that the local inflammation excited by the inoculation
with this matter, is of a very unfavorable nature, and often ends
in a deep sloughing, frequently producing such an adhesion of
the muscles of the arm, as very much to confine its motions;
and some instances have occurred of the mortification spreading, so as to destroy the life of the child; an instance of which
happened in St. George's Fields. The child was inoculated at
the Cow-pox Institution, Salisbury Square, Fleet Street; the inflammation of the arm exceeded its usual boundary; on the
sixth day mortification ensued, which proved fatal to the child."

In the "Medical Observer" for Septemebr, 1810, Dr.
Charles McLean gives a list of sixty cases of vaccinal injuries,
with the names and addresses of ten medical men, including two
professors of anatomy, whose families had suffered, seriously
suffered, from vaccination.

Dr. Scott Tebb, of London, details the following case.—
"A Century of Vaccination," page 282:—

"At an inquest held on December 8, 1882, on the body of
Lilian Ada Williams, born in St. Pancreas Workhouse, and vaccinated on the seventh day after birth, the jury found 'that the
death was caused by suppurating meningitis, following ulceration of vaccine vesicles on the arm, and they were of opinion
from the results of the post-mortem examination that the vaccination of the child ought to have been postponed."

"Such instances are by no means rare, as disclosed in Appendix ix. to Final Report of the Royal Commission, one of the
most flagrant cases there reported being a fatal one of pyaemia
in a 'puny and probably syphilitic' seven months child weigh-
ing 4 pounds 2 ounces, and vaccinated when less than two days
after birth. (No. cxxi).'

The London "Lancet" remarks in a leading article.—Vol.
II, page 35:—

"There is a belief—it may be denounced as a prejudice, but it is not the less a deeply-rooted conviction, and one not confined to the poor or the ignorant—that if the vaccine disease may be transmitted by inoculation, other diseases less beneficial may be propagated in the same manner, and by the same operation. Many a parent of high and low degree dates constitutional disease in her offspring to vaccination with 'bad matter.' Who shall say that this etiological conclusion is always false?" In the number for October 28, 1854, (vol. ii., p. 360), it is stated:—"The poor are told that they must carry their children to be vaccinated by medical men who may be strangers to them. They apprehend—and the apprehension is not altogether unfounded, or unshared by the educated classes—that the vaccine matter employed may carry with it the seeds of other diseases not less loathsome than the one it is intended to prevent."

That cow-pox disease is sufficient to cause death in a weakly child, is shown by a case where calf-lymph was employed, recorded by Dr. Farrar—British Med. Jour., Oct. 13, 1894: "I consider her death to have been due to a constitutional malaise, induced by vaccine virus in a poorly nourished child."

Again, Dr. Tebb writes—"A Century of Vaccination," page 291:—

"A disease of the skin which has been especially referred to by the Vaccination Commissioners is impetigo contagiosa. The frequent occurrence of this malady after vaccination has been remarked on by the late Dr. Tilbury Fox and others. An extensive epidemic of impetigo contagiosa was occasioned by vaccination in the Isle of Rugen in 1885; seventy-nine children were vaccinated on June 11 with humanized thymos-lymph obtained from a government establishment at Stettin; all, with three exceptions, were attacked with impetigo contagiosa. and, by infection, the disease was spread to 320 out of a population of 5,000 inhabitants. A commission of inquiry was appointed by the German government, who reported that they were unanimously of opinion that the outbreak of the disease had been a direct consequence of calf-lymph vaccination."

In Prof. Wallace,—"Wonderful Century," page 232, are the details of a most distressing case:—

"As an example of the dreadful results of vaccination, even where special care was taken, the following case from the Sixth Report of the Royal Commission (P. 128) is worthy of earnest attention. It is the evidence of Dr. Thomas Skinner, of Liverpool:

"'Q. 20,766. Will you give the commission the particulars of the case?—A young lady, fifteen years of age, living at Grove Park, Liverpool, was re-vaccinated by me at her father's request, during an outbreak of small-pox in Liverpool in 1865, as I had re-vaccinated all the girls in the Orphan Girls' Asylum in Myrtle Street, Liverpool (over 200 girls, I believe), and as the young lady's father was chaplain to the asylum, he selected, and I approved of the selection, of a young girl, the picture of health, and whose vaccine vesicle was matured, and as perfect in appearance as it is possible to conceive. On the eighth day I took off the lymph in a capillary glass tube, almost filling the tube with clear, transparent lymph. Next day, 7th March, 1865, I re-vaccinated the young lady from this same tube, and from the same tube and at the same time I re-vaccinated her mother and the cook. Before opening the tube I remember holding it up to the light and requesting the mother to observe how perfectly clear and homogeneous, like water, the lymph was, neither pus nor blood corpuscles were visible to the naked eye. All three operations were successful, and on the eighth day all three vesicles were matured 'like a pearl upon a rose petal,' as Jenner described a perfect specimen. On that day, the eighth day after the operation, I visited my patient, and to all appearance she was in the soundest health and spirits, with her usual bright eyes and ruddy cheeks. Although I was much tempted to take the lymph from so healthy a vesicle and subject, I did not do so, as I have frequently seen erysipelas and other bad consequences follow the opening of a matured vesicle. As I did not open the vesicle that operation could not be the cause of what followed. Between the tenth and the eleventh day after the re-vaccination—that is, about three days after the vesicle had matured and begun to scab over—I was called in haste to my patient, the young lady, whom I found in one of the most severe rigors I ever witnessed, such as generally precedes or ushers in surgical, puerperal, and other forms of fever. This would

be on the 18th of March, 1865. Eight days from the time
of this rigor my patient was dead, and she died of the most
frightful form of blood poisoning that I ever witnessed, and I
have been forty-five years in the active practice of my profession. After the rigor, a low form of acute peritonitis set in, with
incessant vomiting and pain, which defied all means to allay.
At last stercoraceous vomiting, and cold, clammy, deadly sweats
of a sickly odor set in, with pulselessness, collapse, and death,
which closed the terrible scene on the morning of the 26th of
March, 1865. Within twenty minutes of death rapid decomposition set in, and within two hours so great was the bloated and
discolored condition of the whole body, more especially of the
head and face, that there was not a feature of this once lively
girl recognizable. Dr. John Cameron, of 4 Rodney Street, Liverpool, physician to the Royal Southern Hospital at Liverpool,
met me daily in consultation while life lasted. I have a copy of
the certificate of death here.

" 'Q. 20,767. To what do you attribute the death then?—
I can attribute the death there to nothing but vaccination.' "

Prof. Wallace continued:—"In the same report, fifteen eminent medical men gave evidence as to disease, permanent injury, or death caused by vaccination. Two gave evidence of
syphilis and one of leprosy as clearly due to vaccination. And,
as an instance of how the law is applied in the case of the poor,
we have the story told by Mrs. Amelia Whiting (QQ. 21,434-
21,464). To put it in brief:—Mrs. Whiting lost a child, after
terrible suffering, from inflammation supervening upon vaccination. The doctor's bill for the illness £1 12s. 6d.; and a woman
who came in to help was paid 6s. After the first child's death,
proceedings were taken for the non-vaccination of another
child; and though the case was explained in court, a fine of one
shilling was inflicted And through it all, the husband's earn-
ings as a laborer were 11s. a week."

Let us moralize for a moment. Had Mrs. Whiting's child
been injured or killed by a railway train, he could sue the company for heavy damages. But suppose the state not only
quashes this indictment, but arrests and fines Mr. Whiting for
not having already exposed his second child to the same danger.

We should justly conclude that the corporation and the state were in a conspiracy to sacrifice the children of the poor. The case is not quite parallel, I admit; for while we can readily discover an adequate motive in the vaccinator, it would be difficult to find a corresponding motive in the corporation. Here the vaccinator had already killed one child, and not only collected his fee for inoculating the blood with his vaccine poison, but also another fee for treating the fatal symptoms he had occasioned. One would think he ought to be satisfied with this, and so spare the crucified and bereaved parents further sorrow. But no, the vaccinator was not going to stop with any half way sacrifices. Mr. Whiting had failed to show due respect for the vaccinating god in not bringing all he had and placing it upon that vaccine god's accursed altar. And therefore, notwithstanding the day's wages were barely sufficient to keep the family from hunger, he is arrested and fined. There must surely be impending a judgment day for the manifold oppressions which have so long cried to heaven for redress.

Dr. Pickering writes—"Sanitation or Vaccination," pages 73-74:—

'In a census organized by the A. V. Leagues in Scarbro, about four year ago (1888), the results as to cases of injury, the experience of the householders of a certain district were certified to as follows: Cases of injury 74, and of death 37; total 111. An analysis showed them to be composed of skin diseases, more or less severe, 24; scrofula, 2; abscesses, 13; convulsions, 3; ruined health, 16; erysipelas and other forms of blood-poisoning, 18; crippled for life, 7; not stated, 28; total, 111. These results, it must be allowed, are somber and suggestive in detail.

"Other answers, in various towns, have yielded similar results. If Scarbro, a health resort, gives such convicting evidence as to the baneful effects of the complications and sequelae of vaccination, what would 'Whitechapel' say?"

*   *   *   *   *   *   *

"Look at that little child the mother is fondling on her

knees. She how she caresses it; 'tis the loveliest of all earthly gifts. Its skin is white as Alpine snow; its rounded arms and legs are supple, yet firm withal. The eyes are bright as when they first saw Eden. Its sleep is calm and sweet. With a sense of awe and anxiety unknown to man that mother lingers over its fair features, and heaves a sigh pitiful and sad—that child has to undergo a medical operation on the morrow. A medical operation!! The morrow comes, and with it the doctor. He has carefully selected 'good matter,' the incision is made, and the cancerous deed is done. After many assurances, which are not worth a breath—the mother heeded them not—the vaccinator packed up his traps and away he went, dreaming not of what he had left behind to work out its cunning. In a few days the child became ill; the arms were inflamed, the eyes and nose were running sores; it wasted away, and death ended the puny child's career, and that was all! No, it was not. The mother lost her child; her reason went after it, and she was consigned to a mad-house. The father was a widower and childless. This is vaccination! Do you say it is an exceptional case? So far as father and mother are interested, yes; but not so with regard to the child itself. I maintain that for the United Kingdom a folio volume of the size of Dooms-Day Book would be required in which to register the mishaps of a single twelvemonth!

*   *   *   *   *   *   *

"Here is another case of vaccine injury, unique and harrassing in its details. A child was vaccinated, and a short time afterwards it developed sores over the whole body. Infirmaries and their medical staffs were helpless to relieve the sufferer, and it survived for nearly two years; but the skin shrivelled up and resembled that of a mummy. Prior to its decease the parents covered up the face, it was so agonizing to look at.

Here is a case, also related by Dr. Pickering, though not a special case of vaccinal injury, it is nevertheless so full of suggestiveness and common sense, I will insert it here—page 65:—

"During the epidemic years 1871-2, I had the most singular requests made to me. I was sent for to see patients young and old, in all stages of the disease and at all hours of the day and night, both in Leeds and the suburbs. One morning when I was about to leave my house a note was brought from Miss H, the daughter of a soldier, saying that the husband of a sister of her maid, living at Armley, was very bad with the small-pox, and would I kindly go and see him. After reading my letters at the office, I took the train up to Armley, and proceeded to the house of a Mr. Skinner, at the address furnished me by my correspondent. He was in a bad condition truly. I never saw a worse case. The wife was in a state of mind bordering on distraction. She said to me, 'The doctor says my husband can't recover. He came yesterday and said he should not go into the bed-room again, as it was the severest attack he had seen.' I answered, 'You may perhaps save your husband's life if you are prepared to carry out my injunctions with a woman's will.' 'Sir,' she replied, 'tell me what I am to do, and it shall be done.' 'Go, then,' I said, 'at once to the nearest shop, and purchase a piece of mackintosh two yards by two, and some soft soap; place the mackintosh under him, and wash the body well with wash leather, using the soft soap and tepid water; do this five or six times during the day and, when the fever symptoms abate, you can reduce the washings to three or four per day, but the ablution of the body must be continued morning and night for a fortnight. After the second day you can use a bed-room towel instead of the wash leather, but in the present tender state of the skin the wash leather will not irritate it more than he can bear. Let him have milk, oatmeal gruel, and as much cold water as he can drink. Have the windows and doors open, but keep him warm with extra blankets. In a few days—two or three—sponge the body with cold water after the tepid wash, and with this treatment put an additional blanket over him, so as to encourage a healthy re-action. Do this, and you have done your best to save your husband's life.' I repeated my orders again where necessary, and left the two, wife and husband, in charge of the good angel of Sanatory Science.

"In three weeks time that man was at his work, 'sound, wind and limb.' He and his wife have since emigrated to Australia, and I heard, only a month ago, they were doing well in their adopted country. This man had been vaccinated."

That small-pox is such a terrible scourge, is chiefly due to popular ignorance. Drastic drug specifics are not required in its treatment, or will not be when people order their lives in conformity with the physiological laws and rise above the depressing influence of fear. Every year fever slays its thousands. Dr. Pickering lived in the midst of the small-pox for years nursing and caring for those afflicted with the disease, yet the infection never became active in his organization.

In the "Family Physician" issued by Cassell & Co., p. 508, we read: "We know of no cure for small-pox and the disease must be allowed to run its course." Again on page 568: "It must always be borne in mind that we have no specific remedy for any of our common fevers. We cannot hope to cure them and in many cases the object of the treatment is simply to conduct the fever to a favorable termination, and to ward off any inter-current disease." This work is the product of many medical writers and is a compendium of physic up to date. I simply drop these hints, but it is not my present purpose to enter upon a discussion of a rational mode of treating all zymotic affections. But I will state on general principles, if the regular doctors could bring themselves to feel a small fraction of the solicitude for the people to adopt sanitation, hygiene and physiological modes of living, that they do for forcing vaccination on the general public, we should then have prevention on a scale that would amount almost to perfection. If it were not for the shekels associated with vaccination and lack of it in teaching the laws of clean-living,—in other words, if the wampum, to use the Indian's word for cash, could be transferred to the other "bull's horn '—we might then hopefully look for a changed attitude from that fraud of the profession whose main dependence is the calf-lymph infected lancet, and drastic drugs.

William Forbes Laurie, M. D., Edinburgh, St. Saviour's Cancer Hospital, Regent's Park, says: "Being anxious not to do mischief to my fellow-creatures, and being, as regards my own family, liable to fine or imprisonment under the Compulsory Vaccination Act, I lately wrote to some members of Parliament on the subject. I asked them to come here and see for themselves the dismal results of vaccination in cases of paralysis, blindness of both eyes, hip joint disease, consumption and frightful forms of skin disease. Though I received replies they have not yet inspected the cases."

VACCINATION A FRUITFUL CAUSE OF CANCER, ERYSIPELAS AND LOCKJAW.

Cancer in the human system is somewhat analagous to the mistletoe on forest trees, as it grows at the expense of the life or structure upon which it fastens. It is a morbid and foreign growth, converting the cells and tissues of organs in which it has established itself for the growth of its own inversive death-prophesying structure. In its immediate vicinity the tissues deteriorate and die, often leaving a gap or open ulcer between the sound flesh and abnormal growth. It is often hereditary and may remain latent for thirty or forty years, and then suddenly burst forth in its work of destruction. It may be propagated or communicated to the blood of a healthy person through an abrased skin, or from the point of a lancet, somewhat after the manner of the leprosy contagion. In Zurich, Germany, Dr. Hanan succeeded in propagating cancer in rats by inoculation in 1890. It may be readily communicated by means of arm to arm vaccination, since the cancer virus is latent in the blood of many an apparently healthy child. Nor can we be certain that calf-lymph is free from latent hereditary cancer. Indeed, there are not wanting the highest medical authorities who believe vaccination is the principal cause of the alarming increase in cancer during recent years.

Dr. William Hitchman, consulting surgeon to the Cancer

Hospital, Leeds, formerly public vaccinator to the city of Liverpool, stated in 1883, that "syphilis, abdominal pathisis, scrofula,, cancer, erysipelas, and almost all diseases of the skin, have been either conveyed, occasioned, or intensified by vaccination.' —Vac. Inquirer, p. 31.

Dr. Dennis Turnbull, author of "The New Cancer Treatment," says:—

"In my treatment of cancers and tumors during the last 30 years, it has fallen to my lot to come in contact with all grades of society; and, with a view of eliciting the true facts, it is my habit carefully to interrogate my patients, relative to their general habits of life, their antecedents, and the health of their ancestors. I have, therefore, gathered a considerable store of information, which enables me to speak with some authority; and I have no hesitation in stating that, in my judgment, the most frequent predisposing condition for cancerous development is infused into the blood by vaccination and re-vaccination."— The Vegetarian, London, 24th November, 1888.

"Cancer" says Dr. Hitchman, "is a blood disease; so also is cow-pox; and when, to inherited or acquired morbid tendency, vital exhaustion, digestive disorder, and unhealthy surroundings, are added the various complications attending vaccination, the presence of certain growths, or even bony structure in the larynx or any other part, is not surprising to one who believes in casual sequence. Scientifically, whatever tends to a diminution in the natural color and specific gravity, especially of the red corpuscles of the blood, may, sooner or later, lead to serious transformation into tubercular, syphilitic, or cancerous affection."—Vaccination Inquirer, London, February, 1888.

It is also important to note a very peculiar relationship between calf-lymph and human tissue, namely, in their relative rates of organic change. The growth from infancy to adult life in man is extremely slow, while bovine organic processes are very rapid. Hence inoculation of the blood through the skin of a human subject with calf-lymph—however pure—would furnish the conditions for the commencement and growth of cancer, owing to difference in rate of growth of the two sets of plasmic cells. The foreign cells thus introduced would grow in the weaker organ where they would become seated, at the expense of the cells in the surrounding structure; and when we remember that all vaccine matter is a degenerate form of lymph—lymph which has undergone retrograde metamorphosis, putrifaction—the disturbance and ultimate destruction it will occasion by injection into the circulation, will be a hundred-fold greater than if taken into the stomach, where nature could dispose of it without sensible harm.

The lymphatic system is traversed by a far finer network of glands and vessels than is comprised in the veins and arteries, and according to Swedenborg, the lymph that circulates in these vessels is "the true purer blood" of the body. Now, the poison that finds its way through an abrasion or puncture of the skin, is immediately taken up by the lymphatic vessels; and when a cancer begins to grow its little branches and rootlets traverse and ramify in these very vessels, which are specially and immediately invaded by vaccination. We need not therefore, be surprised that so many cases of vaccinal injury occur even when "pure glycerinated calf-lymph" only is used by the vaccinator. For every case of small-pox which vaccination "mitigates" we may be pretty sure there will be ten cases of cancer. Cancer cases are now most rapidly multiplying in those countries where vaccination is well nigh universal—Germany, England, New Zealand, and the United States. It has been stated, re-stated and never denied so far as my knowledge extends, that no Jew or Jewess was ever known to have a cancer unless they had first been vaccinated. It is undeniable that calf-lymph virus —the extract of heifer sores and ulcers—is the cess-pool that breeds blood diseases—the medical wayside weed-patch, on which grows and thrives pimpled faces, ulcerous sores, tumors, cancers, scrofula, and consumption.

Dr. Turnbull, in his book, "The New Treatment," writing on the origin and spread of cancers, after referring to sundry exciting causes—tight lacing, smoking, drinking, etc., says; "Numbers of my patients have expressed themselves as absolutely certain that they never had the slightest sign of cancer until after they submitted to re-vaccination. Let all truly seientific men cease to vaccinate, and, my word for it, the spread of cancer will be materially lessened."

In a carefully written pamphlet on "Cancer and Vaccination," by "Esculapius," the writer concludes as follows:—

"No candid and scientific inquirer who has read the recent works of Drs. Creighton, Edgar Crookshank, and Scott Tebb, can be surprised that an alarming increase in cancer is even now evident. Those who adopt so blindly the brutal practice calf-lymph vaccination are but too surely sowing the wind which they must inevitably reap as the whirlwind, a whirlwind of corruption, disease, and national deterioration. Where the so-called human lymph is employed, syphilis, leprosy, and tuberculosis follow in its train; and wherever calf-lymph is used, tuberculosis and cancer spread like a conflagration."

Erysipelas is one of the most frequent as well as serious effects that follow vaccination. But of late years the deaths resulting from this cause have been classed under different headings. In England and Wales, between the years 1859 and 1880, 379 deaths from erysipelas were directly traceable to vaccination. Indeed the usual inflammation excited by cow-pox virus is erysipelatous in character.

The following table, from Dr. Scott Tebb's work, page 346, gives the number of deaths for each of the intervening years:—

Year.	Deaths from erysipelas after vaccination.	Year.	Deaths from erysipelas after vaccination.
1859	5	1870	20
1860	3	1871	24
1861	2	1872	16
1862	3	1873	19
1863	11	1874	29
1864	13	1875	37
1865	10	1876	21
1866	10	1877	29
1867	4	1878	35
1868	9	1879	32
1869	19	1880	39

In the "Am. Jour. of the Med. Sciences," October, 1850, Mr. W. Moreland, secretary of the Boston Society for Medical Improvement, gives extracts from the records of the society relating to erysipelas following vaccination, and reported on by medical men. Eleven cases were given, three being fatal. Of the eight that did not prove fatal, four were very severe, three of which were attended with extensive sloughing.

In the "Lancet," May 31, 1863, Mr. J. R. Wells relates a case of a lady aged 55 years, who was re-vaccinated. Symptoms of phlegmonous erysipelas set in the following day and in four days after the operation she died.

The "Lancet" of Nov. 24, 1883, relates the cases of two children named Elliston and Griggs, who were vaccinated October 16, and in seven days two other children were vaccinated from lymph taken from the child Elliston. In a short time the Elliston child and the two last children vaccinated, died of erysipelas. The operations were performed at the regular vaccinating station.

"In 1875, there was an official inquiry at Gainsborough by Mr. Netten Radcliffe, of the Local Government Board, into cases of erysipelas following vaccination, of which six died; a searching investigation failed to dissociate the operation from the fatal erysipelas.

"In 1882 another Local Government Board inquiry was held by Mr. Henley and Dr. Airy at Norwich into certain deaths alleged to have been caused by vaccination. It was shown that eight children suffered from erysipelas 'due to some abnormal peculiarity or contamination of the lymph;' of these, four died.

"On the 25th of May, 1883, sixty-eight recruits were vaccinated at Dortrecht, Holland. Of these seven were attacked with erysipelas, and three died. In consequence of these cases, the minister of war, Mr. Weitzel, issued a circular notifying recruits that hereafter re-vaccination was not obligatory in the Netherlands army.

"Before the South Wales and Monmouthshire branch of the British Medical association, on Nov. 15, 1883, Dr. C. T. Vachell, of Cardiff, related a series of cases where erysipelas followed vaccination. On November 1, a child, aged three months, and an adult were vaccinated with lymph obtained from London. On the eighth day the arm of the adult was much swollen and red. On the same day the child presented every appearance of having been successfully vaccinated, and five tubes were charged from it. On November 10, five children were vaccinated from these tubes. On the 11th and 12th all these cases were attacked with erysipelas of the arm vaccinated, and, on inquiry, it was found that the child from whom the vaccine lymph had been taken was attacked with erysipelas on November 9."

—"A Century of Vaccination," page 348.

Among the older records of the Local Government Board are the following:—

"(1). A series of nineteen cases of erysipelas from vaccination at Warrington, with five deaths, in 1871.

"(2). A case of serious erysipelas from vaccination with National Vaccine Establishment lymph at Stoke Newington in 1871, in which inquiry elicited that violent inflammation had occurred in others vaccinated with lymph from the same vaccinifer; the vaccinifer having an inflamed arm on the thirteenth day and a small abscess in the axilla

"(3). Six cases of serious inflammation and three deaths in a series vaccinated with ninth-day lymph from one vaccinifer at Appleby, in 1873.

"(4). Several cases of erysipelas and inflammation, with five deaths, in a series of vaccinations at Chelsea, in 1875.

"(5). Twelve cases of excessive inflammation, six of erysipelas, with three deaths, two cases of axillary abscess, and one large ulcer, in a series of vaccinations at Plomesgate, in 1878.

"(6). Ten cases of erysipelas or abscesses, with four deaths, and several cases of eczema in a series of vaccinations at Clerkenwell, in 1879, in which 'it is clear that the erysipelatous contagion was imparted at the time of vaccination.' These assumed the form of syphilis.

"(7). Three cases of extensive erysipelas from vaccination at Blandford, in 1883.

"(8). Three fatal cases of erysipelas from vaccination at Sudbury, in 1883.

"Between the 1st of November, 1888, and the 30th of November, 1891, one hundred and thirty-two cases of inflammatory or septic disease (mostly erysipelas) following vaccination and terminating fatally, were the subject of inquiry by the Local Government Board. Numerous cases have also been investigated by the Royal Commission on vaccination, and are cited in Appendix ix. to their final report.—Ibid. p. 350, Scott Tebb.

"Dr. Theodore Dimon, St. Louis "Courier of Medicine," 1882, vol. vii., pp. 310-312. Boy, nine years old; vaccinated January 6, 1882, with bovine lymph. Tetanus supervened on January 27; no cause discovered except vaccination, which was followed by an irregular shaped ulcer. Boy died on the tenth day.

"Dr. H. J. Berkeley, 'Maryland Medical Journal,' 1882-83, vol. ix., pp. 241-245. Healthy man, forty years old; vaccinated in the middle of January, 1882. Tetanus supervened on February 7; death on February 13. No lesion discovered except at the point of vaccination, which was occupied by a deep ulcer, with an inflamed and indurated border resembling syphilis.

"Dr. W. T. C. Bates, 'Transactions of the South Carolina Medical Association,' 1882, vol. xxxii., p. 105. Mulatto boy, aged five years; vaccinated February 9, 1882, with humanized lymph. Tetanic symptoms supervened on March 8. No other cause but vaccination discovered. Boy lived fifteen days.

"Dr. R. Garcia Rijo, 'Cronica Medico Quirurgica de la Habana,' 1886, vol. xii., p. 388. White child, two years old; vaccinated in April, 1886. Characteristic tetanus appeared in latter part of May. No lesion beyond vaccination discovered. Death followed on the fourth day.

"Dr. Zahiroodeen Ahmed, 'Indian Medical Gazette,' March, 1889, vol. xxiv., p. 90. Adult, aged twenty-one. The symptoms appeared fourteen days after primary vaccination. He died.

"Local Government Board, Case x., Appendix ix., Final Report, Royal Commission on Vaccination. Female, aged two years; vaccinated on September 10, 1889. Symptoms of tetanus first appeared on October 2, and patient died on the 5th of October.

"Dr. P. A. Morrow, in referring to eruptions incident to vaccination, observes: 'It must be confessed that the profession has manifested a most decided unwillingness to recognize their direct dependence upon vaccination.'

"Again, in the Local Government Board inquiries on erysipelas, held by Mr. Netten Radcliffe at Gainsborough, and by Mr. Henley and Dr. Airy at Norwich, before referred to, there were in all ten deaths, and in only one of these was vaccination mentioned on the certificate of death.

*　　*　　*　　*　　*　　*　　*

"It is impossible to form any accurate estimate of the total amount of serious and fatal injuries produced by vaccination; the following table only gives the deaths recorded by the Registrar-General:—

England and Wales.—Deaths from cow-pox and other effects of vaccination, from 1881 to 1896.

1881	58	1889	58
1882	65	1890	43
1883	55	1891	43
1884	53	1892	58
1885	52	1893	59
1886	45	1894	50
1887	45	1895	56
1888	45	1896	42

DR. S. TEBB.

"This shows that in England and Wales, according to medical death-certificates, one child on an average dies every week from the effects of vaccination. This fatal record, however, does not by any means represent the damage done by the operation, as for every death there must be a very large number of children who are injured, but survive for years with enfeebled constitutions.—Ibid pp. 360-61.

*　　*　　*

"Also, in an inquiry, on behalf of the Royal Commission, on a series of injuries from vaccination at some villages in Norfolk, in 1890, Dr. Barlow found, from the brief provisional investigation he was able to make, that some septic material had been introduced at the time of the insertion of the vaccine lymph, and that this was mainly responsible for the untoward results obtained. There were three deaths and in none of these was the word 'vaccination' mentioned on the death certificate.— Ibed p. 364."

A perusal of the history of vaccination is not calculated to excite our veneration toward the medical profession, the older schools of which sanction a species of blood-poisoning with concentrated animal virus in a manner that contravenes the principles of all true science. Their specifics are largely derived from the traditions and superstitions of an ignorant age. All their theories concerning the preventive and mitigating effects of vaccination belong to the category of pseudo-science. The profession knows this to be pseudo-science, and yet with craft and cunning they shun discussion, shelve complaints, evade and mutilate facts, twist statistics, raise false and irrevelent issues, make false returns of death from vaccinal injuries, dub antivaccinators as pestilent agitators, lobby for compulsory vaccination, persecute the true psychic who restores the sick without medicine, and do many other things which reveal motives foreign to the public welfare.

In this domain—the vaccinating branch of the profession— medical practitioners are inversive, reversive, and subversive; they invert the order of nature by creating disease with the pretence of preventing disease; they revert to an ancient superstition which Jenner borrowed from peasant milk-maids, and which Lady Montagu borrowed from the common folk in Turkey; and they subvert the intention of nature by sowing an extra crop of incurable diseases in the name of health—scrofula, cancer, erysipelas, leprosy, consumption, etc.

No part of the organism requires greater care and attention than the skin. It is the most fatal avenue through which poisons can reach the blood. The venom of the rattlesnake would be comparatively harmless in the stomach, but reaching the blood and nervo-circulation through the skin it is swiftly fatal, while the virus of scrofula, leprosy, or cancer, reaching the blood in the same manner, may lie latent for years and then spring forth with malignant activity. Note also, that the function of the skin is to excrete not to absorb; it is to throw out waste material that has fulfilled its use, not so much to take in material, for this would be "climbing up another way" than the one ordained by nature. Ninety-nine per cent. of all substances that enter the body through the skin are interlopers and enemies which forever war against the original integrity of the man. A mosquito made a minute puncture on the neck of a healthy girl; it had just previously left the cheek of a leper. The following year that maiden revealed the unmistakable symptoms of leprosy. A blue bottle fly inoculated an abrazed surface on the nose of a butcher; a rusty nail pierced the foot of a girl in her stocking feet: a wasp stung a delicate child on her arm. All these died with blood poisoning. Only last Forth of July, about a dozen small boys in various parts of the country received slight skin flesh wounds from gunpowder; all of whom developed lock-jaw in a few days, and died. And not many months since I read accounts in the daily press of one child bitten by a red ant, and another child was stung by a bee, in both of whom blood poisoning supervened, and they died.

Thus we see how the skin is a gateway through which the most subtle and infinitesimal poisons may reach the citadel of life, there to deploy in the work of destruction, either slowly or swiftly, but always surely, having only one goal, which is death. It is through the skin the opium fiend injects the agent of his fantasia, through the skin the viper strikes his venom; aye, through the skin the vaccinator pushes his lance, dipped in the virus that may have traveled from afar, gathering a legion of diseases on the way.

———

RE-VACCINATED HOSPITAL NURSES.

It is frequently asserted by advocates of vaccination, that re-vaccinated hospital nurses very rarely if ever contract small-pox, and still more rarely die of it. While we may admit with Bacon that, "The plague is not easily received by such as are continually about them that have the plague, as keepers of the sick and physicians;" still, such immunitiy as they enjoy is in no wise related to vaccination or re-vaccination. They take the disease and die, the same as other people, but more rarely. Their unifom protection lies in their general health, sanitary habits, and in their cheerful spirits, which are never associated with fear. Dr. Robert Cory officially distributed cards to parents at public vaccinating stations, which stated that: "For fifty years nurses in small-pox hospitals had wholly escaped small-pox, owing to their re-vaccination." This card was originally printed —"Nurses at the small-pox hospital, Highgate." By dropping out "the" and appending an "s" on hospital, a much stronger case for the vaccinator was made out. This same Dr. Cory was the heroic gentleman who inoculated himself with syphilis from a syphilitic child, to prove experimently by vaccination that it could not be thus communicated. But its possibility was duly and painfully demonstrated in his person. The sad sequel need not be related.

I will here append a few reported cases, sufficient to illustrate two or three aspects relating to hospital nurses:

"Dr. C. T. Pearce said to the Parliamentary committee of 1871: 'I yesterday visited the small-pox hospital at Highgate, and (after the statements which have been made in this room that the nurses of that hospital are secure against small-pox by re-vaccination) I confess that I was not a little astonished when the door was opened by a nurse whose face was scarified all over with small-pox. I asked the nurse how many patients there were in the hospital? She said 104. 'Are there many vaccinated?' 'Nearly all, sir, now, and many of them twice over.' 'How many nurses are there?' 'Twelve.' 'How many night nurses?' 'Two.' I went from Highgate to Northumberland Street, and there had an interview with the assistant clerk, who gave me the astounding information that at Stockwell a nurse recently engaged because she was pitted with small-pox, was re-vaccinated on her engagement, and she is now in bed with confluent small-pox!"—London Soc. Tract, p. 6, Hospital Nurses.

"At the Fulham Hospital, three of the re-vaccinated attendants under Dr. Makuna took small-pox."—Small-pox and Vaccination. Dr. W. T. Iliff, p. 10.

"At the same hospital, Dr. Sweeting states that four of his re-vaccinated nurses had taken the disease."

"At the Halifax Hospital, in April, 1881, the matron and a nurse contracted small-pox from a patient; the matron had been previously vaccinated, while the nurse had been re-vaccinated only a week before she was taken ill."—British Medical Journal, May 7, 1881.

"At the Lewes Fever Hospital a nurse was engaged, and re-vaccinated November, 1881. She took small-pox about a week afterwards. and had it badly, but was not marked. She had been vaccinated in infancy, and again when ten years of age."—Vaccination Inquirer, vol. iv., p. 66. Letter, W. T. Martin.

*　*　*　*　*　*　*

"In a letter addressed to Mr. Wm. Tebb, dated January 20, 1882, the late Dr. W. J. Collins states that on the occasion of a recent debate on the vaccination question, at which the house surgeon of the Fulham Hospital was present, he (Dr. Collins) 'had a chat with him afterwards, when he confessed that five of his re-vaccinated nurses had taken small-pox! He (the house surgeon) said he had not considered the difference as regards stating between vaccinated and re-vaccinated.'" (! !)—Ibid.

"Ashton-under-Lyne has just passed through a small-pox scare in consequence of the occurrence of some twenty cases with seven deaths. Nearly all were vaccinated, including two re-vaccinated nurses in the Workhouse Infectious Hospital."—Vaccination Inquirer, v. 10, p. 5.

"The 'Leicester Chronicle,' July 1, 1893, stated that Mr. Clarke, Inspector of Nuisances to the Blaby Union, died of small-pox at the board's 'hospital camp.' In commenting on the case, 'The Vaccination Inquirer' says:—'It was not long before he contracted his own fatal illness that he remarked, in conversation with Mr. Amos Booth, that he considered it impossible for him to take small-pox, so well protected was he.' "

"Writing in 'The Star,' March 1, 1894, in reply to statements in 'The British Medical Journal,' Mr. J. T. Biggs, member of the sanitary committee, Leicester, said:—'During the present outbreak, which began in September last, five of the nurses and attendants at the hospital, all well vaccinated (one of the nurses being re-vaccinated), have been attacked with small-pox. One of these, a very bad case, died of confluent small-pox.'"

"Nurses, being generally advanced in years, habituated to fatigue, and little liable to worry of spirits, do not readily receive infection."—Instructions Relative to Contagious Diseases, London, 1801.

"This well-known phenomenon attending small-pox will appear less singular when we reflect that the same observation has been made respecting the plague, a more virulent contagion, the history of which shows in every invasion of that dreadful malady, that many escape, though constantly employed about the sick, or infants sucking their infected mothers."—(Small-pox) R. Walker, M. A., London, 1790.

"In Buck's 'Treatise on Hygiene and the Public Health,' vol. 2, p. 521 (Art. 'Small-pox and Other Contagious Diseases') we read: 'It is a fact, fully appreciated by medical men, that persons constantly exposed to small-pox very rarely contract the disease. In the case of physicians, health inspectors, nurses, sisters of charity, hospital orderlies, and some others, this is the rule; and of over one hundred persons who have been, to my knowledge constantly exposed, some of them seeing as many as a thousand cases, I have never personally known of more than one who has contracted the disease; but there are many writers who believe perfect immunity to be extremely rare. In this connection, attention may be called to the exemption of certain persons who occupy the same room, and perhaps bed. with the patients, and though sometimes never vaccinated, altogether escape infection."

"The late Dr. W. J. Collins, of London, who had a long experience as a public vaccinator, in his essay entitled 'Have You Been Vaccinated?' writes:—

"'I have had a good deal to do with nurses, and know

their physical capabilities as well as any man. . At one t'me I had a staff that I was in the habit of employing, and they weie so constituted in mind and body as to resist any infection. They were built upon the square, hard as nails, broad as they were long, with plenty of room for the vital organs to play. They had no idea of danger, and seemed to have been born before nerves were invented. They were always in capital spirits, and troubled with a good appetite. * * * These nurses were in constant attendance upon patients who were suffering from small-pox, fever, etc. They had never been vaccinated or had small-pox.' "

"Mr. Thorpe Porter, M. R. C. S., of the Small-pox Hospital, South Dublin Union (see 'Medical Press and Circular, March 2, 1872), says:—

" 'With reference to re-vaccination, I have no faith in it. Not one of the thirty-six attendants at the South Dublin Union Sheds has taken small-pox. Only seven of the number were re-vaccinated. and as the remaining twenty-nine enjoyed the same immunity, wherein is the necessity of the operation?' "— Ibid.

CONSUMPTION AND VACCINATION.

The experiments conducted by M. Toussaint, in France (1881) leave no room for doubt that tuberculosis is due to a specific organism, and may be communicated to a healthy person through vaccination. He vaccinated a tubercular cow with lymph from a vaccine vesicle raised on a healthy child. Then in turn with the lymph from the pocks of the cow he vaccinated four rabbits and a pig. The rabbits were killed two months afterwards and found to be suffering from tuberculosis at the point of inoculation, in the glands and in the lungs. The pig also developed tuberculosis. both local and general. Here we are confronted with a fact of great significance. Toussaint's experiments prove that tuberculosis is communicable through vaccination; and as cows are subject to the disease, both in its latent and active form, we can never be certain that the calf-lymph from the vaccine farms is free from this subtle and insiduous enemy—consumption.

In the preface to Dr. Pickering's large work—"Sanitation or Vaccination"—he presents some significant details from his own family history:—

"My attention was first directed to vaccination by hearing the details of a mishap in my own family circle. The grandfather of my first wife was a surgeon practicing in a town in the East Riding of Yorkshire. About the year 1808 there was some stir amongst the members of the profession as to the duty of vaccinating their own children, I suppose by way of showing their confidence in the operation. Now the surgeon's wife,— a woman remarkable for her strong common sense,—exhibited considerable reluctance to her own children being dragged at the chariot wheels of this new invader. At length her husband said, 'Well, it matters this much to me: if vaccination is not performed in my own family, I am so teazed about it that I must give up my profession, and seek for some other means of gaining a livelihood.' This was an argument the wife was not able to resist; her consent was withheld no longer.

"The next question was where to find a healthy child from whom to gather a small harvest of Jenner's 'pure lymph.' A medical neighbor interested himself in this behalf, and in a few days the opportunity occurred to him, when a young woman, resident in Barnsley, came home with her child, three months old, to visit her parents, and was advised to have vaccination performed by the physician who had attended their own family for many years, and she applied to him accordingly. The child was apparently strong and healthy; vaccination was perpetrated; virus was stored from this vaccinifer; and the two children, ranging from one to three years old, members of the surgeon's family firstly referred to, were vaccinated in due course with the lymph thus acquired.

"There was no taint of hereditary disease in the surgeon's family; his progenitors had been farmers in that part of Yorkshire for two centuries or more; and the wife's family came from a healthy stock.

"Within twelve months after vaccination the two children sickened; the ruddy cheeks became pale; and the whole constitution showed symptoms of some unaccountable yet disastrous change. By a sort of instinct peculiar to woman, the wife insisted that her husband should go to Barnsley to inquire into the antecedents of the parents from whose child the lymph had been abstracted. He went, when, to his dismay, he found that both parents were the offspring of families subject to hereditary consumption

"The cloud of dejection and regret was never lifted from the future careers of either husband or wife; and the two children, a boy and a girl, knew not what health was in their after lives. The two grew up tall and handsome; both married in due time, but the sister only had a family; she had three boys and a girl.

"To cut a long story short, the parents died of consumption before they reached 46 years of age; and of the second generation two of the three boys and the sister died of consumption before they attained their 26th year; the other boy, by emigrating to a warmer climate (Springfield, La., U. S.), added ten more years to a weary and painful existence;—he died of consumption, at 35 years of age.

"The sister above mentioned became my wife; we were first cousins; she left two daughters; one died of consumption, in her 26th year; the other still lives, but she has never known what 'life' is; she has been more trouble in her rearing than all the eight children by my second wife 'put together.'

"Thus the members of a whole family had been hunted —thrust out of existence—by one unfortunate vaccination. How many similar instances there have been in the same period unrecorded, no one will ever know. Some estimate may be formed when I say that, in my journeyings to and fro in the world, I have never met with an individual whose experience did not run on parallel lines with my own; he or she had to recount misadventures in his or her family, or in the family of a friend or neighbor. No exception to this rule has presented itself during an advocacy extending over the third part of a century—a remarkable fact!

If the people of England knew the full meaning of "Vaccination," of the misery and death for 92 years last past, of which it has been the sole exciting cause, and if they could but follow the history of each event with its far reaching consequences, through three generations of people, not a vaccinating station would be standing in England tomorrow night; nor is there a vaccinator who would ever be permitted to refer to the subjcet in any educated family to the end of his days.

It is bad enough in all conscience, that the medical profession recommend a form of blood-poisoning as a prophylactic against a dreaded disease; but to force such a practice on the children of the poor, is a piece of human folly which deserves to be branded as a merciless crime against society. The physieian should be to the people the most reliable oracle, pointing the way to life and health; but instead he sends them the way of disaster and death—even forcing,—compulsorily forcing— them into the path that conducts thither! Professing to stand as guardians and protectors of the little children in seasons of danger, he cuts off every avenue of escape by the device of politic-compulsory laws; then with lance and pus proceeds to poison the fountain of youth by the performance of a rite that was imported from the lowest pit of beastliness, sores on horses heels and cow's teats! Neither the third or fourth generation may atone for the injury thus inflicted. Certainly, the doctors would abandon this dreadful business were not their pecuniary interests so completely interwoven with it. I do not say that vaccinators always sin against transparent knowledge, for I know how prone we all are to nurse opinions and beliefs when they favor our self-interest. The "love of money" is, indeed, the root of this "evil" as of every other, and we must be very watchful if we are not caught compounding with error when our bank account is steadily increasing. If it were possible to separate this practice wholly from pecuniary considerations, it is my firm conviction that the concensus of medical opinion would right soon declare against it.

In the evil times upon which we have fallen, each individual should strive to become "wise as serpents and harmless as doves," for it is now incumbent upon each human unit in the fermenting body politic, to watch and defend his own integrity. Against this integrity all class-interests combine. Production, massed in great trusts which are in possession of the labor-saving machines, sends the individual adrift who depends upon the labor of his hands. The grocer feeds the body with adulterated food; the manufacturer clothes it with shoddy garments; the vaccinator punctures and poisons it with putrid pus —and so on to the end of the chapter. From every direction enemies arise to assail the integrity of the man. We must, therefore, be alert and don our defensive armor. Of these other sinners, I am only making a passing reference to them; it is the chief of sinners—the public vaccinator—the seed-sower of disease—whom these pages are designed to more especially describe. It is my earnest desire to portray his hideous aspect, to depict the "color of his sandals" in a manner that even the little child—the arch enemy of whom he is—will avoid and flee at his approach! Unfortunately, it is not the supreme desire of the average human creature to know the truth and follow it whithersoever it leads. If it was, the question of reform would be a very simple one for solution and adjustment. Persecution of reformers does not arise from the fact that they are conceived in error, but they are hated and persecuted because the proposed reform strikes at the root of class privileges and self-interest.

BLOOD POISONING.

It is no exaggeration to assume that nine-tenths of the diseases that afflict mankind have their origin in some species of blood poisoning; these poisons being chiefly conveyed to the blood through the skin, but also in part through the mucous

surfaces of the mouth, throat, stomach and lungs. In the Registrar General's office, London, there were registered one
thousand diseases that afflict the human body, the larger proportion of which are based on the sequelae or after effects, and
not upon the real disease or its productive cause. Moreover,
if medical men had a predominant and enthusiastlc interest in
the public health as they now have in disease, the facts pertain-
ing to blood poisoning would receive a very different treatment
at their hands.

In the discussion of vaccination as a form of
blood poisoning, practitioners have never gone to the core of
the subject to find a scientific warrant for the support of their
claim. They persistentlv evade the fundamental aspects of the
question, and like a party politician, work upon the fears and
prejudices of the populace to enhance a practice which they
must know neither cures nor prevents disease. In order to promote these interests, the registration department increases
death-causes in general, and others in particular, which are indefinite and so arraigned that vaccine disasters may be screened
or covered up at the vaccinators discretion.

The leaders in the vaccination movement must be perfectly
aware that vaccination stands condemned, but they have no
idea of surrendering it; first and foremost, because of its money
value; secondly, because they do not wish to affect or disturb
the present disease conditions of the country and the world;
and thirdly, they dread the manner in which an awakened conscience and an indignant public would call them to account for
a century of blood poisoning. Disease—kept "booming" by
vaccination—when discontinued and superseded by sanitation,
the death rate will decline so rapidly that the "way faring man
though a fool" will be able to see whereof he has been deceived
bv the rash vaccinating doctor, who thenceforth will be rated at
his proper value. Judas went to his own place and that is where
he ought to have gone. God is just.

Such poisons as nature fails to readily eliminate from the system are stored up in the blood, awaiting the specially exciting cause that shall call them forth,—such as deteriorated vital power, bad habits, exposure, anxiety, disappointment, worry, etc. Any or all of these may rouse the poison into fatal activity. Syphilitic, leprous, or cancerous poison may be vaccinated into a family and there remain inert to the third or fourth generation; hydrophobia poison may lie dormant for a term of years; cancer and scrofula may sleep for a time, but at last each and all of these will usurp the soil in which they have been planted.

Dr. Pickering mentions the case of a syphilitic patient with a bad knee, who, by constant use of mercurial ointment for fifteen years brought on a most deadly salivation, which ran from his mouth day and night. The tongue became knotted and the odor was so intense as to be offensive to pedestrians passing that way.

We may not be able to calculate the results of that first disease taint which the vaccinator introduces through the skin puncture he inflicts on our little ones. Our eye may not follow it in its various paths, through its sure ramification and development in later life; through the children and children's children in whom that blood taint will deploy and accomplish its work of final ruin. It is indeed a serious thing to poison life at its fountain head, even thoughtlessly thinking to avert a possible future danger; but to thus poison the blood—the life forces—deliberately for gain is a most infamous crime against society.

Infection and contagion are in truth one and the same thing; it is a body possessing weight and form, a germ, an egg or sporule containing within it the property of life, which will grow and multiply when sown in a suitable soil, like that of the human blood. Cow-pox pus, broken down cells desquamating from the skin surface of a small-pox patient, and the dissolving tissue of a decaying corpse, contain these poison germs or sporules; and they are so deadly and persistent in their action, that even the boasted "glycerine" with which vaccine calf-pus is mixed, has no potency to destroy.

The presence of these sporules in the blood is blood-poisoning and nothing less, no matter whether the effects become manifest in eight days, in eight years or even until the second or third generation. Yet in the hands of an intelligent and cautious person this infectious matter is comparatively harmless. It may come in contact with the hands, the face or neck, but if not rubbed in, or if it does not reach an abrazed surface, no injurions results may be known to follow. True, a person with a depressed vital tone, with blood corrupted in whom the mucous surfaces of mouth or throat are cankered or slightly abrazed, then there would be danger; the deadly virus might then find ready access to the circulation and infect the person with a specific disease. Probably the most concentrated and deadly animal poison known is found in the female after death from puerperal fever. But even this the dissecting operator may receive on his hands without harm; but dip the point of a cambric needle into this putrifying tissue and puncture the skin with it would be an inevitably fatal procedure.

The crowded and filthy quarters where infectious diseases are generated fill the air of all the contignant country with infectious matter, but in and near these centers the contagion is far more concentrated and active. These disease germs lodge in our garments, enter our lungs, get into dwellings, but they will remain inert until their spring season arrives or in other words, until the human soil is suitably prepared. A healthy person need not fear them as long as that person is positive, free from fear and worry, and who rigorously guards the portals of the skin. The demon of darkness must have been on an active campaign when the vaccinator obtained permission from the state to assail this sacred inclosure—the skin—and befoul the fountain of life with his septic poisons.

In time of small-pox epidemic infection is more than ordinarily dangerous, because it is then more abundant and concentrated, and also because the populace are then more negative and susceptible. Whether they have been vaccinated or re-vaccinated makes no perceptible difference. Small-pox epidemics are nearly always preceded by depressing influences of a general character, like failure of crops, depression in business, lowering of wages and the effects of a grievous war. Then through the mucous surfaces of mouth, throat, stomach and lungs, the germs of disease may crowd and find their way to the circulation. Even here vaccination increases but never mitigates the severity of the disease or conditions of fatal sickness. When a whole people shall learn to live in conformity with the natural laws—ethical as well as physical—these zymotic scourges will practically disappear together with the infectious matter which now develops in consequence of an inverted system of physic.

EPIDEMICS AND FILTH.

During the Middle Ages the nations of Europe were periodically devastated by four distinct forms of plague—the plague proper, the sweating sickness, the black death, and the small-pox. They were each about equally fatal and each most at home in the midst of squalor and filth. During the last century, in consequence of improved sanitation, three of these scourges have practically disappeared in the West, though they continue their hold upon the Orient, where sanitary laws are quite unknown. In the West we have only small-pox left, which should have departed with the other three, and would have departed had the doctors and the state brought to the altar the same disinterested solicitude (?) to secure general sanitation, which they have displayed to enforce vaccination. It cannot be too often repeated: the present home of small-pox, as in times of yore, is where filth abounds; and its proper antidote is not vaccination, but cleanliness. It pays not the slightest respect for a vaccination certificate. but does take full account of dirt and dissipation. To the drunkard and prostitute it says : "I have a mortgage on that man's, that woman's life; they are mine !" and so it moves among the motley crowd, letting its pestilent shadow fall upon the dirtiest and most wretched, gathering these as its pre-ordained harvest. Of the importance of cleaning up these hells of dirt and stench the vaccinator says not a word, but lobbies the legislative bodies to compel every member of these dirty dens to be vaccinated.

Circumcision so long practiced by ⁺he ancient Egyptians and later up ⁺o this day universally insisted upon by the Jews in all countries as well as by many Orientals, is considered cleanly and health inspiring. Phimosis is certainly abnormal and unhealthy often leading, by irritation through the sympathetic nervous system, to the secret vice. It has also indirectly caused death. Why not then, inasmuch as the circumcision-practicing jews are the healthiest and about the longest-lived people on earth—why not, I say, enact a rigid circumcision law? And as this would require a surgical operation, politico-doctors could by persistent lobbying legislators, make it compulsory. And further, it could also be made a fertile source of medical and surgical revenue. This matter has already been favorably agitated in San Francisco, Cal. I should rather favor such a law myself, provided one of the clauses compeled the doctors by way of example, to be the first to submit to the surgical knife. Would not our medical gentlemen pronounce this a menace to personal liberty? Speak out doctors !

Dr. Pickering. in an interview between daily visits among small-pox patients, penned the following paragraph which is inserted in his very important work on "Sanitation or Vaccination," page 47 :—

"Epidemics, and, in fact, all zymotic diseases, may be said

to be filth-diseases. There is no exception to that rule. Whom do they attack? The unclean. What neighborhoods do they visit? The filthiest. What towns do they select? Those where sanitary conditions are the most neglected. Note the last small-pox epidemic, and take Leeds as an example. Who were the victims? The very lowest classes of society, children that were filthy, neglected, and ill-fed, others living in houses that were overcrowded, destitute of proper ventilation, and in courts and alleys where sanitation is a term unknown; adults, who are tramps, drunkards, prostitutes, men and women without homes, wanderers,—with a very modest sprinkling of the very lowest sections of the working classes; these formed seven-tenths of the patients who passed through the hospital of the Leeds Union, and these are the very self-same people, resident in the same houses, streets, and neighborhoods, who would have fallen the first victims to any other epidemic which had sprung up. If they had not yielded to the small-pox they would have suc-cumbed to scarlet fever, typhoid, or the like. If the unsanitary surroundings are there, and the physically deteriorated in health within reach, then the conditions for producing an epidemic are present, and the result cannot fail to be disastrous. The strong and healthy do not take the small-pox." But if they have been vaccinated poisoning the blood, searing the flesh, and depleting the vital forces, they have opened the door and invited small-pox to enter.

A Mr. John Cryer, an ardent anti-vaccinationist, taught school in Bradford, Eng. One day he noticed a lad of about twelve years—a new pupil in school. He questioned him: "Where did you come from?" "Sheffield, sir." "How long have you resided there?" "Six years, sir." "How many are there in the family?" "Six of us, sir." "Then you were in Shef-field during the small-pox epidemic?" "Yes, sir." "Did any of you have the small-pox?" "Oh, no, sir, we lived in a front street." That last sentence tells the whole story. It is worth more than a dozen reports of Local Guardians; worth more than whole columns of statistics. It hits the nail square on the head. and locates the disease. Why didn't the lad say: "Oh, no, sir, we were all vaccinated?" Because children tell the truth, and this was a spontaneous utterance which in one brief sentence gave the facts, the law and the philosophy. "We lived in a front street." When all streets shall be made like unto this front street, and all the people observe hygienic habits; when all shall be washed and made clean; when vaccination stations shall be superseded with free public baths—in that city small-pox will not be able to secure a night's lodging. For that city small-pox epidemics will have been numbered; and no class know this better than the medical profession. But then, what would become of the vaccinating fraternity if the last epidemic of small-pox should bid a final farewell and be no more known about its accustomed haunts? No, for the present the profession must cling to antidotes, specifics and prophylactics as their main chance, while they give to sanitary science a merely formal and tacit recognition. The profession are well aware that such mitigation of zymotic plagues as the civilized world have been able to realize in the last fifty years, is chiefly due to improved sanitation, while prophylactics and antidotes have played but an infinitesimal part, and that part generally working more injury than good.

I never yet met a fever case where the cause was difficult to find; either personal uncleanliness, a vitiated atmosphere, impure water, a cess-pool nuisance, or defective drainage; these or their kind, have invariably been found the exciting cause. When I am called to the bedside of a small-pox patient, I never once inquire whether the person has been vaccinated. What is the state of that patient's skin? Were there any abrazed surfaces about the body through which the disease could gain access to the blood? Is the house well ventilated? No, the atmosphere is foul. I discover, too, that from the convenience off the hall a sewer gas stench proceeds and fills the whole house. The house is in a crowded quarter. I know the rest. It was not neglect of re-vaccination but neglect of the simplest rules of health which caused the small-pox infection to "take." It was in its native soil and the conditions favored its springing forth. Here is a case which illustrates how the small-pox may be communicated through an abrazed skin:—

"In the small-pox epidemic of 1871-2, a lady's housemaid caught the small-pox. It was a mild attack. She did not leave the house. I called to assist the enquiry as to how she had got it. I said to the lady: 1. Is the maid a cleanly girl in her person and habits? Yes. 2. Is the house in a fairly sanitary condition? It is in a good condition, in every respect. 3. Does she offer any explanation? Only today. She said that about ten days before her attack she called at the small-pox hospital for a sister who had had the disease and was discharged that night, and took her home. 4. That circumstance of itself would not account for the small-pox unless the girl had an abrazed skin or spots in process of healing about her where the blood would be directly inoculated by the germs held in the air of the room. Enquire of her if she can bring to mind any incident of that sort? The girl cannot tax her recollection with any such facts. 5. To be more particular, please enquire again—had she scratches on her hands, face, or neck, where a wound of any kind was in a bleeding state? This time, I think, we have got a clue to the mishap. The girl is subject to chapped hands in frosty weather, and they are worse on the washing day. The evening she went to the hospital was during the severe frost in the second week of December; she had a hard day's washing, and she says she remembers that her hands bled very much from 'deep cracks' on the second joints of her fingers on both hands.

"The small-pox is accounted for, I said, and you will be more satisfied now that a cause has been found which explains the phenomenon.

"The attack was mild—1. Because the girl was possessed of a vigorous habit of body. 2. Because the air in the waiting room was constantly changing by persons passing to and fro, and the contagion was not strong enough to infect the system thoroughly. Had she remained there half-an-hour instead of five minutes, her case would have been more severe.

This coincidence shows how careful people should be not to have open wounds in exposed places. Even the scratch of a pin is dangerous in the presence of an infected atmosphere. A piece of Diachylon plaster should be near at hand in every household, or the wound should be covered with a little clean cotton fastened by a bit of thread. It also shows the danger of vaccination. Many of the children of the poor go direct home to an infected atmosphere, the blood is inoculated, and from the supervening fever, or its sequelae, they perish—thousands per annum! * * * The vaccinator never dreams of the danger of blood-inoculation."—Pickering, page 72.

And here is the royal household of small-pox :—

"I called upon the chief constable of Leeds one evening and preferred the following request, viz: 'I want a detective told off to go with me to the common lodging houses. I wish to see how people live, in the small hours of the morning.' 'It shall be as you require. If you call here at 1 a. m., the detective will be in waiting.' I went home and tried to obtain a few hours sleep, but the prospect of my novel undertaking was too engrossing. I slept not. At midnight I wrapped myself in the folds of a Scotch plaid and started for the police office. Arriving there a few minutes before the appointed time, I found my detective ready for business. Of course we took an easterly direction. Detective observed, 'We shall have to be discreet as to the representations we make to hide the real object we have in view; so I shall be on the lookout for a criminal, and you will have to support me in that bit of deceptiveness. It does not do to call these people up at 2 a. m. and search the house from top to bottom without an adequate motive.' 'I understand,' I said, 'and I am pleased to hear that our search is to be from top to bottom.' 'Well,' he answered, 'I suspect you do not want to do it by halves.'

It was in the month of December, a bitterly cold night, the moon shone brightly, and the stars twinkled in their merriest fashion as we knocked loudly at the door of a C. L. H., No. 7, in a narrow street leading out of **Kirkgate**. In turn we woke up the principals of four of these museums of uncleanliness.

"To describe one is to describe them all. The houses were composed of three floors—ground, first, and second—the cellars were only used for coals and lumber. All the rooms were spacions for that class of house, perhaps 15 by 13 feet. Half a century ago the houses were respectably tenanted, no doubt, but they had come down in the world's esteem. The kitchen, which served as a living room for twenty-eight or thirty people from 5 p. m. one day to 10 a m. on the next day, was in a filthy condition—essentially filthy. Pots and pans of all patterns and sizes were thrown on chairs, tables and shelves, unwashed, bearing upon their exterior no evidence of having been cleansed since the day they were made; whilst the stocks in trade of a dozen venders of gimcrack varieties were piled up in a corner. Not a crumb was to be seen. Bones of all sizes and odors, well picked, lay scattered about. There was no waste in that domicile. The window was stuffed with bits of rag to exclude the fresh air and to keep in the warmth. This was a noticeable feature in all the rooms of the house, and very successful it was. But how shall I describe those bedrooms, two on each floor, each one affording sleeping accommodation for seven or eight adults of both sexes, married and single, with sundry 'infants in arms' in addition? The latter don't count as lodgers, they are given in.'

"These children, the very dregs of mankind, head the list in the statistics of the 'Unvaccinated' who perish annually in the periodic outbreaks of small-pox, bronchitis, measles, diarrhoea, syphilis, and their kinsfolk. Unfit for vaccination—nay, unfit for life—they are the 'unhealthy unvaccinated' who picnic in the vital statistics of Dr. Barry and Dr. Buchanan as the 'unvaccinated.' and whose deaths, thus basely certified go to prop the cranky columns on which Jennerism is sustained, and to throw doubt on the veracity of the leaders in the anti-vaccination enterprise who adhere to that representation.

"But to return to my story. On opening the door of the bedroom I met with an atmosphere laden with the exhalations from herrings, onions, and compounds not mentioned in cookery books in various stages of digestion and indigestion. In

sober sadness, if I had remained in that room inhaling the me-
phitic fumes at an elevation of five feet from the floor, there
would have been an end of me and my fads in fifteen minutes.
I feel quite certain on that point. I could only account for life
maintaining itself eight inches from the floor on the principle
that some little fresh air crept into the apartment under the door.
The inmates lay feet to feet, covered with the clothes they wore
in the daytime, with some small article of underclothing
squeezed up into a bundle for a pillow; they were fast asleep,
not one showed any symptoms of life beyond the hard breathing
of those who were semi-asphyxiated as they slept; but I was
destined to learn there was philosophy in the exclusion of fresh
air from each of these dormitories.

"I enquired of our guide, the female owner of this fever
den, why all the bedrooms were so studiously air-proofed. 'Oh,
yer don't know then. It's just 'ere. If they'ev fresh air, when
they waken up they're hungry; but if they ev'nt,—they're not
hungry. D'ye see?' 'Yes,' I said, with a sigh, 'I see.' This was
my first initiation into the patent method of cheating the stomach, and it was a saddening lesson I learnt.

"During the small-pox epidemic of 1871-2 I saw these same
houses and visited them. Each one supplied its quota of victims
to swell the death-rate from the prevailing zymotic, and to demonstrate the fact that the small-pox is a filth disease, connected
strangely with the sin of overcrowding.

"And yet there are Simons, Playfairs, Barrys, and Buchan-
ans in any number, diffused in space, saying, 'Small-pox is not a
disease due to unsanitary conditions,' thus lying in the face of
facts, in the face of Nature, and of God.

"Oh you philosophizing machines, did you ever go, between
2 and 5 a. m., exploiting amongst the fever-stricken outcasts of
society and the dens in which they live, to watch how fevers do
germinate and grow up in first specimens? No, I should not
surprise you at that game. Of what value, then, is your long-
eared theory as to small-pox not being a filth disease. 'Small-
pox is a special disease, needing a special remedy, Vaccination,'
So you say. I know better. Small-pox is a filth disease, it
never was anything else. Do you think you can go on deceiving
this nation, her Queen, her Parliament, her people, and her poor

for ever? Your theories, like Pindar's razors, are made to sell. Vaccination is worth so much, so many hundreds of thousands per annum, to the medical faculty and the observance must be continued, let the consequences be ever so disastrous. The vaccinator has said to Evil, 'Be thou my good.' "—Dr. Pickering, page 74.

* * * * * * * * * * *

"To show that small-pox is a filth disease I call Sheffield into the witness-box. I cling to Sheffield, as Mr. Gladstone clings to Mitchelstown. There's nothing like a big broad fact to hurl at an enemy when you know he is misstating events or statistics to cover his own failures. So I refer to Sheffield, a town where, in 1887-8, there was a fatal epidemic of small-pox; a town reeking in its own filth, vaccinated up to 95 per cent. of the births; a town with, perhaps, ten anti-vaccinators in it, just enough to save it from the fate which befell the Cities of the Plain in the days of 'Abraham; and a town where all who perished were either vaccinated or unfit for vaccination—the last-named were as good as dead to begin with—not one healthy 'unvaccinated' person perished in that epidemic! Not one! What, then, becomes of the official report of the Sheffield epidemic and of the statistics inside? Nothing, the thing—the book,—I mean, like Pindar's razors, was made to sell! 'Tis a report crimson'd in falsehood.

"I call Leicester and Keighley into the witness-box. I could call several other very populous towns if I stood in need of their evidence. Neither of these two towns, in 1887-8, had any filth, any vaccination, and the small-pox, like the Levite, passed by on the other side.

"A thriving trade in filth and vaccine—means plenty of small-pox.

"No trade in filth and vaccine—means no small-pox.

"You Local, but illogical, Government Board, what say you to this indictment?

" 'Ephraim is joined to idols; let him alone.' "—Pickering, pages 73-74.

If one will read a description of the city of London during the early part of the eighteenth century, he need not look any further for the causes which insured a periodical return of the

plague and black death.   In the Appendix to Prof. Wallace's
chapter on Vaccination, he gives quite a lengthy account of
London's unsanitary condition two hundred years ago, a portion of which I will quote and the other portions condense:—

"In the early part of the sixteenth century London was in
a condition of over-crowding and general filth which we can now
hardly realize.   The houses were low and overhung the streets
and almost all had cess-pools close behind or underneath them.
The streets were narrow, the main thoroughfares being paved
with cobble stones, which collected filth and allowed it to soak
into the ground beneath until the soil and the subsoil became
saturated.   Slops and refuse of all kinds were thrown into the
streets at night, and only the larger streets were ever cleaned.
The by-streets and the roads outside London were so bad that
vehicles could only go two or three miles an hour; while even
between London and Kensington, coaches sometimes stuck in
the mud or had to turn back and give up the journey.   The
writers of the time describe the streets as dangerous and often
impassible, while only in the main thoroughfare were there any
footways, which were separated from the narrow roadway by
rows of posts.   Gay, in his Trivia, speaks of the slops thrown
from the overhanging windows, and the frequent dangers of
the night, adding—

'Though expedition bids, yet never stray
Where no ranged posts defend the rugged way.'

And throughout his poem, dirt, mire, mud, slime, are continually
referred to as being the chief characteristics of the streets.
They mostly had a gutter on each side, and with few exceptions
rain alone prevented their being blocked with refuse.   The ef-
feets of a heavy shower in the city are forcibly described by
Swift in his usual plain language,—

'Now from all parts the swelling kennels flow,
And bear their trophies with them as they go;
Filths of all hues and odours seem to tell
What street they sailed from by their sight and smell.
*   *   *   *   *   *
Sweeping from butchers' stalls, dung, guts, and blood,
Drown'd puppies, stinking sprats, all drench'd in mud,
Dead cats, and turnip tops, come tumbling down the flood.'

Macaulay tells us that down to 1726, St. James' Square, though surrounded by houses of the nobility, was a common receptacle for refuse of all kinds, and that it required an act of Parliament to stop its being so used. Hogs were kept in St. George's, Hanover Square, and in 1760 many were seized as a common nuisance.

"The numerous small streams which flowed through London from the northern heights—Langbourne, Wallbrook, Fleet, Tybourne, and Westbourne—which were in earlier times a source of health and water-supply, gradually became noisome open sewers, and one after another were arched over. There were many wells in London, indicated by such names as Holywell, Clerkenwell, and Aldgate Pump, and there were also conduits in Cheapside and Cornhill; but it is certain that, from the filthy streets and house-cesspools, all the water derived from them must have been contaminated, and thus helped to produce the terrible mortality from plague and fevers of the seventeenth century. It has been often suggested that the Great Fire of London in 1666 was the cause of the final disappearance of the plague, but how, except that the new house were for once clean and wholesome, has not, I think, been satisfactorily explained. I believe, however, that it can be found in the action of the fire upon the soil, which for more than a thousand years had been continually saturated with filth, and must, as we now know, have afforded a nidus for every kind of disease-germs. The long continued fire not only destroyed the closely-packed houses, but in doing so must have actually burnt the whole soil to a considerable depth, and thus have destroyed not only the living germs, but all the organic matter in it. The new city for the first time for many centuries, had beneath it a dry and wholesome soil, which to this day has not had time to get fully polluted as before the fire.

When we remember the filthy condition of the streets, and that owing to the cess-pools either under or close behind the houses, the scarcity of water, and the absence of ventilation, the shops and living rooms were always full of foul air, bad smells, and poisonous gases, how can we wonder at the prevalence of zymotic diseases and the dreadful amount of infant and general

mortality? And in many houses there was an additional peril
in the vicinity of church yards. In Nicholl's "Illustrations of
Literary History" (vol. iv. p. 499), Mr. Samuel Gale is quoted
as writing (in 1736,) as follows:—

"In the churchyard of St. Paul, Covent Garden, the burials
are so frequent that the place is not capacious enough to contain
decently the crowds of dead, some of whom are not laid above a
foot under the loose earth. The cemetery is surrounded every
way with close buildings; and an acquaintance of mine, whose
apartments look into the churchyard, hath averred to me, that
the family have often rose in the night time and been forced to
burn frankincense and other perfumes to dissipate and break
the contagious vapor. This is an instance of the danger of infection proceeding from the corrupt effluvia of dead bodies.'

"Many illnesses then originated in churches, and even those
whose houses were exceptionally wholesome were often exposed to a dangerous atmosphere when they went to church on
Sundays.

"The general food of the poor and the middle classes added
greatly to their unhealthiness, and itself caused disease. Owing
to the absence of good roads, it was impossible to supply the
large population of London with fresh food throughout the
year, and, consequently, salt meat and salt fish formed the staple
diet during the winter. For the same reason fresh vegetables
were unattainable; so that meat, cheese, and bread, with beer
as the common drink at all meals, was the regular food, with
chiefly salted meat and fish in winter. As a result, scurvy was
very common. Dr. Cheyne, in 1724, says, 'There is no chroni-
cal distemper more universal, more obstinate, and more fatal in
Britain, than the scurvy.' And it continued to be common down
to 1783, when Dr. Buchanan says, 'The disease most common
in this country is the scurvy.' But very soon afterwards it decreased, owing to the growing use of potatoes and tea, and an
increased supply of fresh vegetables, fruit, milk, etc., which the
improved roads allowed to be brought in quantities from the
surrounding country.

"Now it is quite certain, that the excessively unhealthy conditions of life, as here briefly described, continued with very
partial amelioration throughout the middle portion of the cen-

tury; and we have to consider what were the causes which then came into operation, leading to the great improvement in health that undoubtedly occurred in the latter portions of it and in the early part of our century.

"Beginning with improvements in the streets and houses, we have, in 1762, an act passed for the removal of the overhanging signboards, projecting waterspouts, and other such obstructions. In 1766 the first granite pavements were laid down, which were found so beneficial and in the end economical, that during the next half-century almost all London was thus paved. In 1768 the first Commissioners of Paving, Lighting and Watching were appointed, and by 1780 Dr. Black states that many streets had been widened, sewers made, that there was a better water supply and less crowding. From this date onward, we are told in the 'Encyclopoedia Britannica' (art. 'London'), a rapid rate of progress commenced, and that since 1785 almost the whole of the houses within the city had been rebuilt, with wider streets and much more light and air. In 1795 the western side of Temple Bar and Snowhill were widened and improved, and soon afterwards Butcher's Row, at the back of St. Clement's church, was removed. Of course, these are only indications of changes that were going on over the whole city; and, coincident with these improvements, there was a rapid extension of the inhabited area, which, from a sanitary point of view, was of far greater importance. That agglomeration of streets interspersed with spacious squares and gardens, which extends to the north of Oxford street, was almost wholly built in the period we are discussing. Bloomsbury and Russell Squares and the adjacent streets, occupy the site of Bedford House and grounds, which were sold for building on in 1800. All round London similar extensions were carried out. People went to live in these new suburbs, giving up their city houses to business or offices only. Regent's Park was formed, and Regent street and Portland Place were built before 1820, and the whole intervening area was soon covered with streets and houses, which for some considerable period enjoyed the pure air of the country. At this time the water supply became greatly improved, and the use of iron mains in place of the old wooden ones, and of lead pipes by which water was carried into all the new houses, was of inestimable value from a sanitary point of view.

"Then, just at the same time, began the great improvement in the roads, consequent on the establishment of mail-coaches in 1784. This at once extended the limits of residence for business men, while it facilitated the supply of fresh food to the city."—A. R. Wallace's "Nineteenth Century."

In 1801, London, within the Bills of Mortality, was increased in area by almost fifty per cent. with comparatively very little increase of population, owing to the suburban parishes of St. Luke's, Chelsea, Kensington, Marylebone, Paddington, and St. Pancras being then included; and even in 1821 this whole area had only a million inhabitants, and therefore enjoyed semi-rural conditions of life. This was a powerful sanitary cause which led to the great diminution of mortality, both general and from the zymotic diseases. Then the change of diet from bread, beer, and salted meat, to potatoes, and fresh meat, substituting tea for beer, occasioned a marked change in the death rate. Potatoes were first used in hospital diet in 1767.

Now, the various classes of improvements here briefly indicated—wider and cleaner streets, construction of sewers, better water supply, more wholesome food and especially the spreading out of the population over a much wider area; all occuring simultaneously, are in their combination amply sufficient to account for the remarkable decrease of mortality which occured within the half century from 1775 to 1825. Small-pox is only included with all zymotic diseases in the decrease, yet the Royal Commissioners lay particular stress on the connection of small-pox with vaccination as the cause for the decrease of that particular disease. Prof. Wallace concludes :—

"I have now supplied the last piece of confirmatory evidence which the commissioners declared was not forthcoming; not because I think it at all necessary for the complete condemnation of vaccination, but because it affords another illustration of the curious inability of the commission to recognize any causes as influencing the diminution of small-pox except that vaccine-virus operation. In this, as in all the other cases I have discussed, their report is founded on the opinions and beliefs of the medical and official upholders of vaccination; while the great masses of national experience, embodied in statistics of mortality from various groups of diseases, as well as the well-known facts of the sanitary history of London during the critical half century, 1775-1825, are either neglected, misunderstood or altogether overlooked."

With the vaccinating doctor these pest breeding centers of filth are trivial and unimportant matters in comparison with vaccination. Never mind the dirt and stench, but if you neglect to vaccinate it is at your own peril! It is better that the populace wallow up to their necks in the cess-pools than to neglect to vaccinate and re-vaccinate. Indeed, vaccination is the main prop and dependence of the old outworn school of physic. It is a conservator of old superstitions, of the bank account and an available friend in the period of senility. Not a good thing to mitigate too much. Financial conditions should be kept in a state of equilibrium. When a money center becomes disturbed everything is disturbed. "Hang it," said Thoreau, "if it were not for these pestilent agitators how smooth this business would run."

Small-pox appears and disappears under precisely the same conditions that attend scarlet fever, typhoid, and diarrhoea. It is met with in the streets, in the same haunts and amongst the same people. Vaccination has no more effect to mitigate one than it has upon any other member of the group of zymotics. We shall never stamp out small-pox, cancer, consumption, or leprosy, so long as we continue to stamp them in through the idiotic rite of a vicious cow-pox vaccination. The Germans endeavored to stamp out syphilis by stamping it in with syphilized vaccine pus. They have abandoned that now, and later they will abandon vaccination altogether. It should be a question for every householder to know that his only protection is in personal and domestic cleanliness. Sanitation is the only accessi-

ble agency which God has placed within our reach; and this
agency is full and adequate if we will apply it with religious
fidelity. Let us turn from the idol which the "King" com-
manded us to worship :—

"And a tempest arose, thunders and waves and lightenings,
and the moan of winds; and the dome of the Temple was rent;
and the whirl and the rains rushed in. And behold! a flash, and
it rolled down like a God; and grappling the Image it smote
it from head to foot, and dashed it in fragments; its crown of
jewels was broken; its scepter was a ruin; its law as lies a
blackened corpse; it was stricken into small pieces, and the rain
roared and buffeted its remnants."--Enock.

CHAPTER VII.

SYPHILIS AND LEPROSY TRACEABLE TO VACCI-NATION.

"Vaccination differs, however, from all previous errors of the faculty, in being maintained as the law of the land on the warrant of medical authority. That is the reason why the blow to professional credit can hardly help being severe, and why the efforts to ward it off have been, and will continue to be so ingenious."—Dr. Creighton.

"I want no proof that if I imbibe the causes of disease, I can only disguise the result,—I can never escape it,—by artificially infusing fresh disease. That I can thus escape or lessen it, is the monstrous doctrine to which our wise vaccinators commit themselves."—F. W. Newman, Emeritus Professor, Weston-super-Mare, April, 1876.

The specific vegetable and animal poisons that war against the physiological processes in man have a very wide range in their action, both as regards their relative intensity, and the period after being planted when they commence their work of destruction. Some poisons, conveyed to the blood through the skin, are instantaneously fatal; others will apparently lie dormant for a term of years and then become roused to action, fasten upon some organ—like tubercle in the lungs—disintegrate its tissue and destroy the life. Still others—like leprosy—slowly but surely breaks down the tissue of every organ from nerve to bone, until the entire body falls a mutilated and indescribably repulsive ruin. The vaccine virus proper acts with comparative promptness in producing its specific disease; but is at the same time the most insiduous and dangerous among the poison-fiends on account of the masked, many-sided and multiform properties that lie concealed within its substance. It has traveled a sinuous journey and nested with every conceivable species of infernality, picking up on its way micro-organisms and chemical subtleties which neither bacteriologist or organic chemist are able to detect; but which nevertheless are potent and implacable enemies when sown or cast into the circulating life-stream of a human being. Almost daily we read of vaccinal disasters, of cases that have "gone wrong" though only the "immaculate" and "sterilized" calf-lymph was used in the operation!

All vegetable and animal poisons inoculated through the skin is blood-poisoning. Some of these may be physiologically combated and gotten rid of without serious harm. Other poisons, which the blood cannot expel—like scrofula, cancer and tubercle and vaccine—are sequestered for a season and reduced to a minimum of mischief, a truce having been arranged between the organism and the poison, each waiting for an opportunity to worst the other. Necroscopic poisoning proves fatal in a few days. Syphilis, it were far better to prove fatal and be done with it. The savages of Lamas and Ticunas, South America, extract a subtle vegetable poison by fire from divers plants, and with this they treat their arrow-points, which when they pierce an animal's skin, cause instantaneous death. Yet their flesh is not thereby rejected for food. Mous de la Condamine, of the Royal Academy of Science, Paris, experimented with this poison on dogs, bears, cats, rabbits, birds, etc., and in nearly every case death was instantaneous; but the same amount of the poison introduced into the stomach was inert; inert also when applied to the surface of the skin. It is beneath the skin—where it can reach the circulation—that its fatal effects are manifested. The bite of a musquito, or red ant, or the sting of a bee, or the bite of a rattlesnake, or puncture from a lance tipped with cow-pus, each and all are forms of blood-poisoning. When deliberately inflicted, blood-poisoning is a murderous operation. Vaccination is blood-poisoning with expectations of the fee. How many removes is it from a capital crime against society? The poisons concealed in calf-pus permanently affect the blood; but the effect is often not perceptible until a time arrives when the physical powers are deteriorated by bad habits, exposure, disappointment, or depressing influence of some kind, and then it is that the special poison begins to manifest its fatal effects. Syphilis, cancer, scrofula, or tubercle, borne into the blood with the vaccinal virus, may lie dormant for a series of years, but its opportunity punctually arrives when it will claim and conquer its victim.

VACCINO-SYPHILIS.

In 1862, M. Ricord, one of the most eminent authorities on syphilitic affections, during a lecture in Hotel Dieu, Paris, said: "If ever the transmission of disease with vaccine-lymph is clearly demonstrated, vaccination must be altogether discontinued; for in the present state of science, we are in possession of no criterion which may permit the conscientious practitioner to assert that the lymph with which he inoculates, is perfectly free from admixture."

The following year (May 19, 1863,) standing in the same place, this same eminent authority declared:—

"At first I repelled the idea that syphilis could be transmitted by vaccination. The recurrence of facts appearing more and more confirmatory, I accepted the possibility of this mode of transmission, I should say, with reserve, and even with repugnance; but today I hesitate no more to proclaim their reality. * * * Who, pray, will run such risks to escape the small-pox?"

In 1868, Dr. Ballard, one of the vaccine inspectors for the English government, observed:—

"There can be no reasonable doubt that the vaccine virus and the syphilitic virus may both be drawn at the same time, upon the same instrument, from one and the same vesicle. The vesicle which is thus capable of furnishing both vaccine and syphilitic virus may present, prior to being opened, all the normal and fully developed characters of a true Jennerian vesicle as ordinarily met with."

ESSAY ON VACCINATION.

During the same year (1868) Dr. Cornell, president Homeopathic Society of Pennsylvania, said in his annual address: "To no medium of transmission is the wide spread dissemination of this class of disease so largely indebted as vaccination." Dr. Heim, public vaccinator, Wurtemburg, declared: "I have myself planted syphilis from a child which seemed at the time perfectly healthy."—"Horrors of Vaccination," page 26.

A patient was brought to the class room of the Clinical Society and exhibited to Dr. Hutchinson, when he said:--"We have now emerged from the reign of doubt to one of belief in the possibility of such an untoward occurrence. * * * The facts now before the public will tend to rouse them, if they have not been roused already, from the false security into which they have been lulled."—"Med. Times and Gazette," Feb., 1872.

Here is a record which the heads of every family in the land should carefully read and ponder. The teaching of the medical faculty that blood inoculation, either as a preventive or modifying agent of any disease is a fallacy of the worst type. It is false in principle and pernicious to the last degree in practice. Inoculation for measles, scrofula, and syphilis have all been tried, and abandoned on the fullest proof that the antidote is far worse than the original disease, and that it neither prevented nor modified a second attack. The vaccination folly not only fails to mitigate small-pox, but it is a fearful agent of disease by communicating along with the vaccine virus, diseases far more to be dreaded than the small-pox—diseases which threaten to depopulate tropical archipeligos, and even the continents, if compulsory vaccination were to be enforced for another century. Prof. Germann said in an address to the Diet of the German Empire:

"Above all, the dire fatality, which lately occurred at Lebus, a suburb of Frankfort-on-the-Oder, would alone warrant the abolition of the vaccination laws. Eighteen school girls, averaging twelve years of age, were re-vaccinated, and thereby syphilised, and some of them died. * * * Yet the lymph, the syphilitic lymph, used in this case, was obtained from the Official Royal Establishment, and was the new regenerated or 'animalized' vaccine lymph so warmly recommended for the re-vaccination of schools."

In 1877, Brundenell Carter, surgeon to St. George's Hospital, London, observed: "I think that a large proportion of the cases of apparently inherited syphilis are in reality vaccinal; and that the syphilis in these cases does not show itself until the age of from eight to ten years, by which time the relation between cause and effect are apt to be lost sight of."—Med. Exam., May 24, 1877.

In "Journal d' Hygiene," Aug. 25, 1881, Dr. Desjardins gives a detailed account of the syphilization of the 58 French recruits in Algeria. The most cautious silence was maintained by the military authorities. These soldiers were solaced in a small measure by being granted pensions.

Dr. G. W. Winterburn, physician-in-chief to Manhattan Hospital, gives the details of a very distressing case that came under his observation. In December, 1879, there came to the out-patient department of the hospital, a mother with her little girl, twenty-one months old. The husband had died of pneumonia, leaving mother and three children, which the mother supported by odd jobs at laundry work. Poor but neat, they excited Dr. Winterburn's attention and sympathy. According to the mother's report, the three children seven weeks previously, had been forcibly vaccinated in a house to house visitation. The arms of all her children had remained sore ever since.

For about a week before calling at the hospital she had noticed ulcers on the body of one, and applied salve from the drug-store; but the child grew worse. The day before she noticed places breaking out on the second child—the little girl twenty-one months old—and had brought it to find out what was the matter. Dr. Winterburn says:—

"On examining the child, I found the place of insertion of the vaccine virus, a shallow, cleancut ulcer, filled with a dirty exudation. The cellular tissue round about it was infiltrated and very hard, extending over nearly one-half of the upper arm. The axilla was tender, and the glands swollen. There were six ulcers on the body; four of them very small, just forming that day, and two somewhat larger, having appeared thirty-six hours previously. These ulcers began, like a blister, the size of a split pea, with a swollen indurated base of a copperish hue, and in all respects resembling syphilitic rupia. The ulcers were so characteristic, that I ordered the whole family to appear before me on the morrow. When, on the following day, I saw the infant stripped of its clothes, revealing no less than thirty dreadful ulcers, some of them as large as a silver dime; it made me heart-sick. Some of these had already begun to scab, showing the peculiar watch-crystal formation, so characteristic of this eruption. On the oldest child I found four small blisters on the back, and she also, in a day or two, had a full share of syphilitic sores. Here were three children, which a very careful investigation in the neighborhood, where they lived, showed that they had been, up to the time of their vaccination, in very good health, suddenly stricken with the most incontestible evidences of this dreadful disorder."—"The Value of Vaccination," Winterburn, page 130.

In his appendix to the 37th annual report of the Registrar General of Great Britain, Dr. Farr, page 121, writes: "Syphilis was twice as fatal in the five years, 1870-1874, as it was twenty years ago. Its most fatal recorded forms occur in children under one year of age." The following table gives the relation between vaccination, small-pox and syphilis, from 1850 to 1881. It is from the 11th annual report of Local Government Board, page 346:

Years	Successful Vaccinations at the expense of the Poor Rates.	Deaths from Smallpox.	Deaths from Syphilis.
1851		6,997	598
1852	397,128	7,320	623
1853	366,593	3,151	622
1854	677,886	2,808	964
1855	448,519	2,525	947
1856	422,281	2,277	879
1857	411,268	3,936	957
1858	455,004	6,414	1,006
1859	445,020	3,798	1,089
1860	485,927	2,713	1,067
1861	425,739	1,290	1,177
1862	437,693	1,579	1,245
1863	646,464	5,891	1,386
1864	529,479	7,624	1,550
1865	578,583	6,361	1,647
1866	454,885	2,977	1,662
1867	490,598	2,467	1,698
1868	513,042	1,994	1,886
1869	524,143	1,482	1,859
1870	472,881	2,547	1,858
1871	693,104	23,062	1,742
1872	699,320	19,022	1,831
1873	501,189	2,303	1,843
1874	493.285	2,084	1,997
1875	498.952	849	2,142
1876	566.587	2,408	2,141
1877	529.376	4,278	2,085
1878	513,575	1,856	2,191
1879	519,715	536	2,036
1880	513,283	648	2,162
1881	533,005	3,098	2,069

Thus the average increase of syphilitic fatality has been 50 per year during a period of thirty years, while deaths from small-pox waxes and wanes without any seeming connection with vaccination as affecting its producing cause.

Dr. J. G. Beaney, of Melbourne, says—"Constitutional Syphilis," page 373:—

"And I at once announce at the outset my firm belief that syphilis is in very many instances communicated by means of 'child's vaccine lymph.' This opinion I have deliberately formed and as firmly defend. The evidences of such being the case have, in my practice, been numerous and well-pronounced; so distinct, indeed, that no doubt whatever could exist as to the nature of the eruptions, and the certainty of transmission."

Dr. Scott Tebb, of London, publishes a table giving 700 cases of vaccinal syphilis in countries outside of England. The cases which first attracted serious attention in England, were those of Dr. James Whitehead, of the Clinical Hospital, Manchester, 1857. Out of 1,717 children brought to the hospital, 1,435 had been vaccinated, a large number of whom the mothers blamed vaccination for the persistent and troublesome eruptions which subsequently appeared. Among these Dr. Whitehead found thirty-four children suffering from vaccinal syphilis. I subjoin cases 2, 11 and 56 from Dr. Whitehead's Third Clinical Report:—

"Case 2. An infant, aged nine months, of a bad habit of body. Copper-colored blotches appeared after vaccination. When seen, there was a mixed eruption on the face and scalp and extreme irritability of the whole surface; the vaccinated spots remained unhealed at the end of five months, presenting a well-formed rupia with excavation. The father and mother are described as apparently healthy.

"Case 11. An infant, aged eleven weeks, of medium habit of body. When seen, there were two deep ulcers with hardened bases where the vaccine vesicles were formed three weeks previously; copper-colored roseola on the nates and chin, sallow complexion, mucous tubercles round the anus, eruptions and intertrigo behind the ears, coryza, atrophy, and dysentery. The history of the case is that roseola appeared from twelve to fourteen days after the vaccination, at the age of two months; the mucous tubercles nine weeks after, while under treatment, and atrophy four months after. Father said to be healthy; mother feeble, but apparently free from taint.

"Case 56. An infant, aged seven and a half months, of good habit of body. After the subsidence of the vaccination, the vesicles degenerated into ulcers, surrounded by erythema. When seen, there were erythematous blotches of a copper color on the chest and neck, eczema auris, arthritis of the left elbow joint, and syphilitic pallor. Father said to be healthy; mother apparently healthy."

In Dr. Hutchinson's communication to the Royal Medical and Chirurgical Society, April 25, 1871, among the numerous cases he cites, I select the following:—

"A mother and her two children, one an infant and the other a child of two, were found to be suffering from secondary syphilis. The children were vaccinated in September, 1875, and their vaccination sores had re-opened and for a long time remained unhealed. The mother had contracted a sore on her nipple from the younger child, and her symptoms were two months behind those of the children. The husband subsequently contracted syphilis from his wife."

Scott Tebb writes—"A Century of Vaccination," page 310:

"The disease that cow-pox most resembles is not small-pox, but syphilis. This view of the analogy of cow-pox with syphilis was held by Auzias-Turenne, and in this country it has been advocated by Dr. Creighton. Auzias-Turenne says: 'Between syphilis and cow-pox the analogy may be a long way followed up. The inoculation of cow-pox—a malady with a fixed virus sufficiently well-named pox of the cow (verole de vache)—may, for example, give rise to polymorphic vaccinides, and sometimes to disseminated pathognomonic vesico-pustules, just as the contagion of the mucous patch, symptom of a malady with an equally fixed virus, gives rise to various secondary eruptions, and sometimes to the appearance of disseminated mucous patches. But, happily for the vaccinated, cow-pox passes through a rapid evolution, and does not leave virulent remains for so long a time or so frequently as syphilis.

"The difficulty of distinguishing some cases of cow-pox from syphilis has been recognized by the best authorities. Mr. George Berry, ophthalmic surgeon to the Royal Infirmary,

Edinburgh, in a communication on cow-pox of the eye-lids, says that the main interest in these cases consists in the possibility of the inoculation taking place at all, and in the differential diagnosis between vaccinia and a primary syphilitic sore."

"Emily Maud, a child, was vaccinated on March 26, 1889, and died at the Leeds Infirmary on July 1 of the same year. At the inquest on July 10, four members of the Infirmary staff, Messrs. McGill, Ward, Littlewood, and Dr. Barrs, gave evidence that the child died from vaccino-syphilis, and the verdict of the jury was that she 'died from syphilis acquired at or from vaccination.' "—Ibid.

"If it be a fact, as maintained by Dr. Creighton, that the phenomena of vaccino-syphilis so-called, are due to the inherent, though mostly dormant natural history characters of cow-pox itself, we should expect the same appearances to take place occasionally in cases of calf lymph; and in this connection the experience recorded by Dr. Hutchinson in the 'Archives' for January, 1891, (pp. 213-215), is of interest. He particularises a case of vaccination with calf-lymph presenting certain symptoms simulating syphilis.

"The child was born of healthy parents in July, 1890; was perfectly healthy at birth; was vaccinated at three months of age with Jenner's calf-lymph, at the same time as several others who did well; on the eighth day, only one place seemed to have taken, but later on all three looked satisfactory; at the end of three weeks, the arm was inflamed, and there were large black scabs with pus at their edges; a week later a large slough comprised all the vaccination sores and passed deeply almost to the bone, and there was also a pustule on the nose, and three nodes on the skull.

"Dr. Hutchinson compares this case with another he had described in an earlier number of the 'Archives' (October, 1889, page 110.) These two cases resembled one another, in that in both the infant was perfectly healthy up to the time of vaccination; the lymph used was not taken from the human subject, the skin around the vaccination sores passed into gangrene, with at the time a large granular swelling in the arm-pit. There were also periosteal swellings of considerable size in the skull bones, suspicious sores on the skin; and both patients appeared to be much benefitted by mercurial treatment."—Ibid., page 317.

"Before concluding the evidence under the heading of 'Syphilis,' I wish to allude to the disastrous consequences of vaccination in the American Civil War (1861-65), in which some hundreds of men were affected with a disease presenting all the characteristics of syphilis. The facts are related by Dr. Joseph Jones, and the conditions described were truly frightful.

"The symptoms included phagedenic ulcers, with indurated and everted edges, secondary skin affections, ulcerated throats, loss of hair, and other phenomena distinctive of syphilis. In some cases the gangrenous ulcers caused extensive destruction of tissue, exposing arteries, nerves, and bones, in many cases necessitating amputations.

"Dr. J. T. Gilmore, in a letter to Professor F. Eve, referring to three hundred cases in the Georgia brigades, remarked: 'The cases presented the appearances that are familiar to those of us who were connected with the Confederate army—large rupia-looking sores, sometimes only one; generally several on the arm in which the virus was inserted. In a number of cases these sores extended, or rather appeared on the forearm, and in two cases that I saw, they appeared on the lower extremeties. The men suffered severely from nocturnal rheumatism. Several cases had, to all appearances, syphilitic roseola. I saw enough of the trouble to convince me thoroughly that the virus owed its impurity to a syphilitic contamination.

"Dr. James Bolton testified that 'on careful inspection the ulcers presented the various appearances of genuine chancre. In some instances there was the elevated, cartilaginous, well-cut edge surrounding the indolent, greenish ulcer; in others there was a burrowing ulcer, with ragged edge; in others there was the terrible destructive sloughing process devastating the integuments of the arm. Many of the cases were so situated that their history could be preserved, and in these secondary symptoms appeared, followed in due time by tertiary symptoms. The chancre was followed successively by axillary bubo, sore throat, and various forms of eruption (syphilis dermata), while the system fell into a state of cachexia.'

"Dr. E. A. Flewellen testified that 'while the army of Gen. eral Bragg was at Tullahoma, I was medical director, and I know that very great complaint was made to me as to the character of the vaccination practiced in the army. A large number of men were represented as unfit for duty. I think that one division represented nearly a thousand men as unfit for duty on account of spurious vaccination. I saw a number of cases in the early progress of the vaccination, but they presented nothing abnormal that I could detect. But, as it advanced, the cases seemed to have the appearance very nearly of syphilitic rupia. It diffused itself more or less over the whole surface. A large number of surgeons regarded it as a complication of vaccinia and syphilis."—Dr. Scott Tebb, pp. 320-321.

In April, 1866, Dr. Percival was called to Graniteville, a manufacturing town in South Carolina, to examine and treat 150 cases of syphilis from vaccination. The cases comprised men, women, and children of all ages, from fifty down to one year of age. They all broke out about the same time, and in all the disease was well advanced. The individual first vaccinated was with virus obtained from a man whom it was later learned was suffering from primary syphilis, and one was vaccinated from the other, and so it spread. In every case excoriated ulcers were formed; in some cases abscesses formed on the inside of the arms; in several cases the hair dropped off. The usual treatment for veneral ulcers effected a cure in from three to six weeks. The account from which this is a brief summary, is contained in Dr. Jone's work, "Med. and Surg. Memoirs," vol. iii., p. 478.

Now, with the overwhelming mass of evidence which has been put on record, and notwithstanding the repeated testimonies of the most conscientious and competent medical practitioners, connecting vaccinating and syphilis—yet a majority of the medical profession and medical press affect to treat with contempt this entire mass of evidence. Their day of reckoning is at hand. The people are reading, rising, and the star of truth is already in the ascendency.

So far as possible every mishap resulting from vaccination is discreetly hidden from public view. The average M. D. of the elder school is secretive and mysterious in medical matters. A medical priesthood has grown up which is ineffective, crafty, selfish, persecuting and intolerant toward recent schools of medical reform; implacably savage towards psychic treatment—towards the divine gifts of healing—such as Schlatter displayed—giving a superlative position to drastic drug poisons, and a mean, unimportant and obscure place to sanitation, hygienic laws and habits; and lastly, guarding and defending the most destructive, poisonous, outlawed, and infamous feature in the whole range of medical practice with a jealousy and craftiness which would shame a ward politician or government contractor.

All the authorities I have cited in the foregoing pages stand high, both in their professional practice and in the world of letters; and they have recorded their opinions, and detailed the cases that came under their observation with a most conscientious candor, and certainly without selfish ends in view, inasmuch as their testimony goes to discredit the main pillar of old time medical practice. Nineteen-twentieths of our witnesses that have testified, belong to what is denominated the "Regular Professions," and the majority of them stand at the head of the profession.

Seventeen school girls syphilized at Lebus, near Frankfort, by pure, official, "sterilized" calf-lymph; yet the vaccinator continues to repeat: "Not the slightest danger." * * * "Our lymph is from a well-known source, absolutely pure, glycerinated, sterilized, all germs but the 'vaccine sporule' destroyed, hermetically 'sealed until used,'" and as often as repeated, even so often does the daily press report cases of vaccinal disaster, exposing these hungry second-class-doctor vaccinators.

Again, ponder well the indictment by Dr. Carter, of St. George's Hospital, London, who expresses his firm conviction that a "large proportion of the cases of apparently inherited syphilis are in reality vaccinal." Multitudes of little children under one year of age cursed with syphilis at the hands of the public vaccinator! You fathers and mothers, take this home to your own hearthstones. Think of it—ponder it. It may be your children whose lives will next be blighted; and I know if you realized the full purport of the danger which threatens your home and posterity, you would be calling mass meetings; you would memorialize the legislature; you would raise heaven and earth but that you would get this compulsory curse off the statute books—this unholy compact between the medical-politico priesthood and the state dissolved—forever dissolved.

In the foot-hills of the California mountains, mothers are extremely cautious lest a rattlesnake creeps out from a rock crevice and fangs their little ones; but I warn these mothers that the vaccinator carries something concealed in his vest pocket which menaces the life and welfare of their children and children's children a hundred fold more than all the rattlesnakes along the Coast range of the Sunset State. Rattlesnake venom never reaches more than an infintesimal fraction of one per cent. of the population; but children are poisoned by the hundred thousand at the instance of that unholy conspiracy between the state and old time medicine—compulsory vaccination.

"But we don't vaccinate any longer from arm to arm; we use calf-lymph, glycerinated and sterilized." Very well, gentlemen, but your "calf-lymph" has been tried and convicted in the highest courts of medical opinion. Read Dr. Hutchinson in the "Archives," pages 213-215, for 1891 : A child three months old, perfectly healthy, vaccinated October, 1890. with Jenner's calf-lymph, resulted in three weeks with distinct syphilitic ulcers. Dr. H. also describes other well marked cases which were directly traceable to the much vaunted calf-lymph. Moreover, they do continue to vaccinate whole populations by the old process of arm to arm, with humanized virus. This is notably the case in Hindustan, South Africa, West India Islands, and the Sandwich Islands, and that too, by English and United States officials; and to this fact, I shall presently find the cause for the alarming increase of leprosy in recent years.

Humanity is one, all are units of the great whole. There are many races, yet but one human species. The Occident and the Orient are hand-clasping brothers. The Hindoos and ourselves are of Ayran descent. When in India I feel that I am sojourning among my elder and venerable Brahmanic brothers. If torrid suns have darkened their faces it has illumined their minds. They are thinkers, mystical, metaphysical, yet on the higher planes of life profoundly practical. Already they seek our shores—and all are threads in the web and warp of human life. Vaccination and leprosy, in India, are becoming almost synonomous terms. Leprosy from vaccination has already got a foothold in this country.

In tropical countries animalized and glycerinated lymph has been found to be too irritating, and attended with so much fever and inflammation, that the earlier method has been revived,—revived through vaccinators knowing the awful dangers attending arm to arm vaccination,—revived and made brutally compulsory over those native populations, because mammon takes precedence of humanity, and accustomed revenues must be conserved though this involve the extinction of a race.

LEPROSY AND VACCINATION.

"Leprosy is, perhaps, the most terrible disease that afflicts the human race. It is hideously disfiguring, destructive to the tissues and organs in an unusual degree, and is hopelessly incurable, the fate of its victims being, indeed, the most deplorable that the strongest imagination can conceive, and many years

often passing before death rids the unhappy sufferer from a life
of misery, to which there is scarcely any alleviation. It is not to
be wondered at, then, that the question is one which philanthro-
pists in these enlightened days are taking up actively."—British
Medical Journal, Nov. 19, 1887.

Leprosy has claimed the serious attention of a large number of thoughtful minds of late years and a considerable amount
of literature has accumulated on the subject. One could easily
collect fifty volumes which have appeared in the last twenty
years, besides voluminous reports from hospitals and boards
of health and discussions in the medical journals. But the most
candid, thorough and exhaustive work which I have read was
published by Mr. Wm. Tebb, of London,, "The Recrudescence
of Leprosy," 412 pages. I made the acquaintance of the author
in London nearly a generation ago, and esteem him not only
as a gentleman and scholar of wide attainments, but as a philanthropist and reformer of the most conscientious and persistent type. To him more than to any single reformer in England
is due the passage of the Vaccination Act of 1898, into which
the "Conscience Clause" was inserted. Mr. Tebb has traveled
into every quarter of the globe to make a personal investigation
of leprosy and to study the question in all its aspects,—India,
Ceylon, British Guiana, Venezuela, West Indies, Norway,
United States, Sandwich Islands, Egypt, New Zealand, Australia, South Africa, South America, Greek Archipelago, Syria,
Asia Minor, etc. Upon his thorough researches I shall mainly
depend for the facts presented in this section.

The chief claims which leprosy has on public attention at
the present time, are the dangers which confront the civilized
world by its rapid spread among all classes of society. It
threatens civilization today in a far greater ratio than small-pox,
and is ten-fold more to be dreaded, for upon each and every
victim it sets the seal of an inevitable doom! New germ centers
of leprosy are springing up and the old centers are steadily wid-

ening. Sir Morell Mackensie said in a lecture in 1889: "It is impossible to estimate even approximately the total number of lepers throughout the world, but it is certain they must be counted by millions." Lepers are becoming numerous in all the countries of Europe and there are some in several states of our own commonwealth, but as far as possible these cases are concealed from public observation and scrutiny. The patient and his friends, knowing with what horror the public regard the disease, naturally shun publicity, no one outside save the physician is acquainted with his malady, and he humanely guards the secret. Nor will the leper submit to isolation until his last resource for remaining in touch with his friends is exhausted, since he knows that when isolated he will henceforth be condemned to dwell amidst the most repulsive and saddening surroundings. Mr. Tebb informs us that leper hunting in Hawaii is a dangerous business, as many unfortunate lepers do not hesitate to shoot their pursuers. They would prefer a public execution to confinement in the lazaretto. This statement with similar ones I can personally verify (to say nothing of the lepers I had previously seen in India, Ceylon, Syria, and Egypt), for on my third tour around the world, exchanging steamers per arrangement at Honolulu, I remained over a month in this city and other places in the Sandwich Islands, studying leprosy in all its hideous forms. One or two physicians accompanied me during my investigations. The sights seen were not merely sad; they were sickening. Some from utter hopelessness commit suicide.

That the reader may appreciate the serious gravity of this complaint, I will subjoin a description, from a few eminent authors and practitioners who have had wide experience with lepers. Wm. Tebb observes in the preface to his last painstaking work:—

"Leprosy is one of the most loathsome as it is one of the

most tissue-destructive diseases known, and when going
through the wards of leper hospitals I have frequently noticed
with pain the poor afflicted creatures bending their heads and
covering their hands to conceal from strangers the sight of their
distorted features and mutilated limbs.   It is hardly possible
to conceive, much less describe, the depth of human misery
caused by the spread of this hideous and destructive disease;
but some idea of its nature may be gathered from the following description of leprosy, which may well excite the sympathy
of the philanthropist.   It will be found in a recent work on
leprosy by Dr. Thin, pp. 99-100.   It is translated from Leloir,
an eminent French authority on leprosy, and refers to the
tubercular variety of the disease.   'If the patient,' he remarks,
'does not die of some internal disorder or special complication,
the unhappy leper becomes a terrible object to look on.   The
deformed leonine face is covered with tubercles, ulcers, cicatrices, and crusts.   His sunken, disfigured nose is reduced to a
stump.   His respiration is wheezing and difficult; a sanious,
stinking fluid, which thickens into crusts, pours from his nos-
trils.   The nasal mucous membrane is completely covered with
ulcerations.   A part of the cartilaginous and bony framework is
carious.   The mouth, throat, and larynx are mutilated, deformed, and covered with ulcerated tubercles.   The patient
breathes with the greatest difficulty.   He is threatened with frequent fits of suffocation, which interrupt his sleep.   He has lost
his voice, his eyes are destroyed, and not only his sight but his
sense of smell and taste have completely gone.   Of the five
senses hearing alone is usually preserved.   In consequence of
the great alterations in the skin of the limbs, which are coverd
with ulcerated tubercles, crusts, and cicatrices, the pachydermic
state of skin which gives the limbs the appearance of elephant-
iasis, and of the lesions of the peripheral nerves which are present at this time, and by which occasionally the symptoms of
nerve leprosy are combined with those of tubercular leprosy,
the sense of touch is abolished.   The patient suffers excruciat-
ing pains in the limbs and even in the face, whilst the ravages
of the disease in his legs render walking difficult and even impossible.   From the hypertrophied inguinal and cervical glands
pus flows abundantly from fistulous openings.   In certain cases

the abdomen is increased in size on account of the liver, spleen and mesenteric glands being involved. . With these viscerial lesions the appetite is irregular or lost. There are pains in the stomach, diarrhoea, bronchial pulmonary lesions, intermittent febrile attacks and a hectic state. The peculiar smell, recalling that of the dissecting room, mixed with the odor of goose's feathers, or of a fresh corpse, is indicated but poorly described, by the authors of the Middle Ages who compared it to that of a male goat."

Dr. John Hillis, who spent a number of years in British Guiana, says of the anaesthetic variety:—

"It is known as lenke of the Greeks, baras of the Arabians, jointevil of the West Indies, sunbahiru of the East Indies, and dry leprosy in contradistinction to the other form known as humid leprosy; and is characterized by a diseased condition of the nerves, and a peculiar eruption the primary characteristic of which is the loss of sensation, or anaesthesia; hence its name. After a time ulcerations form, a sort of dry gangrene of the limbs sets in, and joints drop off, and finally there is more or less paralysis. It would take a large volume to describe the signs or symptoms of leprosy, but the preceding account is sufficient to show what an alarming affection we have to deal with."

Surgeon Major G. G. Maclaren, who established Dehra Dun Asylum, writes a chapter in Mrs. Hay's "My Leper Friends," in which he observes :—

"In the many examinations I have made, post-mortem, I can testify that not a single organ in the whole body is exempt from the inroads of this dire and loathsome malady. It invades the brain, spinal nerves, the eyes, tongue, and throat, the lungs, the liver, and other digestive organs. In addition, as is generally known, it maims and deforms the external parts of the body in a manner too revolting to describe. It is painful to witness the amount of deplorable suffering some of these creatures endure!"

The following paragraph from Wm. Tebb will sufficiently indicate my reason for making the discussion of leprosy a leading feature in the present chapter; namely, its close connection with the vaccination outrage which doctors in league with the government, are perpetrating on the victimized and defenceless populations of India and the tropical isles, and which also threatens the very citadel of civilization itself:—

"In the West Indies, in British Guiana, in the Sandwich Islands, and in South Africa, when cases of unvaccinated diseases were related to me, I was urged by the sufferers and by their friends to make known their grievances to English people and to the Imperial Parliament, and, if possible, to bring public opinion to bear upon a mistaken and mischievous system which, without doing the least good, has been the cause of such terrible and far-reaching consequences. Acting upon these entreaties, and upon others contained in communications from various leprous countries, I have prsented to the public through the press, and to members of Parliament, such facts on this subject as came before my personal notice up to July, 1890. I now offer to the public further evidence and testimonies, on behalf especially of the afflicted population of our Crown Colonies and Dependencies, whose grievances have been so long and so flagrantly disregarded. Every attempt to introduce compulsory vaccination in the populous Island of Barbados, British West Indies, has been thwarted, owing to the widespread belief that leprosy and syphilis are communicated by the vaccine virus. In St. Thomas, Danish West Indies, and in Georgetown and other parts of British Guiana. it has, for similar reasons, been found practically impossible to enforce the vaccination law, and, in spite of severe compulsory enactments, entire districts remain unvaccinated by reason of this special danger; while, in the Sandwich Islands, a bill for the repeal of the vaccination law was introduced in the legislative assembly, July, 1890, by J. Kalua Kahookano, a scholarly representative from North Kohala, Island of Hawaii."—"Leprosy and Vaccination," Wm. Tebb, p. 15.

In every civilized community may be found two classes with distinct and opposite interests relating to the public health—two medical schools I may call them. One holds to tradition and dogma, with two cardinal tenets in their medical creed; a drastic drug for the stomach to cure disease and a putrid decoction of decayed animal tissue for inoculation into the blood to prevent disease. The second class—the new higher school—the hard students—places only a secondary reliance upon antidotes and drastic specifies, the main article of their creed being: Sanitary regulation, hygiene, and obedience to the immutable laws of nature. The members of the old style school are like our bankers, who urge that the issuance of money should be relegated exclusively to them. In like manner vaccinators and the conservative class of doctors generally, would like to have all matters affecting the public health left exclusively to them. They want the health conditions of the community under their control, so they can manipulate them as a financier manipulates the stock market. They make no earnest effort to instruct the people how to preserve health and prevent disease. No—no! They have no interests identified with a general and thorough system of public sanitation. They have "de-monetised" air, water, and general hygiene, and set up a sort of "gold standard" of their mysterious drugs, latin-named, and still more mysterious vaccine pus, and secured a law that compels everybody to buy; and if any "divine healer"—like Schlatter, or a psychic like the late Dr. Newton, comes along, even certain of the Homoeopaths and Eclectics would arrest and fine him. Ah, more! If Jesus Christ, the Great Physician, should appear in our midst as of old, long-haired, sandal-footed, and Syrian-clad, curing the leper, making the deaf to hear, the blind to see, the lame to walk, and the dumb to speak, Allopaths, Homeopaths, Osteopaths, and Eclectics of the "baser sort," would quite likely unite, arraign, try, condemn, and jail him! The hydra-headed monster of persecution is not dead. There is if possible more medical than theological idolatry and bigotry in the land. Schools and pathies aside, only the educated, cultured, conscientious, and inspired man or woman that treats and restores the sick—teaching them in the meantime how to keep well—is worthy the name physician!

The second class, or better school of physicians, thoroughly educated, has a real interest in the public health, and a rational and scientific mode of promoting it. They are foremost in urging measures for thorough public sanitation. Where centers of filth and pollution abound they would cleanse and purify. They have a fellow feeling foi the race. They are sympathetic. They are self-sacrificing and they have a keen sense of identity with the common welfare.

In Honolulu, both schools are represented. The vaccinators are continually lobbying for more stringent compulsory laws by which they may be able to compel every unit in the social organism to pay them tribute. A sanitary organization is also laboring for the repeal of those laws, and for the adoption of measures which will prevent zymotic diseases without wrecking the health in other regards, They insist that vaccination shall be left optional with the people. But the vaccinators know full well if they are not permitted to vaccinate with compulsion they cannot vaccinate at all, and their occupation would be gone, for the native population are a unit against the practice, believing the prevalence of syphilis and leprosy in the islands to be mainly due to vaccination. Vaccinating officers, too, are charged with reckless carelessness, operating upon hundreds of persons in succession with no pretence to cleaning the instruments; also that the virus used is a common source of serious inflammation and illness. A determined resistance to vaccination therefore, is spreading throughout the islands, and officials encounter increasing trouble in enforcing the law.

A condensed and much abridged summary of the conclusions to which Mr. Tebb arrives concerning the relation of leprosy to vaccination, in the following:—

1. Leprosy is an inoculable disease, in which the leprous virus usually finds its way to the blood through a punctured or abrazed skin-surface.

2. The most frequent opportunities of inoculating this

virus is afforded in the practice of vaccination, which is the only inoculation that is habitually imposed by law. Note also in this connection that where leprosy most abounds, the mode of vaccination is from arm to arm

3. That the increase of leprosy in the Sandwich Islands, West Indies, Colombia, British Guiana, South Africa, and New Caledonia, has been parallel with the introduction and extension of vaccination in these countries. This fact is neither questioned nor denied.

In some of these—as the Sandwich Islands—there was no leprosy until the natives came in contact with civilization. In these countries, moreover, arm to arm vaccination is all the more dangerous because leprosy is of very slow incubation, and often exists incipiently in apparently healthy persons through whom vaccine virus often passes.

Leprosy is found to be rapidly increasing all over the world, but more especially along the channels of commercial activity. Mr. Tebb devotes 60 pages of his large work with evidence on this point alone. In parts of Russia, particularly the Baltic and Caspian provinces, the disease is spreading. In 1887 Dr. Bergman discovered 37 cases in Riga and 21 cases in its environs. In 1893 the number had increased to 100. In and around Dorpat the disease has reached alarming proportions. In Bokhara and provinces east of the Caspian it is reported as spreading rapidly. Throughout the West India Islands lepers are multiplying altogether beyond the hospital accommodations provided. In 1889 Mr. Tebb visited the làzaretto at Barbados, where from 300 to 400 lepers were congregated from a single parish of 30,000 population. While the population increases at the rate of six per cent. lepers are increasing at the rate of 25 per cent. The report on leprosy in Trinidad in 1891, as given by Dr. Koch, says: "The new infirmary ward, which was finished at the end of 1889, and occupied early in 1890, has been full all the year round. There was a rush of patients to fill it.' In 1805 but three lepers were known in Trinidad; eight years later there was 73, out of a population of 32,000. In 1878 there were 860 out of a population of 120,000; and in 1892, the increase was estimated to be four times more rapid than that of population.

THE SANDWICH ISLANDS.

In the Sandwich Islands leprosy is allowed to be the chief of the destructive forces which are gradually depopulating the native race of this beautiful archipelago. Its rapid increase is by far the most urgent and anxious question of the hour, and successive medical officers of health seem powerless to cope with it. This was fully confirmed when on my third journey around the world studying chronic diseases and their remedies.

Leaving my Australian bound steamer by previous arrangement at Honolulu, I spent much time in Hawaii in the leprosy-receiving hospitals, and at the homes of isolated lepers accompanied by an attending physician. It is admitted here that in many cases the leprous taint is directly traced to vaccination. This is the chief reason why the natives oppose it.

"In a leading article on 'The Nature of Leprosy,' 'The Lancet,' July 30, 1881, p. 186, says: 'The great importance of the subject of the nature and mode of extension of leprosy is evident from the steady increase in certain countries into which it has been introduced. In the Sandwich Islands, for instance, the disease was unknown forty years ago, and now a tenth part of the inhabitants are lepers. In Honolulu, at one time quite free, there are not less than two hundred and fifty cases; and in the United States the number is steadily increasing.

"According to the latest returns handed to me (October, 1890) by Mr. Potter, the secretary to the board of health, Honolulu, 1154 lepers were segregated in Molokai, to which must be added thirty, sent from the Hospital of Suspects at Kalihi to Molokai on the 30th of the same month, while there are probably several hundred secreted by relatives in the various islands. On March 31, 1888, the number officially reported to be at large in the various islands amounted to 644, but efforts have been made during the past three years to capture these afflicted creatures and segregate them at Molokai."—Wm. Tebb, p. 40.

It is estimated by Dr. White, surgeon to the United States Navy, who visited the islands in 1882, that the concealed cases amounted to at least three per cent. of the population. On the origin and spread of leprosy in Hawaii Wm. Tebb writes, pp. 42-43:—

"According to Mr. Dayton, president of the health board, Honolulu, leprosy was discovered in the island in 1840, but Mr. D. W. Meyer, agent for the Honolulu board of health, in the appendix to the report presented to the legislative assembly of Honolulu in 1886, says it was in 1859 or 1860 that he saw the first case of the disease. That 1840 was the date of its introduction is the opinion of Dr. W. B. Emerson, ex-president of the board of health, Honolulu, who, in his report published in 'The Practitioner' of April, 1890, attributes the introduction of the disease to a case reported by the Rev. D. D. Baldwin, M. D., to the Minister of the Interior, May 26, 1864. In 1863 Dr. Baldwin received reports from the deacons of his church at Lahaina with the names of 60 people who were believed to be affected with this disease. In a very few years leprosy increased to an enormous extent, and in 1868 Dr. Hutchinson reported 274 cases. * * * * * * *

"To account for the appalling spread of this terrible scourge of humanity within such a short period of time, the evidence points conclusively to one prominent cause—vaccination. There is no evidence to show that leprosy increased in Hawaii until after the introduction and dissemination of the vaccine virus.

"Small-pox was introduced from San Francisco in the year 1868. In that year a general vaccination took place, spring lancets being used. which the president of the board of health (Mr. David Dayton) informed me were difficult, if not impossible, to disinfect—the operation causing irreparable mischief. The synchronicity of the spread of leprosy with general vaccination is actually a matter beyond discussion, and this terrible disease soon afterwards obtained such a foothold amongst the Hawaiians that the government made a first attempt to control it by means of segregation. Another outbreak of small-pox occurred in 1873, and yet another in 1881, both followed by general arm to arm vaccination and a rapid and alarming development of leprosy, as may be seen in successive reports of the board of health. In 1886 the then president of the board of health recorded his conviction, in an official report, to the effect that that 'to judge by the number of cases in proportion to the population, the disease (leprosy) appears to be more virulent and malignant in the Hawaiian Archipelago than elsewhere on the globe.' Leprosy became then, and is now, the most pressing question in these islands."

In New Caledonia (South Pacific) leprosy was unknown until 1853, when the French formally annexed and converted it into a penal colony. In 1890, 500 cases were reported among the natives and seven of European parentage. Vaccination had been practiced with rigor, and to this a large percentage of the cases are indirectly attributable. But once introduced, it has also spread by means of a peculiar habit the natives have of tattooing and scarifying the skin, making a free channel through which the leprous virus or bacillus can reach the blood. This practice has been with them from time immemorial, and yet no leprosy was known there until they were brought in contact with the vaccination of European civilization.

In India leprosy is estimated to be increasing at the rate of 1,000 per year (British Med. Jour. Sept. 13, 1890.) The Prince of Wales stated in a speech in Marlborough House, June 17, 1889, that there were in India at least 250,000 lepers. In some districts 22 per cent. of the population are afflicted. The leper asylums are totally inadequate to their accomodation. In the city of Bombay, where at least 1,000 lepers are found. they collect in 'dark corners, in gullies where rats and bandicoats have taken their abode, thrown out by their families, neglected and indiscribably wretched."

Whether leprosy is contagious, the greatest diversity of

opinion exists among medical men. As no one has studied this question more carefully and extensively than Mr. Tebb, I consider his opinion entitled to much weight. He does not believe it to be contagious in the ordinary sense in which that term is used; but that the principle mode by which it is communicated is through puncture or abrasion of the skin, that is, by inoculating the blood through the skin with the leprous virus. A sewing needle or pin from the garments of a leper is sufficient, if these penetrate through the skin. Mr. Tebb writes, pp. 80-81:

"In the pursuit of my investigation, I have been confronted on every hand by the most conflicting theories with regard to the causation of leprosy, and particularly with regard to this question of contagion. The contagionists, when pressed, I found invariably included virus inoculation, and interpreted the word in that sense. They admitted that the leprous discharge might be touched with impunity, when the integument is intact, but not otherwise. Every nurse, doctor, attendant, or laundress, in the hospital, is bound to come in repeated contact with pus from ulcerated tubercles. It is only by the insertion of the leprous virus into the blood, through a sore, prick, or abraded surface, that the disease is communicable. This view is now held by the highest authorities in all parts of the world. At the same time, there are others who hold that the disease is transferable in a lesser degree by inhalation, heredity, and cohabitation.

"From personal inquiries made at asylums and lazarettos in various countries where leprosy is endemic, I am convinced that, apart from the risk of inoculation, there is little or no danger of contagion, using the word to mean simple contact between unbroken surfaces of the body. So far as my investigations have extended, the only country where the belief in communication by simple contact prevails to a certain extent is Hawaii; but here also I found much diversity of opinion, not a few using the word contagion to include cow-pox inoculation, both accidental, as in a cut or a sore, and by design, as in vaccination."

The first serious hint from a high medical authority that

leprosy is a frequent result of vaccination, was by Dr. R. Hall Bakewell in 1870. He was vaccinator general of Trinidad and visiting physician of leprosy hospital. He writes:—

"The question is not as simple as it appears. It is not a question of half-a-dozen minute punctures in an infant's arm versus an attack of small-pox. It is a question of performing on every child that is born into the world, and that lives to be three months old, an operation sometimes, though very rarely, fatal; sometimes, but not frequently, attended with severe illness, always accompanied by considerable constitutional disturbance in the form of fever; sometimes, in an unknown proportion of cases, introducing into the system of a healthy child constitutional syphilis, but suspected in the West Indies of introducing a poison even more dreaded than that of syphilis— leprosy. And the parent is required compulsorily by law to subject his child to these evils, most of which are only possible, but one of which is certain (the fever), for the purpose of avoiding the chance of an epidemic of small-pox, which, when it does occur, may or may not attack the child.

"It may be taken as proved that the syphilitic poison may be, and has been, introduced into the system of a previously healthy child by means of vaccination. But we know that leprosy is a constitutional disease, in many respects singularly resembling constitutional syphilis; like it, attended by stainings and diseases of the skin; like it, attacking the mucous membrane of the nose, throat, and mouth; like it, producing falling off of the hair, diseases of the nails and bones; and, like it, hereditary." Why should not the blood of a leprous child, whether the leprosy be developed or not, contaminate a healthy one?

"It seems to me not merely a popular opinion, but a medical one also. In returning to Europe in the spring of this year, I met several medical men from Demerara and other tropical countries, and they all considered that leprosy might be, and is, propagated by vaccination."

Dr. Bakewell was summoned on behalf of the government to give evidence before the Select Vaccination Parliamentary committee in 1871, and testified as follows (Answer 3563, p. 207, Official Report):—

"There is a very strong opinion prevalent in Trinidad, and in the West Indies generally, that leprosy has been introduced into the system by vaccination; and I may say that as vaccinator general of Trinidad, I found that all the medical men, when they had occasion to vaccinate either their own children or those of patients in whom they were specially interested, applied to me for English lymph; and that was so marked that in one instance a man, who had never spoken to me before, wrote me quite a friendly letter, in order to get lymph from England when he had to vaccinate his own child. It is quite evident that the only reason for wanting lymph from England must be that they consider it free or measurably free, from contaminating the system by leprosy; because, of course, there is an equal chance, and probably a greater chance in England, of the lymph being contaminated by syphilis."

Queston 3564 and Dr. Bakewell's answer (pp. 207-8) are as follows:—

"Q.—Have you had experience of any case in which leprosy has been introduced by vaccination?

"A.—I have seen several cases in which it seemed to be the only explanation. I have a case, now under treatment, of the son of a gentleman from India who has contracted leprosy, both the parents being of English origin. I saw the case of a child last year, who, though a Creole of the Island of Trinidad, is born of English parents, and is a leper, and there is no other cause to which it is attributable. Sir Ranald Martin, who is a great authority on these points, agreed with me that the leprosy arose from vaccination."—"Leprosy and Vaccination," pp. 134-135.

In the "British Medical Journal," June 11, 1887, Dr. W. T. Gairdner, professor of medicine in the university, Glasgow, gives a lengthy and sadly interesting account of a case of leprosy which came under his observation in England. As this case resulted from vaccination, I will make an abridged statement of it. The case was a confidential one and hence names and localities are omitted except that the island referred to is one of the group in the British East Indies.

A sea captain and his wife had a little boy with a peculiar eruption on the skin, and took him to Dr. Gairdner who made a thorough diagnosis of the case and pronounced it to be incipient leprosy. The parents had just brought the child from a British tropical island ;they were Scotch and were horrified. As the child continued to grow worse the mother did not accompany the husband on his voyages, but settled down in England where their unfortunate child might have the advantage of good medical advice.

Three years subsequently Dr. G. was lecturing in the town where the lady was stopping and so went to see how the malady was progressing in the little boy, whom he found in the most advanced stage of the disease, proceeding to mutilation of the extremeties and in the last degree of emaciation. It was on the occasion of this visit that Dr. Gairdner learned the history of the case. On the island where the parents temporarily sojourned, the child was vaccinated by a Scotch physician who had been a pupil in Dr. Gairdner's university. This physician took lymph from the arm of his own son, whom a short time previously he had vaccinated with lymph from the arm of a native child which he afterwards learned was from a leprous family and leprosy later developed itself in this child, and as a matter of course the two children—the physician's child and the child of the sea captain—developed it also. The latter died soon after. Dr. Gairdner saw him the second time. In 1887 the physician's son was still alive, sequestered in an English town, but hopelessly afflicted with the terrible and incurable disease.

This was an undoubted case of vaccinal leprosy. It is a fearful indictment against the practice of vaccination, and reveals how grave a danger confronts every parent who submits their children to the perilous ordeal. This case is likewise an other link in that long chain of evidence which confirms the popular belief among the native populations that vaccination is the direct cause of the alarming spread of leprosy. Still, with all these facts before him, the vaccinating doctor—literally the medical lilliputian—not only has no thoughts of quitting his murderous practice, but is continually plotting to make compulsory vaccination more complete and its enforcement more rigorous! Referring to the cases above detailed, the acting surgeon general of Trinidad, Dr. C. B. Pasley, observes: "The fact remains, that an unlucky boy, of undoubted English parentage, acquired a most loathsome disease, and died a miserable death as the result of vaccination."

A sad case of leprosy occurred in the island of St. Kitts, British West Indies, in 1890. The little daughter of a Wesleyan missionary was taken sick and on examination it was found the child had contracted leprosy. Fearing the small-pox, which occasionally visited the isle, the parents in order to save their little girl from a remote and possible danger, inoculated her with the terrible poison that made her existence a living death and source of unfailing sorrow to her parents. The missionary resigned his charge and decided to return to England, hoping he might find some adequate medical skill for his unfortunate child; but a new trouble was encountered in securing passage to England, as the Royal Mail company steamers would not take a leper passenger. The family finally took passage on a sailing craft, but before the vessel got fairly away from the island, it struck a reef, and they barely escaped with their lives. So they remained on the island where their misfortunes began, and where they will perform the offices of love for their stricken one until the authorities tear her asunder from her parents and consign her to the lazaretto, from whence no traveler ever returns. The vaccinator meantime remains abroad, and is not only permitted to pursue his nefarious business, but assisted by the state to hunt down his victims and inflict upon them the curse of all curses—a disease which savages never saw or heard of until the civilized man found him a convenient subject with which to increase his revenues; then he compassionately (?) began to "protect" him.

"While in Trinidad, I made inquiries of a highly intelligent merchant, who has resided forty-three years in the West Indies, and has always been much interested in the public health. He says the belief is general in the islands that leprosy is being extensively disseminated by vaccination, and he furnished me with particulars of a number of healthy families where leprosy and other diseases have broken out after vaccination, of others who, in spite of a law enforcing vaccination, have preferred to undergo the worry and penalties of prosecution to the terrible risks of this hideous and incurable malady. In some instances the children infected with leprosy have been sent by their parents to France and England, where, after treatment by some of the most distinguished physicians, they have either succumbed to the disease or returned to die at home; and in one case the mother died of a broken heart on seeing her eldest son come back a complete wreck, loathsome to the sight. All the victims described by my informant were in good circumstances and none were even sent to the leper hospital, where only the poor are entered. He says that had he kept a record he would have been in a position to have given details of very many cases, with all the attending circumstances, and adds, 'I have come to the conclusion that we are indebted to vaccination for not only this (leprosy) but many other diseases, especially those of a scrofulous nature, as well as syphilis.' "—Wm. Tebb, p. 146.

"Mr Alexander Henry, vice-chairman of the Council of the British and West Indian Alliance, and formerly editor of the St. Kitts Gazette, who has resided some years in the West Indies, and has devoted much attention to the spread and causation of leprosy, writing June 12, 1890, says: 'A medical officer of health cautiously admitted to me that leprosy was contracted by means of careless vaccination. Now, careless vaccination means vaccination from arm to arm, which is almost universal in these islands. I do not believe there is a doctor of any standing in the West Indies who would deny that leprosy can be inoculated. It is admitted that owing to the slow incubation of the disease it is difficult to distinguish a leper; and when you take into account that medical officers are constantly complaining to the government 'that they cannot get a supply of calf-lymph,' and add to this the indiscriminate and careless yet vigorous manner in which they carry out the vaccination laws upon an ignorant and simple people, who have no means of asserting themselves, I think we may safely conclude there is a high probability that leprosy is spread by vaccination."—Ibed. p. 151.

"My own experience has compelled the conviction that leprosy has on numerous occasions been propagated by the vaccinator's lancet in these islands. Children have been brought to me a year or two after vaccination who have shown unmistakable signs of leprosy, and whose parents assured me that such had never been in their family before. On the other hand, inquiry into the antecedents of the child from whom the lymph had been selected revealed the existence of leprous taint either on the paternal or maternal side.

"My own experiences have been confirmed by Dr. Bechtinger, formerly a resident and practising physician here, whose extensive researches entitle his opinion to great weight amongst pathologists.

"The belief, also, in the British West Indies as to the conveyance of leprosy in this way is widespread, and forms one of the strongest grounds against compulsory vaccination that I know of.

"In view of such a fact, and in face of such a terrible danger, it is my conscientious opinion that every physician should hesitate before subscribing to such a doctrine, as compulsory vaccination."—Extract from a letter from Dr. Chas. E. Taylor, of St. Thomas, Danish West Indies, read before Vaccination Commission, Jan. 2, 1890.

Now, the chief secretary of state for the colonies—Lord Kimberly—sent out a circular of inquiry, as to whether there were any grounds for the belief that leprosy was spread by vaccination in the West Indies. A dozen or more of physicians in these islands, who were practically familiar with leprosy, responded to this circular and gave their emphatic testimony that vaccination was causing a vast amount of leprosy. Their evi-

dence was before the College of Physicians. What did this
learned body do with these facts in their possession? Did they
advise Lord Kimberly to relax the rigor of compulsory vaccination in the islands? Did they express sorrow at the leprous
havoc that had already been wrought by the adoption of a mistaken policy? Did they suggest measures whereby a modicum
of justice might be returned to a wronged people for the barbarous practice that had already been wantonly imposed upon
them? Nothing of the kind; but in their answer and advice to
Lord Kimberly they said: "The College of Physicians feel they
can not press too strongly on your lordship the importance of
enforcing the practice of vaccination for the protection of those
who are too ignorant to protect themselves." It is difficult to
say which is the most pronounced in the above passage—bald
hypocrisy, or cold-blooded traffic in the blood of human beings
at one dollar per head! May the day soon dawn when the people—the thinking, toiling people—will be wise enough—enthusiastic enough—to protect themselves from the tender mer-
cies of Colleges of Physicians! Between the members of that
brotherhood of thieves—the commercial agent, the supersti-
tious priest, the scheming lawyer, and the doctor,—the native
populations of all countries, lying near the tropics, are having
a most unequal struggle. Each class manipulates these natives
in a different way, but all have the same purpose—the money
value they make them instrumental in returning to them. All
profess philanthropic motives. The commercial sharper wants
to advance the native's material interests; the priest wants to
rescue their soul from endless hell torments; the lawyer is as
painfully, as self-sacrificingly anxious to assist all the others in
"protecting" him; the doctor, with a heart all tenderness is so
alarmed lest he catch the small-pox! that he invokes the mighty
power of the state and all the resources of the surgical art to
"protect" the poor creature, seeing he is "too ignorant to pro-
teet himself." So between the various "privileged classes" the

civilize, the tropical populations, are being ground to powder. Gold is today's god. It was Rome's before her fall. Civilization, sad to say, worships it however ill-gotten. For it the syndicate is formed—for it the treasure-safe is blown to atoms—for it the highway robber, revolver in hand, boards the railway train—and for it the hungrier, leaner class of doctors will fight —persistently and politically—fight for compulsory vaccination. When, oh when, will the world come to understand that God is just, that all, here or hereafter, will reap what they have sown— that compensation is as certain as the needle to the pole—that sin brings suffering in all worlds, and that heaven is attained only by being right and doing right—only by living the upright, Christlike life.

Dr Edward Arning made a thorough bacteriological study of leprosy in the Sandwich Islands; and in a letter to Wm. Tebb dated Sept. 6, 1889, he says:—

"During my stay on the Hawaiian Islands for the bacteriological study of leprosy, I was naturally drawn to a scrutiny of the question whether leprosy is transmissible, and had been there transmitted by vaccination; all the more so as there is a general opinion prevailing on these islands that the unusually rapid spread of the disease about thirty years ago may probably be attributed to the great amount of indiscriminate vaccination there carried on about that period. And there is no mistake about the actual synchronicity of the spread of vaccination and of leprosy in the Hawaiian Islands; but many a mistake is possible as to the real casual relation between the two.

"I could trace the first authenticated cases of leprosy back to about 1830, but the terrible spread all over the islands did not take place until very nearly thirty years later, at a time when an epidemic of small-pox had given rise to very general and very careless vaccinations throughout the group. * * * * * I attach far more importance to an instance of an increase of leprosy soon after vaccination on a much smaller scale, and during a much more recent period than the above. I have it on good authority that a very remarkable new crop of leprosy cases sprang up at Lahaina, on the island of Maui, about a year after vaccination had been practiced there.

"The impossibility of detecting leprosy in its early stages is a matter of common notoriety amongst physicians, so that many who believe in the prophylaxis of vaccination refuse to incur the terrible risks involved by its practice in leprous countries."—"Leprosy and Vaccination," p. 157.

Dr. F. B. Sutliff, of Sacramento, Cal., who has studied the disease as government physician on the Island of Maui, says:—

"I very seldom visited a school without excluding some (children), while the spots just beginning to show in others made it only too probable that they would not long be doubtful cases. It did not seem to me a difficult task to read the fate of Hawaii in the little dark faces that looked up from their books."—"Occidental Medical Times," April, 1889.

It is the general opinion of all residents in Honolulu, that the remarkable spread of leprosy subsequent to 1853 was due to indiscriminate and general vaccination in that year. Alarmed by an invasion of small-pox, a vaccination of the whole population was ordered, and as physicians were few, non-professionals aided in the work. This heterogeneous and indiscriminate arm to arm vaccination, soon sowed a bountiful crop of both leprosy and syphilis. But Mr. Walter M. Gibson, president board of health in Honolulu, has expressed the opinion that the chief cause of leprosy and secondary syphilis, was the indiscriminate and careless practice of vaccination in 1868. After this general vaccination, numerous leprous centers sprang up in various parts of the islands where the disease had previously been unknown.

A remarkable outbreak of fresh leprous cases occurred at Lahaima in 1871-72, Island of Maui. This was one year after a general vaccination. Sixty cases occured suddenly in a locality which up to that time had been almost entirely free from the disease.

When Capt. Cook visited the islands their population was

estimated at 400,000; and in 1900 a population of 35,000 would be a very liberal estimate,—a race literally swept off the face of the earth, that the business of the vaccinator may continue to yield an unfailing annual revenue. A race "protected" by the murderous practice of professedly civilized men on the pretence that they are "too ignorant to protect themselves." Notwithstanding these appalling facts confronting them in their midst and on every side, what do they do? What redress or mitigation of wrongs already committed do the doctors propose? Just what the College of Physicians proposed on another occasion. They heap insult upon injury!

In the biennial report of the president of the board of health to the Hawaii legislature of 1888, the said legislature was informed and advised, "that the work of vaccination had been pushed with vigor," and that "the board would recommend the passage of a more stringent law, imposing heavier penalties and giving vaccinating authorities all necessary authority." If this is not deliberate, cold-blooded, and demoniac cruelty, perpetrated against a defenceless native race, some of which prominent white men have married, it would be difficult to find an example. And who is it behind the board and largely constituting it? Who is it urging on this infamous work? They are the doctors who run vaccination on "business principles;" doctors who seemingly place no higher value on the "Kanucks" than their vaccination fee will yield them,—on a West India native, or Afrikander, or Hindoo. How the legislature must be "impressed" with the vaccinator's philanthropy when he is so persistently lobbying their body for a more "stringent law." Nor can we suppose that the legislature is quite so "verdant" when passing vaccination acts that they are simply aiding these self-sacrificing, kind-hearted (?) doctors in the "protection of those who are too ignorant to protect themselves."

In Cape Colony vaccination was made compulsory in 1882. A large number of cases of vaccinal injury soon followed, which

the London "Daily News" attributed to "impure lymph." But
a most vigorous vaccination of the natives was prosecuted; and
on Sept. 6, 1883, an additional act was passed by the local legislature, in which Section 60 reads:—"No person who has not
been vaccinated shall be appointed, or if appointed prior to the
taking effect of this act, promoted to any office in the public
service." A penalty of £2 was provided for non-vaccination of
children. Nothing was either said or done to remove the real
cause that was breeding the pestilence—the "long continued
filth, neglect, and scarcity of water, foul, unkempt streets, seas
of mud in the winter, of dust in the summer, and a population
ignorant of the commonest instincts of decency." What did
the vaccinators care for sanitation? They had not invested in
that direction. As a natural consequence, in 1884, after the
wholesale vaccination of 1882-3, there was an epidemic of small-
pox, and leprosy was increasing at a fearful rate. In 1885 the
medical officer for Herbert reported:—"During the year small-
pox, syphilis of a particular type, and leprosy, have been the
prevailing epidemics. The last two named are still prevailing
to an alarming extent."

In summing up the evidence for Cape Colony, Mr. Tebb
observes:—

"One experienced district surgeon told me that he had,
again and again, year after year, called the attention of the
board of health to proofs of this terrible havoc wrought by arm
to arm vaccination, and had advocated its suppression in the interests of public health. A careful examination of the official
documents would show that the facts incriminating vaccination
have not been allowed to appear."—Tebb, p. 245.

"When making inquiries regarding etiology and spread of
leprosy in South Africa, I was generally referred to the Rev.
Canon Baker, of Kalk Bay, Cape Colony, as a high authority
on the subject, and one who had probably devoted more attention to it than any other resident in the colony. Canon Baker
had in 1883 given evidence before the select committee of the

House of Assembly, Cape Town, and presented a statement of his views, which appeared in Appendix A, pp. 1-9. Since then he has continued his investigations and accumulated a considerable body of facts bearing on the subject. Vaccination, he says, is carried out in the colonies in a most careless and perfunctory manner. He has seen the operator pass his lancet from one arm to another without the smallest attempt to disinfeet the instrument or discriminate between the diseased and the healthy, in districts where both leprosy and syphilis are endemic. From other reliable sources I am satisfied that this is the rule rather than the exception. Canon Baker believes that leprosy is chiefly communicated by means of inoculation, and that arm to arm vaccination is a prolific cause of the spread of this fearful plague in South Africa.

"The Colony of Natal passed Vaccination Law No. 3 in 1882, and Law No. 10 in 1885. Penalties for non-vaccination £5. In a communication from Archdeacon Colley, (I have the honor of personally knowing Archdeacon Colley, meeting him not only in Natal and Cape Town, South Africa, but later, frequently in London. The Archdeacon is not only a most reliable witness, but personally a most scholarly, broad-minded English clergyman,) dated Natal, August 25, 1885, I learn that hundreds of summonses were issued in vain upon the colonists, but the natives were vaccinated by thousands; one operator would get through two hundred a day.

"While the vaccination laws for several years have not been enforced against the white population in Natal, all the natives are vaccinated either under persuasion or threats, the operation being carried out in the usual careless manner, with arm to arm virus taken from native children without previous examination, and not the slightest attempt is made to clean or disinfect the lancets after each operation. Hundreds of natives, as I am informed on unimpeachable authority, have died of blood-poisoning and of inoculated diseases.

"A member of the Legislative Council, Sir John Bisset, reported in Parliament that many were 'blood-poisoned, presenting a horrible sight, and dying masses of corruption.' In January, 1891, leprosy disseminated in this way was discovered in fifty kraals in one electoral division alone. The natives in their simplicity submit to vaccination, being told that it was the 'In-cosi' (King) that ordered it, and this was the way the white man secured himself against the plague of small-pox.

"As the government of Natal does not publish reports from the district surgeons, and appears to be indifferent as to the suffering and mischief caused by the vaccinators, I found it difficult to obtain further details."—"Leprosy and Vaccination," pp. 273-75.

CHAPTER VIII.

MISCELLANEOUS FEATURES OF VACCINATION.

"Science is in the main most useful, but is sometimes proud, wild and erratic, and has lately proposed a desperate device for the prevention of infectious perils. She proposes to prevent one peril by setting up another. She would inoculate new diseases into our old stock, in the anticipation that the new will put out the old. I pray you be not led away by this conceit. This manufacture of spick and span new diseases in our human, bovine, equine, ovine, canine, and perhaps feline species is too much to endure the thought of, especially when we know that purity of life is all-sufficient to remove what exists, without invoking what is not."—Sir. B. W. Richardson, M. D., LL. D., F. R. S.

In the foregoing pages I have frequently coupled a large percentage of the medical profession—and especially the vaccinating fraternity—with a species of commercialism whose major purpose of pecuniary gain is in direct antagonism with the public health and welfare. And as I propose to continue the discussion somewhat along similar lines, I will here offer a word of qualification.

I do not arraign the profession for violation of the higher ethical law in any different sense than I arraign all professions and occupations embraced in our modern politico-selfish and competitive life. The entire structure of existing society—social, religious, professional, political, and commercial—is one in which all the parts are in mutual antagonism. Every form of social movement is an inversion of the higher normal order. The normal order finds its expression in love and reciprocity. The inversive order, in which we live, is one whose actuating force is self-interest, and hence one in which jealousy, rivalry, competitive strife, fraud, deceit, hypocrisy, injustice, oppression,, murder, war, conquest, etc., are abundantly interwoven with the social movement. The root out of which these hydra-headed antagonisms spring is the intense "love of money." This is the prime motive which impulses nearly every detail of human activity. The age is culminating; all lines are converging toward the "golden calf," wherein the specialties of the "Devil's" form of order will be bound in an apocalyptic "bundle" preliminary to its final destruction. Error is mortal and must die; truth alone is immortal, eternal.

The general system by which each individual and each class are able to promote their apparent welfare is one of competition and strife, not the best but the worst motives are accordingly brought to the front and kept there. This inversive system, general menstrum, or social environment prompts the groceryman to water his syrup, the manufacturer to put shoddy in his goods and to undersell his rival by a species of deception. It prompts the vaccinator to puncture and poison with putrid pus, while he swears it is the very "savor of life unto life;" prompts the lawyer to multiply contentions and quarrels, while to put an end to frauds and all quarrels would serve him poorly. Each individual and each class find their environment already provided when they arrive on the stage. The "rules of the game" are established, and they find it far easier to adopt these rules than to induce mankind to abandon them; so they take up the struggle and the strife where their fathers left it.

It is beyond the power, I fear, of any class of reformers to change the scheme by which society moves like a mighty avalanche toward the vortex of an impending revolution! While this system continues to remain it is absolutely certain that the majority will apply it in the prosecution of their daily business affairs. The old order is a broad highway which is crowded with "soldiers of fortune," the strong treading down the weak, and each intent on gaining a vantage ground where they may compel the less fortunate to pay them tribute. The new and prospective order is as yet but a narrow lane, in which the tall grass is seldom trodden down by the weary feet of solitary pilgrims who keep their integrity.

It is not my purpose therefore to unjustly condemn or criticise the doctor, lawyer, priest, manufacturer or trader, who feels compelled to use the tools bequeathed them by their ancestors. To each of these I am willing to concede they would practice the law of love under a more beneficent scheme of living—a scheme based upon justice and benevolence—a scheme in which self-interest would not antagonize the general welfare. It is the corporate greed, fraud and injustice I am aiming at, not the individual. While we are under the law of "struggle for existence and survival of the fittest" it must needs be that "offences come," yet nevertheless, "woe unto him through whom they come!" God is just. Nature knows no forgiveness. The "Good Law" holds each individual to account. You are humane men whom I meet on the street or in the public assembly, being neither strangers to pity nor generosity. You are moved by the spectacle of suffering, and put your hands deep into your pockets to relieve individual cases of distress. But when you combine with other men in a corporate capacity; I know then that the system will take precedence of the man; I know that you will then scheme for money and place and power, wholly indifferent to the disease, poverty, suffering and widespread disaster you may occasion. Thus banded together, your only concern for the "goose" is that she shall continue to lay golden eggs. It is your corporate character I am trying to introduce to my readers. I want them to realize how crafty, hypocritical, untruthful and utterly disregardful of the common good corporate bodies are in general, and the Vaccinating Syndi-

cate in particular.   It shall be with me a purpose—a persistent
endeavor to clip the claws of this medical monster and so diminish its capacity for harm.

Now, the heads of the medical profession having hastily
committed themselves to vaccination as an unquestioned prophylactic against small-pox, and having induced Parliament to
award Jenner £30,000 from the public treasury, and also to en-
dow a National Vaccine Establishment at £3,000 a year, henceforth reputations and vested interests were at stake, and so the
vaccination delusion soon petrified into a dogma which both
the profession and the state had a powerful motive to defend.
In this way vaccination became one of those time-honored institutions, which courts and classes and professions conserva-
tively guarded as a sort of heirloom of the race.   It was therefore as reprehensible to neglect vaccination as to neglect baptism; far more so indeed, since to the former were attached
fines and imprisonment in this world, while neglect of the latter
was mercifully left to be adjudicated in the next world.   To this
giant evil the reformer stood like David before Goliah.   The little handful of reformers who at first organized the London Anti-Vaccination Society began their work with much the same
appearance and prospects as the little band in Boston, headed
by Garrison, when they commenced their assault on the great
institution of American slavery in the United States.   This little coterie in London, with the noble Wm. Tebb at their head,
were regarded as insane fanatics, and handled by the profession
much as a householder handles a polecat that has found its way
into his cellar.   For them contempt, misrepresentation, and persecution by the corrupt ring of feed and salaried professionals
and officials who "stand in" with the state to reap their monthly
and annual harvest at the expense and pain and protracted misery of the poorly informed and crucified public.

We know somewhat the kind of spirit that actuates a party

machine which has long feasted on public spoils; how con-
scienceless and infamously corrupt they become; how they
carry their measures by subsidizing the press, falsifying facts,
and twisting statistics; hot, cruel, and unscrupulous they are,
in crushing those, whom they cannot use or appropriate; with
craft and cunning they pose before the people as guardians and
defenders of the public safety. It is indeed high time the public should be made aware of the animus which is behind the
whole vaccination business. Vaccination as a therapeutic is
the pivotal from of inversion, the keystone in the arch which
carries the full weight of old-time mercurial, blood-letting practice. It is the barometer, the indicator, which shows the financial outlook for medical practice from year to year. When
boards of health can be spurred up to "enforce the law;" when
the public schools are closed against those who refuse to submit; and when a fresh "set-back" can be given to advanced
practitioners, then business is good and old-school medical
stock is at par. To attack vaccination, therefore, is to run up
against the "Wall Street" interest and syndicate trusts of value
in the medical profession.

The medical profession, including the three more prominent schools, with a few exceptions, individually and collectively
are either tacitly or expressly pledged to resist all attacks; to
stand by the vaccination rite as persistently as a hard-shell Bap-
tist stands by immersion as the only door into the Kingdom,
or as a Catholic stands by the Pope's infallibility. Not only will
the profession carry the fight to the last ditch in defence of their
vaccine dogma, but they will push their disgusting practice under our noses, in season and out of season, with a standing prospect of a small-pox cyclone just ahead! Health boards are the
principle means for the enforcement of such legislation as the
vaccinators have been able to secure. The vaccinating "trust"
has a prominent place in the structure of that "Old Dragon"

whose slimy trail marks a path of desolation over which the victims of disease and poverty are hopelessly treading toward their untimely graves. A few reformers—fellow sufferers with the masses—conscientious royal-souled reformers—are trying to make the householders of this country—the parents and guardians of the rising generation—realize that the old vaccine virus monster, notwithstanding his flattering promises of salvation from disease, is really a disease-breeder—a parasite fastened upon their vitals, poisoning their life-blood and slowly but surely undermining the integrity of their bodily structure.

Be assured dear readers, vaccination is not your friend, but rather your insidious and implacable enemy, compared with which prosecutions, fines, and imprisonment are light penalties. Martyrs in the coming time wear crowns. It is far better that your children have the doors of the public school slammed in their faces than that you submit their bodies to be inoculated with the virus of detestable and incurable diseases.

It is not flattering to the voting population of the United States that they have permitted every state legislature to frame and pass a compulsory vaccination act. If the majority—or any less number—think vaccination a good thing, they are free to adopt it without any compulsory legislation, when, if the claim of the vaccinator were valid, they at least would be safe, whether their neighbor was vaccinated or not. It should concern the neighbor alone whether he choose to adopt vaccination, sanitation or any other form of protection.

Bushmen of Australia, may eat, as they do, mice if they choose; the Basutos of Africa may eat spotted adders, as they do, if they choose; the Digger Indians of California, may eat dried and finely-powdered grasshoppers, as they do, if they choose, and gormandizing gluttons may eat market-hung fowls till they are bluing and purpling into rottenness if they choose— but I will not do it, and I insist that there will not be no such un-

American statute-law enacted as will compulsorily compel me to subsist upon such abominable stuff. Mildly drawn, I should consider it a daring—a most audacious menace to personal liberty! And yet, better, almost infinitely better, have mice and grasshoppers in the digestive apparatus than cow-pox virus in the circulatory system, poisoning the blood and breeding such diseases as eczema, boils, eruptions, erysipelas, cancers, scrofula, tumors and sluggish syphilitic sores.

Once educate, once raise people above poverty, dependence,dirt and wretchedness, and they will discover a sufficient motive to live, as to voluntarily adopt real and efficient means of protection against every form of epidemic disease. But the American citizen and sovereign has surrendered his liberty to class privilege and power. He has permitted the vaccinator to enter his household and plant the most filthy diseases in the pure and tender bodies of his children. A whole nation consents to be put under compulsion to submit to the barbarous practice of the vaccinator whose only interest in the rite is the ready and unfailing revenue which the legislative guarantee of vaccination affords. Our fathers who laid the foundation of the state had better conception of liberty than their weak descendants, and it is the voter's own fault·that compulsory vaccination was ever permitted, and once permitted and proved to be an unmitigated curse, that it is any longer tolerated. The general community have not informed themselves on this question which vitally concerns their welfare and their children's welfare, and so have quietly submitted to be bound and handed over to the executioner. As a people we have regarded with apathy and indifference the compulsory legislation which has conferred upon doctors and boards of health arbitrary powers by which they may compel parents to submit their children to the merciless vaccinator or otherwise incur dreaded penalties. Through ignorance, dear readers, you have permitted a "rob-

ber's roost" to be established over your front entrance, where
t nclean birds may congregate and poison the airs of your home
sanctuary.

ANTI-VACCINATION LITERATURE.

The amount of anti-vaccination literature which has been
put in circulation, is a fair indication and measure of the popular protest aroused against the practice. A catalogue of anti-
vaccination literature, printed in 1882, showed:—

	Writers.	Publications.
British	100	205
American	17	36
German	39	104
French and Belgium	8	29
Dutch	2	4
Swedish	3	7
	169	385

Since 1882 both the number of writers and publications
have greatly multiplied, until now it may fairly be assumed that
500 publications, books and pamphlets have been put into circulation against the vaccination delusion, and particularly
against compulsory legislation. The uniform attitude of the
medical profession toward this literature has been one of contempt. A standing reproach has been levelled against the anti-
vaccination literature as being intrinsically "poor stuff." A
similar reproach was levelled against Garrisonian literature during anti-slavery agitation in the fifties. When abuses cry to
heaven for redress, reformers do not study an elegant and refined mode of writing and speaking, but address themselves
primarily to the work in hand. It is quite true that previous to

1880 but few medical men from the old school of physic championed anti-vaccination reform. It would be folly to expect them to do so. Popular reform does not originate among the members of a privileged class who can obtain from government anything they ask for; a class moreover, who readily secure appointment to official positions, and who reap pecuniary benefits from the oppressive measures complained of. Popular reforms are generally espoused for the benefit of the poor, since the poor being defenceless are the principal victims of compulsory and oppressive laws. In this agitation the reformers are principally physicians from the new schools of medicine—Homeopaths, Eclectics, Hydropaths, and Osteopaths. But in 1887 and 1889 two eminent names were added to the reform list from the old Allopathic school—Dr. Creighton and Prof. Crookshank, who have treated the whole subject of vaccination so scientifically, thoroughly and conclusively, that old school doctors generally are conspicuously silent touching their labors in this field. Some, however, are anti-vaccinationists, and many do not believe in making it compulsory. Then the distinguished naturalist, Dr. Alfred Russell Wallace, has more recently made most important contributions to anti-vaccine literature, which not only materially assisted the London society in securing the "Conscience Clause" in the vaccination act of 1898, but also constitutes a powerful factor in the reform agitation in the United States.

Progressive new school physicians being far more numerous in this country than in Europe, they are almost to a man opposed to the vaccination scourge, and from this class scores of pamphlets on various phases of the subject are published and sent forth every year. Moreover, in every municipality where health boards close the public schools against unvaccinated children, these progressive, broad-minded physicians open the fight to secure their rights and are foremost in the organization of anti-vaccination leagues.

ATTITUDE OF THE PRESS.

One of the chief difficulties that stands in the way of those who desire the repeal of oppressive laws, is the attitude of the press. The great dailies, and to some extent, the popular magazines, are owned and managed by pivotal minds who represent class interests and leading party organizations. Their existence is for the promotion of these interests—place, power, and wealth. They each and all profess complete and undying devotion to the common interest and welfare, but these they unhesitatingly and invariably subordinate—and, if necessary, sacrifice—to the aforesaid class and corporate interests. Their professions are usually a hollow mockery and hypocritical pretense. We know they have no interest in reform or reformers, and further than they can turn them to lucrative and popular account. The real reform journal is round the corner, in a back alley, whose editor is also both typo and printer. But the "press," the political press, which I am writing about is located in a twelve-story building with marble front which it owns. The "press" does not hesitate to send the reformers to jail; to brand him as a malefactor, an anarchist, an insane fanatic, a troublesome disturber of the peace. What the privileged classes hate the press hates.

The great newspaper is the mouth-piece and defender of chief inversions that characterize modern society; it is part and parcel of that "Old Dragon" which has been made the conquest of the world; which has fenced itself in with privilege and place and power. Once the great newspaper represented a principle; now it represents a corporation, and therefore has no soul. When Horace Greeley launched the "Tribune" it became a living exponent of a living and breathing man. The modern "Tribune" is the organ of a corporate interest; its editorial page is anonymous; its writers are paid to run the machine under its corporate management.

The great newspaper is on good terms with the vaccinator and upholds compulsory vaccination laws. When it makes mention of the anti-vaccinator it is with an air of flippancy and arrogance, styling him as an "advocate of free trade in small-pox." (St. James Gazette, London.) It uniformly excludes communications that contain statements to the discredit of vaccination. This was the case with the San Diego "Union," and the "Tribune," both water syndicate sheets. The "London Times," as another for example, displayed gross unfairness two weeks before the report of the Royal Commission on Vaccination was published, by printing a lengthy article, "Professional Criticism on Non-professional Evidence of Opponents of Vaccination;" said article evidently being the work of a medical member, hiding under a fictitious name, of the Commission and designed to prejudice the public in advance in favor of vaccination, which the Commission was trying to bolster up. This article passed over in absolute silence the most important evidence that came before the Commission, namely, that of Prof. Crookshank, which occupied the Commission nine days and embraced 110 printed pages; being by far the fullest and most complete indictment of vaccination on scientific grounds which has ever been made. It is not difficult to find a motive for this silence; for what the "Times" does not notice, the average well-to-do Englishman regards as of little account. The legislators who make laws for the vaccinators, and the justices who send protestors who refuse to be vaccinated to prison, get their knowledge of current events from the "Times." As the "Times" did not deign to notice the terrible indictment of vaccination contained in Prof. Crookshank's evidence, the legislators and justices who make and execute vaccination laws, will never trouble themselves to go to the Blue Book and look up the evidence. Then magazine editors are very careful not to admit articles which might offend a haughty aristocracy or medical orthodoxy. So with current journalism, truth and falsehood are trivial and unimportant matters; but to stand well with that portion of the public that gives patronage and offers pelf are matters of vital concern.

In the Normal Order the daily press would be the great exponent of truth and righteousness, but in the existing order its general moral rottenness is so manifest that the careful thinking public has come to regard it as the liar par excellence. No great newspaper hesitates to destroy the reputation of any man who dares to offend, or who advocates an unpopular cause. Had not Capt. Dreyfus been a son of a member of one of the millionaire firms of Alsace, it is very doubtful whether the daily press outside of France would have expended the eloquence and employed the machinery of hundreds of publishing houses in his behalf. There are thousands of innocent men under condemnation—thousands who are wronged and defrauded whom the great daily papers do not work for. Millionaire press-corporations do newspaper work, not in the interests of humanity, not that justice and mercy may abound on the earth, but to secure the same ends for which all trusts are organized in the inverse order—the gratification of corporate greed. Moral consideration is wholly ignored by corporate press combinations. Personal responsibility and individual conscience have quite disappeared from the modern newspaper. Its editorial page is anonymous; its backing is aggregated wealth; its character is compositely infernal; its purpose is to possess and dominate the world. It is persistently, deliberately and systematically employed in fostering class hatreds, race hatreds, and this very often by falsehood and malicious provocation. It never champions reform except as the Pharisee and hypocrite champions reform. It is not in the reform business, only as the style of selfish business can be made to serve its purpose. As well expect to gather figs from the thistle stalk, as to find a candid conscientious and important discussion of class encroachments upon the people's liberties by the metropolitan press.

It will thus be seen that reform of public abuses and class encroachments, has no champion or defender in the popular press located in the great commercial centers. The reformer knows by oft repeated experiences that he has no friend or ally in the millionaire newspaper; knows, too, that when the press uncovers scandal or exposes fraud in high places, it does this with party motives or as a paid detective or attorney; knows moreover, that in its daily record of current events it has but a slight regard for truth, which is most conspicuously manifest in its publication of war news. Consider, therefore, what a difficult task lies before the regal-souled reformer in his endeavor to reach the masses with the facts and the truth which vitally concern their welfare.

MAMMON AND VACCINATION.

I have already made frequent mention of the "Mammon" feature associated with the practice of vaccination, and doubtless many readers will think I have made it too prominent; but the more I reflect on the history of legislation which the vaccinating fraternity have been instrumental in bringing about, the more thoroughly convinced I am that they are actuated by the same motives that impel business combinations in every sphere in life. Moreover, each class has a code of morals adapted to its particular form of self-interest which is wholly different from that of practical life. War, politics, trade, law, medicine, each have their so-called moral code, which is modified from year to year in a manner to conform to local circumstances. The Golden Rule is good doctrine to profess and adapt to Sunday worship, but in practical life it is construed in

a "Pickwickian" sense and not permitted to interfere with business.

While modern "civilized" warfare discards poisoned arrows
and explosive bullets, it is nevertheless compatible with war-
morals to employ explosive shells, concealed mines, torpedoes,
ambuscades, starvation, cutting off the water supply, fabricating
lying dispatches, employing spies, spreading false reports, dis-
playing false signals, etc.

In law again, the "code" is adapted to the interests that are
to be subserved. By common usage an advocate is pledged
to "defend his client," whether his cause be just or unjust. The
only end he has in view is to win the case, to do which he is
justified in suppressing or discounting the facts on the other
side. If he prosecutes, his object is to hang the prisoner—innocent or guilty. If he is on the defence, then the prisoner must
be cleared, though not a doubt exists as to his guilt. No man
can enter a chancery suit with a reasonable hope of being alive
when a final decision is reached, if he has a determined adver-
sary.

The medical profession, perhaps more than any other, is
interwoven with the misfortunes of mankind. The pecuniary
feature of medical practice is associated with disease, not with
health. Old school physic has a similar stake in disease that
the law has in private and public disagreements and quarrels.
Neither war, law nor medicine will waive pecuniary interest,
office or power to mitigate human suffering, but in further-
ance of these interests they would not hesitate to lay waste
the fairest fields that industry and thrift ever conquered from
rude nature.

Dr. Pickering (New School), who has fought the vaccinators the last thirty years, and who knows the fraternity better
than almost any other writer, says in preface to his large work:
"Vaccination with the faculty is purely a money question.

I shall drive this nail home at every point; it is the bone and sinew of the practice. Every argument employed, every statistic requisitioned, finds its inspiration in the money value of the observance. There is no craze so absurd that it could not be legalized with the aid of similar endowments pains, and penalties.

"If the faculty deny the charge I make, then I challenge them to surrender the public monies and grants they receive, and to let vaccination stand or fall on its own merits. They know too well the truth of what I allege. If vaccination were left to fight its own way in the world it would die of 'atrophy and debility' within a twelvemonth—and medical men know it—hence it is not very likely they will trust their craft to the perils of an open sea."

Walking out one morning in the city of Leeds, Dr. Pickering met a physician with whom he was well acquainted. Personally this doctor possessed the virtues and sympathies of a kind-hearted man, but professionally his actions conformed to the current methods in business affairs. When passed on the pecuniary side of vaccination, the physician observed:—

"It is absurd saying that medical men have no money interest in vaccination. Let both parties discuss the subject honestly. Lately I was requested by letter to re-vaccinate the girls in a ladies' seminary where a limited number only are under tuition. I was occupied less than an hour. Every one was prepared for the operation at the time I called. I took home with me ten guineas—20 at 10s. 6d. fee for each pupil. Can I conscientiously say that I have no pecuniary interest in vaccination? The thing is absurd. I hate "cant." There are public vaccinators who earn £100 per annum by vaccination under the Local Boards of Guardians, in addition to that they may obtain a bonus of £100 to £300 a year for supplying charged vaccination points to the authorities, and they may further gain £50 or

£100 a year by private vaccinations. Have these men no pecuniary interest to subserve? If the vaccination question is to
be thrashed out, by all means let it be done on fair principles.
I admit, I must admit that medical men have a strong pecuniary interest in vaccination and that this interest is a factor in
determining the retention or surrender of the observance."—
"Sanitation or Vaccination," p. 44.

"I emphatically assert that the money product is the common sense definition of vaccination; it is not susceptible of any
other interpretation, and it accounts fully for all the efforts put
forth by the faculty, or rather the medical officers of the Local
Government Board, to retain it. The money value of vaccination is its only value. It never had any other appraisement."

Dr. James Braithwaite, editor of the "Retrospect of Medicine," wrote in 1872:—"As for the faculty, what I say for myself I say for each one—vaccination is viewed by us as a thing
to be done; it is a law, and we carry it out without making
many serious injuries. We do not admit responsibility for the
legal enactment."—(Pickering, p. 30.)

Neither does the lawyer admit responsibility when using
his legal art and subtlety to defeat the ends of justice; nor does
the army scout admit responsibility when he succeeds in in-
veigling the enemy upon the mine prepared for his destruction.
Certainly, this admission of Dr. Braithwaite illustrates and sup-
ports my contention, that few people in our modern life—especially in a professional capacity—act with a sense of personal
responsibility in the prosecution of their calling, any further
than the efficiency required for success. If their acts involve
suffering, they do not consider it any affair of theirs. Their
conscience is not troubled.

The profession find it far easier to conserve and defend a
"good thing" like vaccination, than to let that go and adopt
some other form of blood poisoning. Letting go of "inoculation" and substituting therefor vaccination, cost much labor and

time and money. Experience has taught the profession wisdom in matters relating to vaccination as a business enterprise, since this is the only business firm in this country which has state endorsement to the extent of compeling the people to buy their goods. In England the vaccinator's annual bonuses amount to $100,000, and their doles through Boards of Guardians to $500,-000. But their various benefactions, of which no account is taken, is estimated to reach $10,000,000 a year. The profession will hardly consent to part with a friend like that.

The old school doctors, with their vaccine virus and false promises have robbed the people of all nations during the last hundred years—civilized and uncivilized—to the extent of hundreds of millions of dollars, and what have they given them in return? A long catalogue of filthy, loathsome and incurable diseases among the poorer classes of civilized nations, and a wholesale spread of eczema, syphilis, and leprosy among the native races in tropical lands, by which they are rapidly verging toward final extinction; and this under the pretense of "proteeting people who are too ignorant to protect themselves." There is no cunning, no infernal device, no infamous craft, no false array of statistics they have not put under contribution in their efforts to conceal the real truth from the government and the people. They well know their practice has not the valid warrant of science. They know that the introduction of putrifying animal tissue into the delicate blood vessels of a human being is an operation against which not only psychic science, but the instincts of humanity revolt and for which every victim is liable to pay a fearful penalty.

"Some two years since a retired officer, lately holding an important appointment in the Queen's army, took his son to a well-known surgeon in London for his opinion as to certain symptoms which affected the youth's health. The father is a staunch advocate of non-vaccination views and loses no opportunity of improving his knowledge. As he was leaving the consulting-room he turned to the surgeon and inquired, 'Doctor may I ask, are you opposed to vaccination?' 'No,' the doctor replied, 'I should think not, indeed, when I consider that it brings me in £400 a year.' Four hundred pounds a year from surgical cases due to complications following the vaccine fever which Jenner called 'vaccination.' 'This fever runs its course.' And you answer, 'Yes, for eight days.' Aye, and sometimes for 80 and 800 days after that, and occasionally it accompanies each heart-beat till that poor heart ceases its beating. I have seen many such instances. My third illustration is an example—the disease communicated with the vaccine virus 'ran its course' for 5,000 days, only killing its victim after nearly twelve years of cruel suffering.

"If one surgeon in London estimates that his income from his practice is increased by £400 every year, dependant upon vaccination, it would be an interesting statistic if we could ascertain how many surgeons there are in London, and throughout the country, who derive similar advantages 'from public and private vaccination!"—Dr. Pickering, p. 338.

The annual revenue from vaccination in India, South Africa and British West Indies, where the practice is enforced by compulsory laws, must be much greater than that derived in England. So far as the United States are concerned, I have no present access to information on this point, but the annual revenue from vaccination, and for treatment of diseases incidentally growing out of the practice, certainly mounts up into the millions, and from a business point of view, constitutes one of the most lucrative branches of medical practice.

THE ROYAL COMMISSION AGAIN.

The appointment of a royal commission on Vaccination and Parliament (1889) has played so important a part in discussions of the subject, in England, upon the continent, and in the United States, that the reader will pardon some further comments on its appointment and proceedings.

While this commission was appointed to silence popular clamor, yet that portion of the public who protested against compulsory laws, had no voice in selecting members who were to com- se it. It was appointed to shelve a troublesome subject, and provide a way to dispose of the interminable series of questions which came before Parliament as to the administration of vaccination laws. Its appointment was wholly in the hands of those who had an interest and stake in the practice. Medical men were represented on the Commission by six to one in favor of vaccination. Of the eight laymen appointed, none of them has expressed a definite opinion on the subject, but as might have been expected, these naturally deferred to the medical experts upon a subject so largely medical in its character.

Suppose a municipality, like Chicago, should appoint a Commission to enquire into the fouling of Chicago River by the manufacturing industries, and the appointing power—which the people have no direct voice in—should select six to one from the very manufacturers who are perpetrating the evil complained of, to sit on the Commission. The people would justly conclude that this farce of a Commission was merely a "sop" to silence their murmurings, while the nuisance would be in no wise abated as a result of the Commission's findings. For a similar reason the medical profession had no occasion to fear a final report at the Royal Commission. In theory we do not allow a magistrate having a large property interest in public houses to adjudicate licenses; nor one who has railway shares to sit on Railway Committees. But when the people want to know the truth about vaccination; how it may affect their households; what protection may be expected and what dangers may be feared from a practice to which the law compels them to submit, this commonsense rule is reversed: The doctors have their own way: They appoint themselves to adjudicate the momentous issue.

"A Commission or committee of enquiiy into this momentons question should have consisted wholly, or almost wholly, of statisticians, who should hear medical as well as official and independent evidence, would have all existing official statistics at their command, and would be able to tell us, with some show of authority, exactly what the figures proved, and what they only rendered probable on one side and on the other. But instead of such a body of experts, the Royal Commission, which for more than six years was occupied in hearing evidence and cross-examining witnesses, consisted wholly of medical men, lawyers, politicians, and country gentlemen, none of whom were trained statisticians, while the majority came to the enquiry more or less prejudiced in favor of vaccination. The report of such a body can have but little value, and I hope to satisfy my readers that it (the Majority Report) is not in accordance with the facts."—Prof. A. R. Wallace— Wonderful Cen. p. 235.

In their eagerness—as interested parties—to defend vaccination as the sole protection and safeguard against small-pox, this Royal Commission totally ignores all other forms of liability, as age, over-crowding, poverty, notoriously unsanitary conditions, etc. The distinctions of rich and poor, or of cleanliness and filth they never notice. Vaccination alone is the qualifying factor. The Commissioners say: "Those, therefore, who are selected as being vaccinated persons might just as well be so many persons chosen out of the total number attacked. So far as any connection with the incidence of, or the mortality from, small-pox is concerned, the choice of persons might as well have been made according to the color of the clothes they wore." (Final Report, par. 213). Now, there are extant exhaustive statistical tables which show that about one-seventh of all small-pox mortality occur in the first six months of life, and more than half of these again occurs in the first three months. Small-pox is especially a childhood disease, infants being far more liable to it than the adult population. Many children have their vaccination delayed on account of ill-health. Hence the "unvaccinated" always include a large proportion of those who, merely because they are infants, supply a much larger proportion of deaths from small-pox than at any other age. How inaccurate and misleading, therefore, the statement of the Commissioners, that the unvaccinated might as well be chosen at random, or by the color of their clothes, as far as any liability to small-pox is concerned.

Again, any man with a grain of commonsense and a scintilla of conscience knows, that independent of the question of vaccination, the liability to an attack of small-pox is vastly increased by bad habits and unsanitary surroundings. Take the epidemic of Gloucester in 1895-6. Divide the city by a line running east and west through St. Michael's Square, into the clean, well-to-do northern quarter, and the South Hamlet which is crowded, poor, filthy, extremely deficient in water supply, and most abominable in its drainage. Would not any unprejudiced medical man say that the chances for taking the small-pox were increased tenfold in this Drouth District? What were the facts? As we saw in a previous chapter, both quarters were about equally vaccinated. The northen half had the largest population; yet the number of fatal cases in the South Hamlet were 2,036, while those in the North District were 214,—ninety per cent of the fatality fell in the crowded, filthy and unsanitary quarter of the City. The most of these, too, had been vaccinated. These facts were before the Commission, but were considered by them too trivial and unimportant to even mention. Well, the medical members of the Commission were the "attorneys" on the defense, and saw only what would contribute to the acquittal of the accused.

In their examination of evidence, the Commission treated witnesses whom they knew to be opposed to vaccination very much as President McKinley's Commission on the army beef scandal treated all witnesses who complained of its bad quality. The policy was to worry, badger, harass, and if possible, render the testimony contradictory and worthless. The work of the Commission was an enquiry which it was desirable the public should follow from day to day, yet the majority decided its proceedings should be conducted with closed doors—mark this closed doors—and so its hundreds of columns of printed matter was sequestered in the Parliamentary Blue Books which none but students and professional men ever examine. In this way, the general public, which should have been instructed regarding the practical workings of vaccination throughout the Kingdom, were not a whit better enlightened than they were before.

But the accumulating wrath of the people might in some degree be appeased. The Commission in their Final Report, while they acquitted vaccination and hesitatingly voted to retain it, conceded the propriety of a "Conscience Clause" to be inserted in the Compulsory Vaccination Act. In the United States we have not even secured that; and although the State Supreme Court in several States have decided compulsory vaccination to violate both State and Federal constitutions, yet State and Municipal Boards continue to close the Public Schools to unvaccinated children, whose parents refuse to obey the pseudo-vaccination laws. Oh, for a little of that spinal stiffening—that stalwart spirit of liberty which actuated our forefathers in 1776, to infuse into the weak-kneed house-dawn of a new century; the rank and file of our American citizenship; the feeble folk whose once vigorous young sap has been contaminated, poisoned, and rendered well-nigh worthless by a century of vaccination!

MISSTATING FIGURES.

A vast amount of misconception has arisen in the public

mind from the unfair and misleading mannei in which vaccination promoters, and physicians who have a pecuniary interest
in vaccination, handle facts, and figures. From the first the
National Vaccine Establishment of Great Britain has exhibited
the usual traits which characterize a heartless, soulless corporation. Supported by Government grants, it has issued periodical
reports which were printed by order of the House of Commons. In 1812 and again :n 1818 it was stated: "Previous to
the discovery of vaccination the average number of deaths by
small-pox with the (London) Bills of Mortality were 2,000 annually, whereas, in the last year 751 persons have died of the
disease." Again, in 1826, the report stated: "But when we
reflect that before the introduction of vacci:nation the average
deaths from small-pox within the Bills of Mortality (London)
was annually about 4,000, no stronger argument can reasonably
be demanded in favor of the value of this important discovery."

This malicious, misleading, and grossly exaggerated figure
was repeated in 1834; and then again in 18ƒ6 there was added
another thousand thus: "The annual loss of life by·small-pox
in the metropolis and within the Bills of Mortality only, before
vaccination was established, exceeded 5,000, whereas in the
course of last year only 300 died of the distemper." In 1838
this lie—this doctor's lie—was again repeated; and this sort of
advertising by the medical profession was sanctioned and paid
for by the Government. A patent medicine vender has to pay
for his own advertising and depend on the good will of the
public for the disposal of his wares; but the government has
adopted a system of "paternalism" toward the vaccinator unheard of before, giving him offices and salaries, advertising his
goods, and guaranteeing their prompt and ready sale by
compelling every house-holder to become a purchaser. We
should not be surprised to see some heavy twisting, turning,
and pettifogging to retain a sysem that can boast such unpar-

alleled backing and Government guarantees as vaccination.

Now, 2,000 was the average annual small-pox mortality in London for the whole of the eighteenth century. So the number in the alleged fact is multiplied by two, plus one thousand; while the misleading features of the report is, "Whereas in the course of last year only 300 died of the distemper;" leaving the inference that as 300 is to 5,000, so is the average annual difference that should be set down to the credit of vaccination. No regard is here paid to the epidemic and periodical character of small-pox—to the fact that a series of years intervene between the periods when small-pox becomes epidemic, when the small-pox mortality reaches but a few hundred annually. But as a sort of rebuke and masterly irony on the last lie above cited, immediately after the report was published, small-pox broke out in vaccinated London with epidemic violence, and carried their boasted figure up from 300 to 4,500. This was the London epidemic of 1838. Vaccinationists for a time, at least, were ashamed of their misstatements.

Again, Dr. Letson—a public vaccinator—testified before the Parliamentary Commission in 1802, that before vaccination the annual small-pox fatality in London was 3,000, and in Great Britain and Ireland 36,000. In this way: The population of Britain and Ireland was estimated to be twelve times greater than that of London. Assuming small-pox fatality to be 3,000 in London, he multiplied by 12—36,000. He first takes the London death rate for small-pox at one thousand above its average, and then assumes that the town, village, and country populations have the same proportional amount of small-pox as over-crowded and superlative filthy London. We have here once more illustrated the fact that the vaccinating syndicate, from the Royal Commission down to the scrub-doctor, totally ignore sanitation and every species of personal habit and environment as factors concerned in the relative liability to contract small-pox. The whole question is made to turn on the vaccinated and unvaccinated. Sir Gilman Blanc tells us that in many parts of the country small-pox was "quite unknown for periods of twenty, thirty, and forty years." In 1782 a surgeon at Seaford, in Sussex, knew of only one small-pox death in eleven years. Hence, to compute the small pox fatality of the country from that of London in order to show what vaccination had done toward "utterly stamping out the disease," is, to say the least, a species of dishonest, if not disgraceful, pettifogging.

Dr. W. B. Carpenter—author of a well-known work on physiology, but whose word no literary man in England could be induced to swear by—in a letter to the "Spectator" of April, 1881, says: "A hundred years ago the Small-pox fatality of London alone, with its then population of under a million, was often greater in a six months' epidemic than that of the twenty million of England and Wales now is in any whole year." Now the facts, known to every well-informed enquirer, are,—that the highest small-pox mortality in London in any single year, for twenty years before vaccination came into vogue, was in 1772, when it reached 3,992; while in the London epidemic in 1871 it reached 7,912—in a thoroughly vaccinated population. (See Won. Cen. p. 226.) I have good authority that this amazing mistake was pointed out to Dr. Carpenter and acknowledged by him privately, but it was never withdrawn publicly.

Mr. Earnest Hart, editor of the "British Medical Journal," in his work, "The Truth About Vaccination," p. 35, states that in forty years from 1728 the average small-pox mortality for London was 18,000 per million living, which was the correct figure multiplied by nine, and this was triumphantly dwelt upon and compared with modern rates, which vaccination has reduced to a minimum. Then the local Government Board has authorized, published and distributed in thousands of families, such statements as the following: "Before the introduction of vaccination, small-pox killed 40,000 persons annually in this country. This was in 1884. In later issues of this tract the language is slightly modified: "Before its discovery (vaccination) the mortality from small-pox in London was forty times greater than it is now."

It is such "official" figures, such demonstrations of moral dishonesty as I have here cited, that our local lillipution doctors draw upon when they get down off their professional stilts to demolish the "erroneous" statments of Anti-Vaccinators.

FALSE MEDICAL RETURNS.

It is no uncommon thing to hear a public vaccinator assert that his practice has extended through a series of years; that he has vaccinated a certain number of thousands, and has never seen the slightest evil results therefrom. Interested men have wonderful power and aptness of not seeing what they have decided should not interfere with their business. One need not see the sun while he resolutely shuts his eyes. Public vaccinators, it is true, do not see the result except by accident. Those who get small-pox go to the hospital, and cases of vaccinal injury are usually treated by other physicians. The vaccinator goes his way and is never interested in the results of his practice. Medical men, like other men, have a habit of covering up and prevaricating when the facts look ugly. The end in view is the important matter, means are secondary and subservient. In strategy, a lie generally serves the end more effectively, than does the truth.

Prof. Wallace—"Wonderful Century," p. 228—gives a list of 785 deaths in fifteen years directly traceable to vaccination, yet which were officially returned as deaths from erysipelas.

But now and then we find a public vaccinatɔr with a spark of conscience left. Dr. Henry May, in an article published in the Birmingham "Medical Review," January, 1874, says:

"In certificates given by us voluntarily, and to which the public have access, it is scarcely to be expected that a medical man will give opinions which may tẽll against or reflect upon himself in any way, or which are likely to cause annoyance or injury to the survivors. In such cases he will most likely tell the truth, but not the whole truth, and assign some prominent symptom of the disease as the cause of death. As instances of cases which may tell against the medical man himself, I will mention erysipelas from vaccination, and puerperal fever. A death from the first cause occurred not long ago in my practice, and although I had not vaccinated the child, yet in my desire to preserve vaccination from reproach, I omittẽd all mention of it from my certificate of death."

While there may be many, here was ceitainly one honest, conscientious doctor. The omen is a good one. The millenium must be at our doors!

That this style of suppression has been going on during the whole period of the vaccine practice, is rendered more than probable by the statement of Dr. Maslean, who says: "Very few deaths from cow-pox appear in the Bills of Mortality, owing to the means which have been used to suppress a knowledge of them. Neither were deaths, diseases, and failures transmitted in great abundance from the country, not because they did not happen, but because some petitioners were interested in not seeing them, and others who did see them were afraid of announcing what they knew."—Quoted by Dr. Wallace (Won. Cen. p. 229).

Dr. Charles Fox, of Cardiff, published 56 cases of vaccinal injury, 17 of which resulted fatally; but in the medical returns only two were mentioned in connection with vaccination. Among those which survived, some were permanently injured, and others were crippled for life. The sufferings of some of the children were so great and so prolonged that their mothers were obliged to endure mental tortures for years on their account. And this is the account of only one medical man. If all the medical men, in all the civilized coutries of the earth, should by some inscrutable providence go to the confessional and make a full disclosure of things they now declare they have not seen, we should then have something of a picture—a gennine picture—of the cost price of the disease and suffering occasioned by a century of vacccination; a picture of the ruined temples which God made divinely fair; of native races in tropical lands verging toward extinction with the curse of scrofula, syphilis, and leprosy, which the vaccinator has sown broadcast among them.

Mr. Alfred Milnes, a statistician who has paid special attention to this subject, expresses the deliberate opinion, that if the officially admitted deaths were multiplied by twelve, it would come much nearer representing the actual number of deaths resulting from vaccination. After a most thorough review of the misstatements, special pleading, and deliberate falsifying by the medical profession, Professor Wallace sums up the case against them:

"The facts and figures of the medical profession and of Government officials, in regard to the question of vaccination, must never be accepted without verification. And when we consider that these misstatements, and concealments, and denials of injury, have been going on throughout the whole of the century; that penal legislation has been founded on them; that homes of the poor have been broken up; that thousands have been harried by police and magistrates, have been imprisoned and treated in every way as felons; and that, at the rate now officially admitted, a thousand children have been certainly killed by vaccination during the last twenty years, and an unknown but probably much larger number injured for life, we are driven to the conclusion that those responsible for these reckless misstatements and their terrible results have, thoughtlessly and ignorantly, but none the less certainly, been guilty of a crime—a terrible crime—against liberty, against health, and against humanity, which will, before many years have passed, be universally held to be one of the foulest blots on the civilization of the nineteenth century."

—The Wonderful Century, p. 232.

In notes on the Small-pox Epidemic at Birkenhead, 1877, (p. 7), Dr. F. Vacher says: "Those entered as not vaccinated were admittedly unvaccinated or without the faintest mark. The mere assertion of patients or their friends that they were vaccinated counted for nothing." Another medical practitioner justifies this method of making statistics as follows: "I have always classed those as 'unvaccinated,' when no scar, presumably arising from vaccination, could be discovered. Individuals are constantly seen who state that they have been vaccinated, but upon whom no cicatrices can be traced. In a prognostic and a statistic point of view, it is better, and I think, necessary, to class them as unvaccinated."

—Dr. Gayton's Report for the Homerton Hospital for 1871-2-3.

This method, which is so general as to be well nigh universal, is such a falsification of the real facts as to render them worthless for statistical purposes, and bears out Prof. Wallace's contention that "there is much evidence to show that doctors are bad statisticians, and have a special faculty for misstating figures."

"I know one gentleman, a manufacturer in Lancashire, who has a family of 13 children, not one of them has been vaccinated, and a certificate of successful vaccination was handed in to the authorities in proper form, and within the prescribed period after the birth of each child. 'How can that be?' do you ask? Ah, the ways of the vaccinator are past finding out. 'Do you mean to infer that the medical men signed those certificates knowing them to be false?' Do not repeat that question I implore you, lest I should say, 'Yes, I do!'

* * * *

"I am acquainted with a physician in a northern town, one who is honored with a government appointment. I hold a letter from him in my hand now, dated Dec. 3, 1889, who says that,

'whilst in practice in London I frequently filled up death certificates of children as Marasmus, Debility, etc, when I felt perfectly certain that such cases of wasting and debility in delicate
children had been induced by vaccination,—or, aggravated by
vaccination."

—Pickering's Sanitation or Vaccination, p. 165.

"When I know that the deaths from atrophy and debility,
diarrhoea, and convulsions, a total of 54,344 deaths annually,
are wrongly certified; that they are symptomatic, not caustive,
I am justified in saying that the whole system of registration
and certification requires to be remodelled and reformed. Medicine will never reform itself. Certification should be in the hands
of an independent authority.

"Again, when I contemplate the resources of infection
in its power to spread epidemic and fever miasmata all around,
and know, at the same time,, that all fever contagiousness given
off by the patient is the result of bald-headed ignorance in the
treatment, I am not surprised that Medicine should seek to hide
some death causes under misleading symptoms, and that a con-
tinned warfare should be kept up between itself and the other
three rival systems, all of which are immeasurably in advance
of Allopathic practice."

—Ibed, p. 194.

"Within the last four or five years the mortality from
typhus has dropped from 7,000 to 300 and 160. This is to be accounted for by the fact of some sudden eruption, or instruction,
either from the Registration Department, or from the Royal
College of Physicians. It is not claimed to be in consequence
of the discovery of some andidote, or some violent national ex-
penditude, counteracting the conditions which give rise to this
fever. No, it is too sudden to be real. It is, on the whole,
entirely a change in certification. Instead of being found under
the heading 'Typhus,' the deaths have been transferred, I should
say, by authority, to other death-causes which are similar or
symptomatic. It was necessary to show a change somewhere
in the dull, continuous, mortality from fevers, and typhus was
selected. Fashion rules even in certification. Query, Is it
fashion?

"Sanitarians know that typhus has not much chance of ever

becoming epidemic again.

"We still have epidemics, plenty of them, such as phthisis, bronchitis, pneumonia, atrcphy, diarrhoea convulsions, other diseases of circulatory system, cancer, etc.; but these are quiet and permanent epidemics, they come and go without observation, Death retains his power and popularity, and as he conducts his victims off the stage, he saunters on with discursive step to mark his contempt for the impotency of physic."—Ibid, p. 213.

DECADENCE OF OLD SCHOOL CONSERVATIVE DOCTORS.

The startling assertion is made by an expert in inebriety in a paper read before the Connecticut Medical Association, that morphinism is being spead among the people of the United States by the example and advice of medical men themselves, ten per cent. of whom are now opium drunkards. The assertions and deductions of the author, Dr. T. I. Crothers, of Hartford, and thus summarized in the Memphis "Appeal." (Dec. 4, 1899):

"According to Dr. Crothers, twenty-one per cent.—or one in five—of the physicians of the Middle and Eastern States use spirits or opium to excess; and he concludes that from six to ten per cent. of all medical men are opium inebriates. It is estimated that there are 150,000 opiumists in the United States; and this fact in connection with the prevalence of the opium or morphine habit among doctors presents one of the greatest problems for solution before the American people. It would seem a fair inference that the responsibility for the spread of morphinism among the people rests largely with those doctors who are addicted to its use. It would never occur to an uninformed person to contract the opium habit. This can only come from example or from constant prescription by a doctor, and if the latter is addicted to the use of the drug he is more apt to be reckless in prescribing it. Thus the spread of the habit is no doubt largely due to that part of the profession which has become cursed with morphinism. Physicians have the reputation of being very strict in the observance of the etiquette of the profession, and very rigorous in their hostility against the quacks, whose capacity of harm is readily understood. Certainly then it would seem that the medical profession ought to protect itself as well as the people at large from the opiumists among the doctors. Unless something is done to stop the growth of inebriety in its various forms among physicians, it may be necessary to invoke the aid of the law, and have doctors examined once a year to ascertain whether they are addicted to any of the habits which are so utterly incompatible with the proper discharge of their professional duties. There is no calling which makes such a demand for a clear head and a steady hand as that of the doctor."

If the bad habit could be confined to the old-style drug doctors, the public might in the end be the gainer; but since every doctor who is an opium fiend will be instrumental in fastcuing the habit on scores of his patients, he thus becomes a "center of contagion," from which the curse will spread and ramify through society. At least nine-tenths of the opium, the morphine disease, with much of the drunkenness in this country is directly traceable to practicing physicians. Whom could the world spare better than the old-school drastic-drug doctor?

MORE LOCAL TESTIMONIES.

J. W. Hodge, M. D., at Niagara Falls, N. Y., contributes a vigorous paper on vaccination to "Light of Truth," published in its issue of September 16th, 1899, from which I extract the following:

"To affirm that there never has been any scientific warranty for a belief in the alleged protective virtues of vaccination and that its practice is backed by ignorance and indifference, is a sorry charge to make against the medical profession at the close of the nineteenth century; but the charge, I regret to say, is only too true. I know whereof I affirm, for I, too, must plead guilty to the charge. Before discovering my mistake I had vaccinated more than 3,000 victims, ignorantly supposing the disease I was propagating to be a preventative of small-pox. Having taken for granted what my teachers had asserted, I was a staunch believer in the alleged efficacy of vaccination as a prophylactic against small-pox. I remained in this blind and blissful state of ignorance for several years, and not until I acquired a little experience in the school of observation and reflection did I discover my faith was pinned to a shameful fraud. The first real eye-opener I received upon the subject was in the year 1882, while practicing my profession in the city of Lockport. At that time small-pox made its appearance in this city and soon attained the proportions of an epidemic. At the outbreak of the disease general vaccination was ordered by the department of health and the writer was officially appointed public vaccinator. My duty was to go from house to house and vaccinate all persons who could not present vaccination scars on their bodies, and to re-vaccinate all those who could not give assurance of having been vaccinated within a period of two years. Just before and during the prevalence of this epidemic I operated upon nearly 3,000 victims, using the so-called 'pure calf iymph' obtained every third day 'fresh' from the vaccine farm of the New York city board of health. Much to the disgust of the people, and more to my own surprise and chagrin, I was confronted with a large number of cases of vaccinal erysipelas, as well as several cases of phlegmonous axillary abscesses following as results of my work. One death occurred from blood poisoning, the result of vaccination. This was not all. A number of those vaccinated were attacked with confluent small-pox at periods varying from twelve days to three weeks, after having been rendered 'immune' by cowpox.

"These astounding facts, so contrary to my preconceived notions about vaccination and small-pox I was unable to account for, and they worried me not a little, as I was unable to see where the 'protection' came in.

"With Pascal, 'I considered the affirmation of facts as more powerful than the assertions of men,' and began a careful study of the relations existing between small-pox and vaccination, with the ultimate result that I was forced to entirely abandon all faith in the medical dogma of vaccinal protection against small-pox. During the epidemic I had under inspection 28 small-pox patients, all of whom, with one exception, (a very mild case), had been 'successfully vaccinated,' as attested by vaccinal scars on their bodies. Several of these patients have been revaccinated before contracting the disease. Thus was I forced through the stern logic of disagreeable facts to the unwelcome conclusion that vaccination had not 'protected' these victims of small-pox.

"After the remarkable revelations of this dismal experience had dawned upon me I determined to make a careful study of the literature on small-pox and vaccination, and accordingly procured all the works I could find on these topics. After a thorough investigation of the statistics of small-pox epidemiology collected from various parts of the world, I was treated to another great surprise, namely, the world's greatest statisticians on small-pox and vaccination fully corroborated the experience that I had met in the Lockport epidemic. Previous to this disappointing experience I had read only orthodox literature as is usually found in the medical libraries of physicians. I had heard only the exparte testimony of the provaccinists. I knew (?) but one side of the question, and was like him of whom John Stuart Mill said: 'He who knows only his own side of the case knows little of that.' After a careful study of the history of vaccination and an extensive experience in its use, I am thoroughly convinced that it is utterly useless as a preventive against small-pox, that millions of vaccinated persons have died of small-pox—that the practice of this degrading rite is enforced by doctors as a dogma without being understood. That like that other infamous dogma (inoculation) it is only good for 'fees." That inoculation was unanimously believed in and practiced by the 'regular' doctors for 100 years in multiplying small-pox cases by spreading the contagion. That small-pox epidemics were checked by the cessation of inoculation, not by the introduction of vaccination. That small-pox continued to increase under vaccination until sanitation came into more general use. That sanitation and isolation have controlled small-pox, and vaccination has claimed the credit.

That vaccination protects from small-pox only by killing the persons 'protected." That vaccination has been the means of disseminating consumption, cancer, syphilis and many other fatal and loathsome diseases. . That consumption follows in the footsteps of vaccination as directly as an effect can follow a cause. That tuberculosis is a disease common to cattle and to human beings, and has frequently been conveyed by vaccination from the former to the latter. That Edward Jenner saddled a legacy of disease and death on the human race and incidentally made $150,000 by the transaction. That many doctors and some editors are making money by propagating this curse. That vaccination is called 'successful' when it makes a healthy person diseased. That disease as the result of vaccination is the legitimate harvest from the seed sown. That vaccination has no scientific basis upon which to rest its claims and no analogy in any ascertained principle or law in nature. That 'spontaneous cow-pox' is a myth, the disease so-called being tubercular or syphilitic in its nature. That when vaccination kills its victims the facts are suppressed and health (?) boards return death certificates so made out. That compulsory vaccination has recently been abolished in England and Switzerland, while laws sanctioning this crime still disgrace the statute books of 'free' America. That vaccination is one of the foulest blots on the escutcheon of the 'noble art of healing.' " A portion of the above article appears in a previous page of this volume; but this vaccination subject, so notorious in results, deserves line upon line of condemnation.

Prof. Thomas D. Wood, of the Stanford University, recently said in a lecture:

"Tuberculosis bacilli is a rod-shaped plant, the 1-5000th part of an inch in length. It is a parasite on animals, and does not exist outside of the warm-blooded animals. It will penetrate almost every tissue of human beings or of animals. It will die at 175 degrees Fah., may be killed in sunshine, and objects to the air. It may be killed by certain forms of chemistry, but it cannot be frozen. It hibernates, too; dries up, remains quiescent on your mantel, awaiting to be taken into the system, Consumption has been developed in the human system by occupying rooms in which no consumptive had lived for five

years. It effects human beings, especially when crowded together in large cities of big buildings. It is partial to the do-
mesticated animals, but rarely attacks the horse, and more
rarely the dog. Swine are most affected. Next to these are
cows and heifers."

Now mark—tuberculosis in cows and heifers; and from
these we get the cow-pox lymph which vaccinationists thrust
into human arms, which is tantamount to inocculating them with
consumption or tuberculosis tendencies. It is generally admitted that both consumption and cancers have increased in the
world since the introduction of Jenner's cow pox system.

It is said that these heifers are entirely healthy. How do
you know? Did the officials look at their tongues and feel of
the pulse? Cows, heifers are dumb. They can not tell you
whether they have a kidney complaint, or indigestion, or any
other disease. And then—think of it—they take supposed
healthy heifers from the fields, confine them in 'sterilized stables' (a phrase used by a San Diego doctor), rope them, throw
them, shave their abdomens, puncture this portion of the hairless body with 'small-pox pustular poison,' and then watch the
irritation, watch the animal's thirst, the increasing inflammation
up to the point of puss-rottening—and now call the brute
healthy, do you? Would you consider your own body healthy
if half covered with inflamed pustules and discharging sores?
Then watch the applied clamps as they squeeze out the putrid,
mucus-like pus, mingled with a little of the animal's inflamed
blood, to be manipulated into 'pus-lymph'—rather impure poison!

WHY NOT HAVE A LITTLE PURE CATARRH LYMPH?

"How would it do to take catarrh mucus from the nose of

some otherwise healthy young lady and manipulating it up to
the point of pure catarrh lymph, introduce it compulsorily into
the school children's arms as a preventive, say against the grip,
erysipelas, or some kind of eczema?

"These half-fledged medical scientists forget, however, that
a heifer may have the germs of tuberculosis or some other malady in its blood before such disease is visible in its tissues, or
before it could be detected by a postmortem examination. Indeed, the opinion of eminent chemists is that whatever lurking
and latent disease there may be in a heifer, is drawn out by the
violent poisoning to which a small-pox inoculated animal is subject and that it commingles with the so-called 'pure pus' which is
squeezed out of the poor creatures' 'running sores!'"—J. M. P.
in San Diego Daily Sun.

Here is a sample of the practical working of this "specially
prepared," "pure" vaccine matter—some that was guaranteed
to have been secured by the latest and most improved methods.
In the early part of 1894, the Iowa State Board of Health sent
out a decree that all the school children in the state should be
vaccinated and amongst the other children so maltreated was little Alma O. Peihn, daughter of L. H .Peihn, president of the
First National Bank of Nora Springs—a beautiful little girl six
years of age and unusually healthy. Shortly after her vaccination with this "pure" pus, her arm swelled and became inflamed
and was soon covered with black spots. No pains or expense
was spared to give her the best medical attention, but all to no
purpose. In a few days her whole body was covered with similar spots; then they became putrid and loathsome sores, and in
less than a week thereafter her sufferings were ended by death.
The doctor who performed the operation, probably, in all his
practice extending to thousands of cases, "never saw a case of
vaccinal injury follow vaccination."

Early in 1899, a whole family in New York contracted
syphilis from vaccination. The St. Louis "Medical Gazette"
says:

"The New York 'Medical Journal' of March 26th last, records an epidemic of syphilis in which the disease was introduced into the family, according to the history, by vaccination, and in which every member of the family of eight was ultimately infected. The first case was a child of two years; then the mother, aged 32; then two girls aged 9 and 14 respectively; then a boy of 4; then a girl of 7, and then a nursling, aged 6 months. The father escaped until the last, but late in the spring he came to the clinic with a characteristic eruption, alopecia, etc. The cases were all severe. There were several irites, all had obstinate and some very extensive mucous patches, and the two-year-old child had syphilis pneumonia. The site of inoculation was discoverable in two cases only, probably on account of the lateness and irregularity with which patients were brought to the clinic. In the other it was upon the center of the cheek, and in one girl it was upon the eyelid."

The Board of Health, of Winona, Minn., made a vaccination order and furnished vaccine virus to the surgeons. P. Von Lackum was appointed vaccinator for the Third district. After the epidemic had subsided he returned the virus which had been furnished him and proved he had used pure cream instead. He also showed that his district did not have a single case of small-pox, and that the general health was good, while in the other districts there were many cases of small-pox and much sickness and many deaths. This occurred in 1873. Until the detestable compulsory law is repealed, we will pray that the "Von Lackum's" will multiply in the land.

I presume I may be excused if I refer to the City of Leicester once more. It is the city of standing reference with Anti-Vacccinators. It is the champion city in the world for its successful and practical protest against compulsory vaccination and in finding a better way. For the sake of once more reasserting its position, a member of its Boa·d of Guardians last year moved "that this Board resolve to continue the policy of the three previous Boards in not instituting proceedings against parents under the vaccination act." This was adopted by forty yeas—no nays. This means that Leicester has tried ignoring vaccination and is abundantly satisfied with the result, not by a majority merely, but unanimously. We saw in a preceding chapter that Leicester's Board of Guardians has been elected for many years by a unanimous anti-vaccine constituency.. That city will always be accorded the proud position of having held the foremost place in the agitation against compulsory vaccination, and especially for havng risen en-masse in open defiance of the vaccination act. It has a noble record of sacrifice and labor, its protesting citizens having paid over $100,000 in fines for refusing to submit to vaccination. Over 7,000 cases have been brought before the magistrates. The cost and loss of time exclusive of fines represent a sum equal to $50,000. Seventy persons have been sent to prison for "conscience sake."

For over twenty years Leicester has made a specialty of sanitation, and has practically demonstrated the fact for the whole world, that to be free from small-pox, and all other filth disease, the person, the house, the street must be clean. This is their form of prevention; this their secret of safety. Walt Whitman must have had some such city in mind when he wrote:

"Where no monuments exist to heroes, but in the common
    words and deeds,
Where thrift is in its place, and prudence is in its place,
Where the men and women think lightly of the laws,
Where the slave ceases, and the master of the slave ceases,
Where the populace arise at once against the never ending
    audacity of elected persons."

The Atlanta Constitution, a vigorous broad-minded Southern Journal, recently had the following:

"At Americus (Ga) several Christian Scientists, who refused to be vaccinated, were sentenced to an imprisonment for thirty days, and a fine of $15.

"This in free America, sounds like autocratic rule in Russia, or the semi-barbaric methods of China. The despatches tell us that many of those thus sentenced belong to the best families in the place. The refusal to be vaccinated therefore, can not be charged to ignorance. Call it rather elightenment. They have read of the fatalities, and the disease which follows the use of the vaccine lance, and in self-protection, they are defying an unjust and arbitrary law.

"The course pursued by the authorities of this Georgia town, wlll have an effect entirely contrary to that intended. It will be looked upon as persecution, as an attempt to deprive people of rights and liberties, which are inherit to America.

"It will arouse a hostility which will give a strong impetus to the anti-vaccination movement—a movement that is surely growing in all civilized and enlightened countries." Yes, it is growing and all the powers of earth and hades can not check it. Let the doctor consider, let the conservative beware when science let loose a great truth.

"Swing inward, O gates of the future!
Swing outward, ye doors of the past,
For the soul of the people is moving
And rising from slumber at last;
The black 'rites' are retreating,
The white peaks have signaled the day,
And freedom her long roll is beating,
And calling her sons to the fray."

AN EMINENT DOCTOR'S CONFESSION.

The eloquent and cultured Dr. E. M Ripley, of Unionville, Conn., said in a public address delivered in New Britain, Conn.:

"Never in the history of medicine has there been produced so false a theory, such fraudulent assumptions, such disastrous and damning results, as have followed the practice of this disgusting rite; it is the ultima thule of learned quackery, and lacks, and has ever lacked, the faintest shadow of a scientific basis. The fears of the whole people have been played upon as to the dangers of small-pox, and the sure prevention by vaccination, until nearly the whole civilized world has become phys ically corrupted by its practice.

"The life-blood of nations has become the cesspool of vaccinators, wherein they have poured the foul excretions that are thrown off from diseased beasts, nature adjudging it too vile to contaminate the system of any living creature. Scrofula, that hydra-headed monster of pathology, whose ramifications extend into and complicate nearly all the diseases that flesh is heir to, and whose victims are as the sands of the seashore in number, is one of the oldest children of vaccine poisoning. Syphilis, that disreputable disorder, that sinks its victims below the scale of decency, and hounds them to dishonorable graves, has been carried by the vaccinator's lance into the homes of the innocent and the virtuous, and there the blighting curse has been left to consummate a work of disease and death, with consequent suffering that defies the imagination of man to depict."

When a mad dog enters a community and bites a child, the whole people rise up and demand the death of the creature, and desire that all available means be immediately used to eliminate from the system of the child the virus that has been so cruelly inserted. The action of the people in this case is a very natural one; but let me tell you that where the bite of a mad dog has caused death in one case, the mad doctor, with his calf-lymph poisoned lance, has caused his tens of thousands.

It is the most outrageous insult that can be offered to any pure-minded man or woman. It is the boldest and most impious attempt to mar the works of God that has been attempted for ages. This stupid blunder of doctor-craft has wrought all the evil that it ought, and it is time that free American citizens arise in their might and blot out this whole blood-poisoning business.

"It is a sorry charge to make against a learned profession to say the that the cause of vaccination is backed by ignorance, but so it is. I know whereof I affirm, for I, too, must plead guilty to the charge. I vaccinated for five years, ignorantly supposing that it was a preventive of small-pox. I took for granted what my medical teachers had affirmed. I came near being a murderer, and in my own family, too. For weeks my child, vaccinated by my own hand with pure vaccine lymph, and from the calf, too, was tended upon a pillow by his faithful mother; and when not in a stupor he suffered as only the damned can suffer. After a time the crisis passed and he came back to life; and I then and there took a solemn oath never, so long as God would let me live, would I poison another human being with vaccine virus, and I have kept my vow.

From that time on I studied the subject, as I should have done before, and as all doctors should before commencing medical practice, and I was appalled to find how fearfully I had been deluded."

In consonance with Dr. Ripley's above address, it may be said, that vaccination is a moral cancer, a santanic contagion, invading all the sanctities of human life. Masquerading as sanitary science, it is the champion harlequin of our time, and while a source of revenue to medical boodlers, at last it "biteth like a serpent and stingeth like an adder."

The English physician, Dr. John Pickering, F. R. G. S., F. S.S., F. S. A., etc., says:

"Wherever you have no vaccination you have the best health. The moment you give up vaccination you do away with small-pox; it will die out."

The late Dr. William Hitchman, Consulting Surgeon to the Cancer Hospital, Leeds, and formerly public vaccinator to the City of Liverpool, expressly stated, in 1883, that "Syphilis, Abdominal Phthisis, Scrofula, Cancer, Erysipelas, and almost all diseases of the skin, have been either conveyed, occasioned, or intensified by vaccination."—(Transactions of the Makuna Vaccination Inquiry, p. 31, London, 1883.

Dr. Hitchman further says: "Cancer may be generated anew whenever the necessary conditions are present. And here a strong indictment is again furnished against both 'calf-lymph' and 'arm-to-arm' vaccination. Cancer," says Dr. Hitchman, "is a blood disease; so also is cow-pox; and when, to inherited or acquired morbid tendency, vital exhaustion, digestive disorder, and unhealthy surroundings, are added the various complications attending vaccination, the presence of certain growths, or even bony structure in the larynx or any other part, is not surprising to one who believes in causal sequence. Scientifically, whatever tends to a diminution in the natural color and specific gravity, especially of the red corpuscles of the blood, may, sooner or later, lead to serious transformation into tubercular, syphilitic, or cancerous affection."—Vaccination Inquirer, London, February, 1888.

To introduce any animal substance directly into the human lymphatic system is perilous, especially as the lymph is, to use Swedenborg's forcible and scientific definition, "the true, purer blood." So that, even were the actual lymph of a perfectly healthy calf to be introduced into the lymphatic system of a healthy child, the conditions sufficient for the generation of a cancer would then be present; owing simply to the mere difference in the rate of growth in the representative cells of calf and human being, or in that of the protoplasm out of which they are respectively formed.

W. H. Burr, a clear-headed student, historian, writer and author, residing in Washington, D. C., says: "I gave the following English statistics to the New York Daily Sun, fourteen years ago:"

"Vaccination was made compulsory in England in 1853, again in 1867, and still more stringent in 1871. Now mark the result as given in the vital statistics authorized by Parliament. Since the first year named England has been visited with three epidemics of small-pox, each more severe than the preceding, as appears from the following figures:

Epidemic of	Deaths.
1857-58-59	14,194
1863-64-65	19,816
1870-71-72	44,631

"And you tell us that in New York City (August, 1885), where vaccination is not yet compulsory, the disease has almost disappeared, while in London, where most stringent compulsory laws prevail, the small-pox is raging.

"All the foregoing facts appeared in the Sun of August 21, 1884, with the editor's own heading in these words: 'Vaccination a Fraud—New York Healthier Without It' * * *

"It is sanitary regulations, and not vaccination which abate the ravages of small-pox.

"The anti-vaccinationists have always been able to demolish the pretensions of their adversaries. I don't wish to say any more on the subject. Let Brother Peebles come forth with his 'pen-gatling.' "   W. H BURR.

The Chicago Inter Ocean of recent date prints the following special from Fort Wayne, Ind., concerning the evil effects of vaccination:

"Indiscriminate vaccination has caused many children here to suffer seriously. This morning the seven-year-old son of William Maddux, foreman of the New York, Chicago and St. Louis Railway wrecking gang, died suddenly from blood poisoning, superinduced by vaccination. There are six other cases where chidren are afflicted with blood poisoning from the same cause, and children were vaccinated who were unable to stand the shock, and some physicians have not used fresh vaccine points, but have used virus from the arms of other children."

In the Transvaal, where war is now raging, vaccination, says Dr. Bond, is enforced with a cat-o-ninetails. In Algiers soldiers if refusing vaccination, are bound with cords and then legally poisoned. The fee here is $5. when it "takes."

The Abyssinian Emperor Menelik had encouraged vaccination for a long time; but seeing the bad effect he became disgusted with the results. Dr. Wurtz reports the following—see p. 124 Life in Abyssinia: "A rich Abyssinian refused vaccine lymph offered him by Dr. Wurtz and insisted on having eight young female servants inoculated with the result that they all died of small-pox. In 1896 a French trader of Addis-Abada, had nine servants inoculated with the result that each of them soon afterward had a sphilitic sore on some part of their bodies and one of them, a chancre-like ulcer on the wrist. Three other neigboring children were vaccinated with what was termed pure calf-lymph. One of these exhibited scrofula immediately after and the two others syphilitic symptoms."

The erudite Dr. A. Wilder, of New York, physician and author, assures us that if vaccination has any influence, it is that of changing the body from a natural and normal condition to an unnatural and diseased one; in which case, repeated vaccinating can be but an endeavor to make this unnatural and diseased condition permanent. The individual is thus rendered sickly, and placed in a state of chronic aptitude to contract other diseases."

The doctor further says that Lorenzo Dow was once challenged to preach from a text to be given him by a minister just as he was about to begin. The text assigned was from Numbers xxii., 21: "And Balaam rose up in the morning and saddled his ass."

"This text," said Dow, "embraces three distinct ideas, which I will explain. First, Balaam, the wicked prophet; he denotes your minister. Second, the saddle, which is the salary which he receives. Third, the ass; this means the people of his congregation. The improvement is this: that your minister has his saddle fastened upon you, and is riding you to inevitable destruction."

"Of our friends in Brooklyn I say, as Chatham said of the American colonists: "I am glad that they have resisted." It may be that martyrdom is in store for the friends of personal freedom and pure bodies; we shall see. We read that when the apostle cast the Python-spirit out of the soothsaying girl (Acts xiii.) "her masters saw that the hope of their gains was gone," and in the mad fury of their disappointed cupidity, caught Paul and Silas and dragged them to the agora, under the charge of teaching illegal and pernicious customs. The multitude—the majority—rose up en masse, and the magistrates beat them and cast them into prison. Doctor-craft is about as malignant and obstreperous today. It abides no law, no constitutional safeguard that conflicts with its selfish ends."

During the Civil War, 1863-4-5, Mr. C. C. Watkins, a
solid, substantial citizen of San Diego, Cal., 125 Grand Avenue,
was with other soldiers exposed to the small-pox. Soon there
were exhibited symptoms of the disease. And including Mr.
Watkins, nearly a dozen of them were put into a pest-house
in Tennessee. Seven of them had been vaccinated and every
one of them died, while C. C. Watkins, who had not been vaccinated, was the only one that fully recovered from the terrible
disease. And yet there are physicians, either ignorant enough
or impudent enough, to declare that calf-lymph vaccination
is a preventive of small-pox. It is strange that thinking cultured people are losing faith in the average doctor? Many
of them had better drop their profession and become black-
smiths or daily tillers of the soil.

Dr. Johnson, of Newburyport, Mass., says: "We have five
children, all of whom have been exposed to the disease. The
only one who took it was the one who had been vaccinated."

The Hon. A. B. Gaston, present member of Congress
from Meadsville, Pa., writes as follows in the monthly Cassa-
dagan: "Americans unfortunately have some of the most
tyrannical laws that could possibly disgrace any statute books.
Among the numerous vicious laws of my own state. I may name,
the compulsory vaccination law, as it is at present being en-
iorced in my own city, a benefit to physicians, and hundreds
of filthy poisonings for the victims. This vaccination fad carries a thousand dollars into the pockets of the doctors, and two
thousand bits of health-destroying virus into the systems of
our children, to vitiate and curse their rich young blood.
Every intelligent reader knows that the best preventive of
small-pox, or of any contagious disease rests, in sanitary regulations, in personal and municipal cleanliness, by fortifying the
system with pure air, pure food, pure diink, pure habits of
thought and of living, and entire abstinence from excesses and
over indulgence in all directions."

The Washington Star informs us that Congress has made
an appropriation of $100,000 to be expended in an effort to ex-

terminate tuberculosis among the cattle in the United States. What appropriation will it make to exterminate the tuberculosis—imparted virus—or the cow-pox virus—that doctors are strenuously, selfishly and compulsorily putting into our children's arms under the baseless pretence that it will prevent small-pox?

Cows and heifers are known by the well-informed to be very many of them unhealthy. "A herd ten days ago," (says Public Opinion, Jan. 14, 1891), "on a farm in this district, was found to have 80 per cent. of its animals infected; and a few days before that no fewer than 90 animals in a herd numbering 125 near Richmond, Va., were discovered to be diseased. These are extreme and unusual cases, it is true; but occurring synchronously within a narrow radius, they were enough to rouse the Government to a sense of the danger to which the country is exposed from this source. An experiment performed by one of the scientists attached to the animal industry laboratory about the same time tended in the same direction of alarm. Ascertaining from test experiments which he had been making with the milk supply of the Capital that it was tainted with tubercle, he inoculated a guinea pig with the milk; and, sure enough, after a few days when the tubercle bacilli contained in the milk had had time to plant itself and develop in his system, the rodent exhibited unmistakable tuberculosis. Concurrent circumstances like these, forced on the attention of the Government, produced the belief that it was about time a general investigation of diseased cattle should be made, if the danger to human health so portended would be avoided.

Sores or ulcers on these tuberculosis cows, heifers or calves, are tapped and the discharged pus—virus manipulated, is forced compulsorily into the arms of our children. How long—oh how long will our suffering countrymen permit this outrage!

The following is from the Rev. Isaac L. Peebles, a prominent preacher in the Methodist Episcopal church, Mississippi. It is an exhibition of not only high-grade Scotch grit, but of southern chivalry on a religious plane. He thus writes in his able pamphlet on Vaccination: "The virus that Dr. Jenner, the accredited father of vaccination, used first was from a sore on the hand of a young woman. This sore, she claimed, was produced by matter from the sores on the teats and udders of the cows, while milking them. This was the filth start of vaccination, but the extreme nastiness of its filthiness will appear more clearly when we remember that the sores on the cow's udders and teats were caused by an oozing matter called grease from the diseased heel of badly kept horses. Persons attending the horses would milk the cows without washing. It almost makes us vomit to think of such filth, and yet to think that human beings would have it compulsorily thrust into their children's bodies. Although this was the beginning of Jenner's vaccination, yet it was not its limit. Two years after his first vaccination, he vaccinated his own son with the virus of hog-pox. Indeed, he vaccinated with the putrid matter from the disease of horses'·heels. He further by way of experiment vaccinated with horse-pox, cow-pox, goat-pox and hog-pox, and it is a wonder that some of his disciples have not completed his list by taking filth from some dirty mangy dog and vaccinating some poor ignorant fellow and calling it dog-pox. Jenner contended that all these poxes were of the same origin."

Some claim that it is produced by vaccinating a cow with a virus of small-pox, while others of equal ability claim that the virus of small-pox will produce small-pox, and not cow-pox, and that cow-pox must appear of itself in the cow. The doctrine of spontaneous cow-pox is without foundation. Indeed, it is contrary to reason and the nature of things, unless it can be proven that the good Lord, through special regard for the ladies, made the cow of such peculiar sensitive nature that the pox develops in her, and her only, so that the nice term "cow-pox" could be used, instead of the gross term "bull-pox." * * * Fifty years from now, there will rise up a well-informed generation, who will look back on this time of vaccination and forced vaccination with wonder and pity. Let those who love the darling, filthy, butchering business practice it on themselves as much as they choose, but for humanity's sake, if for nothing else, let others alone."

What becomes of the heifers and calves after they have yielded their harvest of Pustular and poison pus Lymph?

This question, legitimately asked, is a very serious one;— what becomes of them? Are they killed and their shaven, sore and pus-scarred bodies buried from human gaze? This would be a waste of beef, not "embalmed beef," but rather veal from a calf-lymph producing farm. No, these pus, or pustule-tapped heifers, are returned to the farmers or sold in city meat markets. Such facts the more deeply intensify vegetarians in their vegetarianism.

The Philadelphia Daily Item, Nov. 22nd, 1899, has the following trifle condensed: "Some more interesting facts are coming to the surface in connection with the fight inaugurated by the Anti-Compulsory Vaccination Society of America against the law which was passed at the last session of the Legislature, and Attorney C. Oscar Beasley is willing to tell his experience in getting matters into shape for what he says will be one of the greatest legal battles ever waged in the State.

In the Sunday Item he said that there were only twelve farms, or "factories," as he called them, in the country for the production of vaccine virus.

"We have abundant evidence," said Attorney Beasley, "direct from the people who have seen the calves, after they. had been used for the purpose of producing the virus, taken from these farms full of poisonous vaccine matter and sold.

"Naturally, everyone interested in this matter wants to know what becomes of these poor animals. What I have just told you is only part of the story, but we also know that they have been sold to the public as veal after the virus has been put into them. We can prove that, and if such action is preventing the spread of disease, I, at least, would like to be informed how the authorities reconcile the facts.

"The people who run these cow-pox farms rent the calves from the farmers. After the calves are kept the proper time they are sent back to the farmers. Now, the question is, 'What do the farmers do with them?' I have already told what we know—and what we can prove.

"There are a number of mattters which will be brought out before this affair is concluded, and I want you to understand that I will be responsible for everything that I tell you.

TO MAKE A TEST CASE.

"There are hundreds of children who are kept away by the enforcement of this law from public, private and Sunday schools, and it is not unlikely that the League may arrest some of the Sunday school superintendents on the charge of preventing the children from attending the school because they are not vaccinated. A test case will be made and then we will see where we stand on that phase ot the case."

At this point in his talk, Mr. Beasley referred to a letter which he had received from a Catholic priest who was a resident of this city. He was immune from small-pox and during the terrible epidemic of the winter of 1872 and 1873 was one of the Catholic clergymen who were detailed by the Archbishop of the diocese to visit the poor and afflicted in all parts of the city and give them extreme unction, the last rite of the church.

This reverend gentleman says he is positive that the disease caused by the inoculation of vaccine virus is at best a very vile one. It not unfrequently causes death. The virus, he says, is sure to fasten upon the weak portion of a child's system. These are still more greatly weakened by the virus often with fatal results. He concludes by saying that he hopes the League will be successful in having the bill repealed."

The April number of Frank D. Blue's Vaccination, published in Terre Haute, Ind., has the following:

"David Mackay, M. D., Surgeon General of the Grand Army of the Republic, in sending a subscription to Vaccination says: 'The abominable practice is only one of the horrible delusions arising from filth, and from a false dietary,—flesh-eating. Until that ceases man will go on his crazy method of 'curing' a disease, by creating a worse one.'"

HASTENING TO A CLIMAX.

As I write January 15th, 1900—the evening mail brings to my desk an item from the Los Angeles East Side News, giving the latest phase of the Vaccination Question in Chicago:

"A small-pox case escaped from the chief medical inspector of the health department and ran into a crowd of people. The inspector called a half dozen policemen to his aid, rounded up seventeen persons supposed to have been touched by the small-pox patient, and in spite of protests, threats and resistance, vaccinated the lot. The Tribune says:

"With his back to the side of a house Dr. Spalding seized his patients as fast as they were pushed toward him by the police and applied the virus in record-breaking time."

Now, dear reader, I shall have to "take back" the assertion I made in the fourth chapter that "no person has yet been vaccinated in the United States by applying actual physical force." The Chicago incident inaugurates that phase and makes the compulsion of the "Code" a concrete fact. We now stand on a par with Germany in the mode of enforcing the law. The same paper from which 1 clip the above casually mentions that recently 2,500 medical students in Chicago mobbed a preacher for criticising the drug practice. The doctors are evidently numerous in Chicago—indeed, so numerous that quite a large army of them must needs be numbered among the "unemployed." The unemployed "vag" holds the citizen up in Chicago as he returns late from business or pleasure, and if caught is "sent up." And why should not the unemployed doctors "round up" a few citizens occasionally and vaccinate them, when the law says they may do that very thing? At this season of the year—since the "Appendicitis" racket is about played out—many doctors must find but a scanty demand for their "professional" services in that city. With office rent falling due and no "revenue" with which to buy coal, we should not be surprised to learn that they are arming with the lancet, with tubes, or a phial of calf-pus and taking to the street, physically enforce vaccination. They well understand that the Legislature gave them leave to vaccinate all "goers and comers," and agreed to help them do it up to the point of efficiency.

Now, by lending to the doctors the services of the police, we may be assured the Government is faithfully performing its part of the contract. Why should we not hope and pray that the State Legislature and the doctors shall carry out their mutual "understanding" that the common people shall be "protected," seeing that they are "too ignorant to protect themselves."

I would suggest (seriously) that on the next election day in Chicago, the doctors charter a sufficient force of police to "round up" a few hundred voters, and that the doctors be ready for duty with "pure" glycerinated and "sterilized" calf-lymph to duly "protect" the aforesaid voters; and that this operation be repeated on each successive election day, until American "sovereigns" are aroused to the point of rising en masse to break and repeal this infamous compact between the doctors and lobbied legislatures—legislatures that are bought and sold by unprincipled multi-millionaires.

COMPULSORY VACCINATION AND THE MILITIA.

The Militia called out! Such was a recent heading in the Hudson Journal, June 15th. Called out for what? Here's the paragraph—it speaks for itself:

"The Hudson company of militia, ninety men strong, went to Stockport today to aid in enforcing quarantine regulations against a number of persons who have refused to be vaccinated.

"An epidemic of small-pox has prevailed among 500 colored brickyard laborers at Walsh & Company's yard, Stockport, for some time. About fifty, white and colored, refused to submit to vaccination, so a company of the State Militia was ordered to Stockport to enforce the quarantine rules."

And this is the free America, is it? This, a land of personal liberty, is it? This a country of inalienable rights, is it? No—it is rather an oligarchy manned by certain "professsional" doctors, the repulsive dules and unconstitutional laws of which, are to be enforced by the militia.

There's not a thoroughly-read, intelligent physician in America but that knows, and if honest, will frankly admit that cow-pox vaccination is not an invariable preventative of small-pox. They know from the most unimpeachable testimony that thousands vaccinated and re-vaccinated have died and still die every year of small-pox. And yet in Hudson the militia is called out to enforce the blood-poisoning process of vaccination—compulsory vaccination—with fire-arms behind it! Think of this, freedom-loving American citizens, and blush for your country!

Soon after their arrival Miss Nora Donahue, Worcester, Mass., was reported by the Health Board to be suffering from small pox and was sent to the pest-house. The Steamboat Company, bestirring itself, the Boston Board of Health went to Worcester and after due investigation and examination decided that the case was not small-pox. In the meantime it came out that this young woman had been twice vaccinated, once when she left Queenstown and again as she entered the harbor of New York, but that "neither took"—when the plain truth was it took too well, producing "a new disease," said the Rockland (Mass.) Independent, "worse than the small-pox." This is what we have all along contended for, that vaccination creates new diseases, as well as sows the seeds and lays the foundation for eczema, erysipelas, ulcers, tumors, cancers, and other of the filthiest, festering diseases known to the human race.

BUBONIC PLAGUE FROM VACCINATION.

Dr. R. M. Leverson, of Fort Hamilton, gave his views on vaccination before the Brooklyn Philadelphia Association in Williamsburg, Jan. 14th, 1900. He said: "Should small-pox be discovered in your family, do not be foolish enough to send for your doctor or any other one who would notify the Board of—well, some call it Health. Do not, I say, resort to that. All this talk about the danger of the disease is exaggerated. It is easily treated and not in any way formidable. The importance of vaccination as a subject of discussion is increased now, because of the prevalence of bubonic plague in many sections. It is the disease which a generation ago was predicted by those who opposed vaccination. Scientifically we say the cow-pox was really the specific disease of an animal. Vaccination means the inoculation of the dreaded taint, and the bubonic plague is nothing more nor less than the result, is a sporadic form, of this evil specific disease."—New York Tri-Weekly, Jan. 15th, 1900.

The above is a note of warning—I do not say timely warning, for the time is past. A century of vaccination over the civilized world has fully prepared the soil for the crop which we must now reap. It has been prepared in India, where for two generations compulsory vaccination has been forced on the native population—mostly arm to arm vaccination, which has given rise to a distinct diathesis, and to new and before unheard of diseases, as set forth at the beginning of this chapter. Bubonic plague is undoubtedly one of these new species, which will abundantly flourish during the first quarter of the twentieth century.

The wholesale vaccination on the Hawaiian Islands since 1853 has prepared the soil there, and as I write—January, 1900—the dreaded plague has gained a strong foothold there, and will undoubtedly reach the Pacific Coast during the ensuing summer. At any rate, sooner or later it is bound to come and ravage the United States, for a poorly-informed public have submitted themselves to be made merchandise of by a class of semi-consciousless physicians, until sloth and ignorance will exact a sterner mode of teaching. The object lessons which the plague, with varied zymotic diseases, will furnish, may have the effect of opening the eyes of an apathetic public to the grave violations of physiological law to which they have so long blindly submitted.

Unlike the yellow fever, bubonic plague is most virulent in winter, but like all zymotic diseases, its home is where filth abounds. It continues to spread in India, and in the city of

Bombay it acts fatally within a few hours. The natives refuse European aid, remembering well the sad lesson taught them by the vaccinators. Nearly all cases prove fatal. Everywhere there are little puddles of water, especially in the suburbs, amidst the most filthy surroundings, and the water is used by the natives, they preferring it to the water supplied by the city authorities. Last winter (1899) there were 250 deaths daily in Bombay, sometimes 2,500 a week. The epidemic recedes for a few weeks during the hottest season; then reappears with destructive violence when the cooler weather sets in.

THE VACCINATION DOCTOR'S DOOM.

Just as "inoculation" was prohibited by law in England, so will vaccination in both England and America soon be strenuously prohibited by law. Its death knell is already being sounded. All honor to Covington, Ky., for pronouncing vaccination "felony" for physicians. This, bear in mind, is one of the highest classes of offenses with a severe penalty attached thereto. Here is what the Cincinnnati Times-Star, May 2nd, says:

"At the meeting of the Covington City Council Monday night the ordinance demanding compulsory vaccination was repealed. Mr. Evans, from the Third ward, introduced an ordinance making it a felony for any physician to vaccinate a person under any circumstances and provided a fine therefor of $100 and four months' imprisonment."

The English inoculation fad had its reign in Britain and died. The cow-pox lymph, the serum and the anti-toxin will pass away with the increased intelligence characterizing this era of thought and profound research.

Just now, there is a bubonic-plague scare in San Francisco, originating, the Press says, among the doctors and directed towards the Chinese. On my third journey to and through the great cities of India, I was brought into close connection with this plague, which, like the small-pox, is a disease of dirt and filth. It first appeared in Bombay among the underground rats and then among the poorest and dirtiest portion of the lower caste. It seldom affects the cleanly, and if it did, it would be comparatively harmless. Those treated with drastic drugs generally died. Those placed under cleanly sanitary conditions lived. This disease should have been called the glandular rather than bubonic plague. Those previously tainted with syphilis, gonorrhea, and whose blood had been poisoned with calf-lymph virus, were the first attacked by this oriental disease. Women were seldom seriously affected by it. The San Fran·isco Press of May 20th, says: "There are several cases of bubonic plague in the city and that portion of the city ocenpied by the Chinese." The San Diego Sun of May 24th publishes the following: "A great number of Japanese have voluntarily presented themselves for inoculation with serum, and a few, but not many, Chinese have submitted to treatment."

Inspection of the Chinese quarters is in progress, and sanitary measures are being enforced.

The Chronicle editorially declares that there has been no real cases of bubonic plague, and said the cry was raised by the city board of health, some of which are physicians, to compel the supervisors to appropriate a large sum of money to hire an army of guards and inspectors, and that the whole scheme is a political conspiracy."

No doubt, this scare and scheme was "a conspiracy" between the politicians and physicians for selfish ends, all of which is painfully deplorable, in this boasting, self-assertive age of civilization and moral enlightenment.

MORE MEDICAL TESTIMONY.

The Homeo Envoy, Philadelphia, Pa., records the case of a man, who in the category of a good compulsory law-abiding citizen, was vaccinated with pure glycerinated lymph and "it took"—took so well that the doctor got frightened and had him quarantined for the reason that the vaccination had actually developed into a full-fledged case of pronounced small-pox. The family physician, with a great degree of gravity, said: "This is unaccountable—unaccountable!"

Recently, says that eminent physician, J. W. Hodge, M. D., Niagara Falls, N. Y., "The Buffalo Courier printed a statement taken from the records of the surgeon general's office at Manila showing the number of fatalities and their causes among our troops up to the second of last June.

"According to this compilation," says the editor of the Courier, "of 699 privates, 294 died of wounds received in action, 9 killed accidentally, 23 were drowned, 7 committed suicide, 106 died of typhoid fever, 89 of small-pox and 14 of meningitis."

By examining the above tabulation we find that the deaths from small-pox among our troops (all of whom, without exception, have been repeatedly vaccinated since leaving this country) constitute 317, nearly 50 per cent, of the entire number of deaths from all diseases.

The Courier frankly and truthfully says: "Opponents of vaccination find a good argument in this condition of affairs at Manila."

In many of the old countries where vaccination has been tried long and faithfully, its compulsion has been abandoned from the army. In Sweden, Norway, Belgium, Holland and Switzerland no soldier is now obliged to be vaccinated. The prevalence and fatality of small-pox among our much vaccinated troops in the Philippines is no unique experience and does not at all surprise those who are familiar with the history of vaccination. The London Morning Advertiser of Nov. 24, 1870, reported as follows: "Small-pox is making great havoc in the ranks of the Prussian army, which is reported to have 30,000 small-pox patients in its hospitals. These were all vaccinated and re-vaccinated."

And yet there are doctors—rather non-studious medical professionals (complimentarily called "physicians"), who persistently tell the people that vaccination prevents small-pox. They either do, or they do not know better Do they think—do they observe—do they investigate—do they study and reason? It has been wisely said that he who will not reason is a bigot, he who dare not is coward, and he who can not is an idiot. Each back-chapter physician, touching this all-important matter of small-pox, vaccination and anti-vaccination, must necessarily pose upon one of the points of the above trilemma. Take your positions, Physicians! The people constitute the jury.

AN INSISTENT FALSEHOOD.

"He who said the age of myths was past was surely unacquainted with the suspicious ways of certain doctors in sustaining the tottering vaccine idol. Perhaps the most remarkable of the many fables invented by the advocates of vaccination to bolster up the Jennerian dogma, surely the basest and most insistent is that known as the "Franco-German war statistic."

Along in 1872 the following falsehood first appeared in English print, in the British Medical Journal. In June, 1883, it was used by Sir Lyon Playfair in a debate in the Commons and challenged by Mr. P. A. Taylor. Sir Lyon Playfair, waving Dr. Colon's book, La Variola, said, "I got it from the Physician General of the French army," but he did not, for investigation showed it was not in the book, nor was Colon ever

physician general of the army. In the official report of the
speech Playfair had it put "I give these figures on the authority of Dr. Philenus of the German Reichstag, and of similar figures of the statistical congress in St. Petersburg." This started
a new line of investigation which revealed the fact, that it first
appeared as a stray newspaper paragraph in an Austrian journal.
So here in brief we have a fanciful tale involved in the imag-
inative brain of an unknown newspaper man, through an Aus-
trian-Russian-German-English source to prove a French statistic that never did have any foundation in truth.

The matter was not allowed to rest here. Earl Granvillle in
Paris was appealed to by Dr. Carpenter, (who was very active
in disseminating the lie) and Granville reported that the French
authorities stated the deaths from small-pox were unknown,
that the confusion was too great for registry, thus effectually
disposing of the French part of it. The story was publicly re-
tracted in the London News, August, 1883.* And the German part fared no better for Herr Lisouke, in a letter to Geo.
S. Gibbs, dated July 20th, 1883, expressed regret that during
the twelve months of the war the deaths from small-pox were
not recorded. So followed the German ha'f of the lie.

Herr Steiger, February, 1883, at Berne, gave the German
loss from small-pox as 3,162, the French as 23,469; by June,
1883, Playfair got it down to 261 and by the time the British
Medical Journal published it the second time in 1898 it had
dropped to 49, and 23,400 respectively. The French army was
perfectly vaccinated, but a part of it was not re-vaccinated before this campaign. Dr. Bayard says, "Re-vaccination originated in France, and every soldier is revaccinated on his entrance
into the regiment—our army knows no exceptions."

Dr. Oidtmann, staff surgeon, says: "Shortly before the
war the whole French army was re-vaccinated. This general
re-vaccination tended rather to extend small-pox than to protect

---

*The first edition of "Vaccination Vindicated, by Dr. McVail contained this falsehood,
but in the second edition (1898) it is dropped. And it is well that it was, for infamy in
sustaining a bad cause could not have well gone further.

against it." Dr. Colon, in charge of the small-pox hospital Bicetre, says: "The mortality was much less in the militia who were not re-vaccinated than in the regular army which was re-vaccinated." Dr. Jehner in Etiology of Variola, says: "The French prisoners were not sick on their arrival, but small-pox in epidemic form broke out among them after they were placed in German camps; all measures to repress it, even the daily re-vaccination in mass were useless. Even the German guards took sick." The soldiers were finally washed and their clothes steamed, and from that time the epidemic rapidly declined. (Phys. Jl., 1873).

It is no new thing to go to Germany for proofs of the value of vaccination. I have a copy of Hall's Journal of Health, October, 1860, that says, "The Prussian more than any government in existence, practices vaccination, every soldier is re-vaccinated upon entering the army.

Early in 1870, Dr. Seaton, of the English local government board, before the Commons, declared that Prussia was well protected, and that that country was safe, yet inside a year 59,839 persons died from small-pox in Prussia; 2,083 in Berlin alone. Nor did the well vaccinated army fare any better. Dr. Creighton, the great epidemiologist, says: "Evidence as to re-vaccination on a large scale comes from the army. The rate from small-pox in the German army, was 60 per cent. more than among the civil population of the same age. The Bavarian contingent, re-vaccinated without exception, had five times the death rate from small-pox that the civil population of the same age had, though vaccination is not obligatory among the latter. The statistics of Prof. Vogt, of Berne, prove the same facts.

Severe epidemics are not unknown in Germany in these days. Nor are deaths and injuries from vaccination uncommon. So true is this that in 1896 the German Imperial Health

Board, alarmed at the increasing anti-vaccinationists, and their growing influence, issued a pamphlet of 192 pages confessedly for the purpose of meeting their ever increasing attacks. As the annual income of the doctors from vaccination is over 40,-000,000 marks this zeal is easily understood. Even forcible vaccination of all children is advocated, of course, at State rates.

The pamphlet was at once attacked by the anti-vaccinationists, and charges made that the German mortality list contained no column for deaths from vaccination; and that all such deaths are covered up under secondary causes, such as erysipelas, pyemia, etc., that it is a written rule in the army that even in severe cases of small-pox, such illness is entered as skin eruption, and Col. Spohr, 48 years in service, testified to hearing army surgeons censured for entering recruits as suffering from small-pox, and that small-pox cases were always entered under some "appropriate illness."

Dr. J. A. Hensel, late surgeon in the German army, in an address delivered in Salt Lake City, Feb. 2nd, 1900, said in brief: "In June, 1888, I was on duty in Strasburg, and over 2,000 small-pox cases were in the pest house; every one successfully vaccinated but three months before, for the third time. I myself, was laid up for five weeks, although I had been vaccinated for the seventh time, successfully. In 1898 I witnessed the amputation of three arms and the discharge of four men from the army for general disability, all from vaccination. After this experience I am convinced that vaccination is no protection against small-pox. Dirty barracks started the epidemic."

December, 1899, R. Gerding was held before the Berlin Criminal Court for making these charges in his book on small-pox and found guilty, but the supreme court promptly reversed the ease and ordered the State treasury to pay all the cost. A German corespondent in December, 1897, wrote:

"We must not lose sight of the fact that the German doctors are experts at making statistics. Fine sounding new names, as 'variolides,' etc., are invented for diseases from which people die, but by no recording deaths, small-pox is made to appear as stamped out." So after all the abscence of German army small-pox is simply a case of logic, for vaccination prevents small-pox; these men are vaccinated and can not take small-pox; therefore, there is, and can be, no small-pox in the German army.

It is a too common habit of the vaccinators to pick up figures anywhere and vouch for them as authentic, just because they happen to lie in favor of vaccination.

In June, 1898, the British Medical Journal again started the same old lie, and it began the round of the American press. From Maine to California has it circulated, appearing in all state health bulletins, including the Government bulletins and quoted as gospel by Surgeon General Sternberg in defense of his frequent poisoning of the poor soldier boys in the far East, who continue to die of small-pox, despite the assertions of Surgeon Lippincott, that our army is the best vaccinated army ever put in the field.

There is some excuse for the laity not knowing these facts, but there is, at this late day, no good excuse for all physicians not knowing the truth, and with them it is either a case of woeful ignorance or wilful lying."—F. D. Blue.

All medical journalists, or doctors, who have published or mouthed this falsehood—malicious falsehood—should, if professed Christians, read upon their knees Revelations xxi. VIII.: "But the fearful, the abominable, the murderers, the whoremongers (the abortionists) and all liars"—mark these last words —"and all liars, shall have their part in the lake which burneth with fire and brimstone: which is the second death."

And why this terrible doom? Possible because, as the Scripture saith, they have put the "mark of the beast"—(cow-pox lymph)—upon our children's arms and limbs; and further, before God and men they have repeatedly lied for the glory of vaccine virus—the curse of the century!

———

SUMMARY AND CONCLUSION.

In the foregoing pages I have endeavored to bring into prominence the following features of the Vaccination question:

(1.) That Vaccination was neither a scientific discovery, nor is its claim as a prophylactic against small-pox valid or philosophical. Vaccination with sphilitic virus to prevent the "bad" disease would be just as rational; but that has been tried and abandoned. Dr. Koch's much vaunted tuberculin has been tried in almost every country on the globe, and proved to be worse than useless. Indeed, if the principle on which vaccination is predicted was founded in physiological laws, then every zymotic disease might be similarly prevented.

(2.) That the vaccine virus is invariably a form of putrefying animal tissue which, while its substance and quality may in part be determined by the microscope and chemical analysis, it nevertheless declares by its effects that it contains subtle potencies which present day analysis is utterly unable to detect; and therefore that its inoculation in the blood of a human being is always attended with grave danger and often plants in the body the most loathsome and incurable diseases known to men. Vaccination is always a form of blood-poisoning, while the vaccine virus is often the vehicle of specific occult qualities and seeds of disease which defies all present powers of detection. Moreover, such poisons are a hundredfold more dangerous when introduced through a skin puncture than if taken into the stomach.

(3.) That the much vaunted rite of Vaccination fails to "protect." I have adduced ample evidence that the vaccinated are just as liable to an attack of small-pox as the unvaccinated —especially during a small-pox epidemic; that epidemic outbreaks of the disease have nothing to do with the question of vaccination, but everything to do with habits and modes of living. The quarter in a great city where the people are clean, healthy and vigorous, never suffers severely from small-pox, even in epidemic years. On the other hand, small-pox has its home and breeding ground in filth, poverty, wretchedness, intemperance, and over-crowding—a fact about which vaccinators are uniformly silent. All that is needed to avert an attack of small-pox is uniform obedience to hygienic and sanitary laws; and should small-pox symptoms appear when one is thus fortified, it need not be feared more than a mild attack of measles. Then a rational procedure is not to resort to a drug spcific but suggests a wise use of the natural accessories of air, water a cool temperature and a spare diet. Then the disease need never pass even into the confluent form. Generally, if people had small-pox under the same circumstances that induce cow-pox, it would rarely assume the malignant form, except where it has its own natural breeding ground—filth. Epidemic small-pox is the cyclonic culmination of causes that have become ripe for expression; and those causes might be scientifically anticipated and effectually removed before they reach the typhus or the small-pox stage of epidemic intensity.

(4.) I have pointed out that vaccination—destructive and desolating as it has proved to be—has become the curse par-excellence of civilization through its alliance with the politico-state. No man has a right to disease another against his will.

It is indeed a most intolerable tyranny to compel vaccination by law. It is un-American. It is unconstitutional. It is dangerous, often causing death. No privileged class ever before formed so unholy a compact with the state as has the medical profession in respect to vaccination. Compulsory vaccination is the most flagrant—the most dastard crime ever perpetrated against the liberty of the citizen, and its permission of toleration on the statute books of the states in these United States, raises a serious query whether democratic populations are intelligent enough to govern themselves. The permission given by American voters to their servants—the Legislators—to frame and enact into law such an infamous statute, is a pretty sure prophecy that the people's liberties will at last fall something as Rome's fell, before the miserly schemes of the privileged classes.

(5.) I have pointed out how the populace is becoming aroused in various towns and municipalities where Boards of Health have closed the public schools to unvaccinated children; but these local contents, being fractional and scattered, will bear but little fruit toward securing the repeal of the compulsory law. There is no general uprising of the whole people, no aroused public seniment to thunder at the doors of the State Legislatures, no well-informed populace regarding the real status and respect of this vital question. Therefore, the repeal of compulsory vaccination laws in this country belongs to the indefinite future.

6. That vaccination has been convicted as the vile parent and direct cause of a long list of incurable diseases, such as scrofula, syphilis, erysipelas, eczema, cancer, consumption, leprosy, boils, tumors, and other diseases for which science has not as yet found a name. From a very large recorded list of vaccinal injuries, fatalities and deaths, I have cited a few cases, enough, however, to indicate the menacing danger which constantly threatens ,and which ought to be sufficient to deter fath-

ers ard mothers of children from subjecting them to be poisoned with the vaccinator's lance, whatever the legal penalties might be. Defy the compulsory law, stamp it in the dust, pay fines, be imprisoned if needs be, die the martyr's death—do anything rather than have your children's blood poisoned and their health wrecked for life.

(7.) That the root and inciting cause of all this vaccination tyranny centers in the inordinary "love of money"—the mad lust for gold. Money is the universal solvent. It is the symbol of everything which the earthly natural man desires, and will procure everything which he desires, power, privilege, office, emoluments, ease, luxury, flattery, worldly honor, the favors of women, unholy gratifications, etc. The love of money impulses every class, whether in law, theology, politics, trade, or especially the medical vaccinator—to plot against the liberty of the citizen, i. e., to reduce the citizen to a condition of dependence where tribute may be exacted of him.

It was along these lines the medical profession lobbied governments and legislatures and secured a compulsory vaccination law, for which they promised the most and fulfilled the least, of any corrupt ring that ever formed a league with the state, or cursed a country—and all to "protect" the dear people from an attack of small-pox (?) Reader, friend and fellow-citizen, your protection never occupied the smallest corner in the vaccinator's heart. He sows calf-lymph virus to reap a harvest today, and larger, richer harvest in the future. Let us think, study, pray, write, vote and remove this compulsory curse from our statute books; then the vaccination delusion will speedily disappear, and Americans enjoy the freedom for which their foremothers prayed and their forefathers fought and died. Henceforth—toil on—vote for men, not politicians. Your homes are your castles, defend them against the aggressions of the deadly vaccinator. Fight with pen and tongue and ballot for the right, and though the evening be gray, and the night dark, morning will come.

> "Look up, look up, desponding soul,
>   The clouds are only seeming,
> The light behind the darkening scroll,
>   Eternally is beaming.
>
> The warm glad glow of deathless youth,
>   Shall crown the true endeavor;
> The tide of God's immortal truth,
>   Climbs up and on forever."

Three Journeys Around the World.

Or Travels in the Pacific Islands, New Zealand, Australia, Ceylon, India, Egypt and other Oriental Countries. In one volume. During Dr. Peebles' late (and third) trip around the world, he studied and noted the laws, customs and religions of nations and peoples, giving special attention to Psychism Magic, Theosophy and reform movements. He visited Ceylon, India, Persia, Egypt, Syria and the Continent of Europe, and secured much material which has been embodied in a large octavo volume. The volume contains thirty-five chapters, and treats on the following subjects:—Home life in California; My Third Voyage, the Sandwich Islands; The Pacific Island Races; Ocean Bound towards Auckland; New Zealand; Melbourne; Australia; From New Zealand Onward; A Series of Seances upon the Ocean; The Chinese Orient; Chinese Religions and Institutions; Cochin-China to Singapore; Malacca to India; Spiritual Seances on the Indian Ocean; India; Its History and Treasures; India's Religious Morals and Social Characteristics; The Rise of Buddhism in India; The Brahmo-Somaj and Parsees; Spiritualism in India; From India to Arabia; Aden and the Arabs; the City of Cairo, Egypt; Egypt's Catacombs and Pyramids; Appearance of the Egyptians; Study of the Pyramids; Sight of the Great Pyramid; Ancient Science in Egypt; Astronomy of the Egyptians; From Alexandria to Joppa and Jerusalem; the City of Joppa; City of Prophets and Apostles; Jesus and Jerusalem; Present Gospels; the Christianity of the Ages; Plato and Jesus in Contrast; Turkey in Asia; Ionia and the Greeks; Athens; Europe and its Cities; Ceylon and its Buddhists; The India of today; Hindoo Doctrines of the Dead; The Mediterranean Sea; Egypt and Antiquity. Not only the liberal press, but the phrenological journals pronounce this the most interesting and instructive volume upon foreign nations, races and religions ever published. Illustrated with Oriental faces. Large 8vo, cloth gilt sides and back. Nearly 500 pages. Price, $1.50, postage 20 cents.

Was a Soul--Did it Pre-Exist?

From whence the Immortal Soul ? This question of the nature and the origin of the human soul has occupied the thought of the world's best thinkers through all the ages. Did it begin to exist with the body? Is it evolved from the body? Did it ascend up through all the lower orders of creation, or is it a potentialized portion of God? What relation does pre-existence bear—if any, to transmigration, re-incarnation or re-embodiment. Price 25 cents.

India and her Magic.

A lecture delivered by Dr. Peebles' before the medical students of the College of Science in San Francisco, January, 1895. Astounding wonders described that he witnessed during his three journeys around the world. Price 10 cents.

Immortality.

A handsomely bound book of 300 pages, showing the proofs of a future existence from consciousness, intuition, reason and Psychic demonstrations. Price $1.00; paper, 50 cents.

The Christ Question Settled.

A magnificently bound volume of 400 pages—a very symposium by Rabbi Wise, J. S. Loveland, Hudson Tuttle, W. E. Coleman, Colonel Ingersol, J. R. Buchanan and others, treating of the existence of Jesus, His Conception, His Manhood or Godhead. What the Grostics said of Him. What the Talmud said of Him. What the learned Rabbi I. M. Wise and other erudite Jews said of Him. What Cerinthus, Celsus, Julian and Pagan philosophers said of Him. What ministering angels through intermediaries said of Him. Notwithstanding the Atheism and the icy Materialism rampant in some portions of the world, it is conceded by those competent to form a sound judgment that this book absolutely settles the question of Jesus' existence, and His mission to this world. Price $1.25.

Hell.

Its import and duration, a review of the Rev. Dr. Kipp's sermon delivered in the Presbyterian church, San Diego, Cal., upon "What is Hell?" by Dr. J. M. Peebles. A pamphlet of 25 pages. Price 10 cents.

The Seers of the Ages.

This large volume (9th edition) treats exhaustively of the Seers, Sages, Prophets and Inspired Men of the past, with records of their visions, trances, and intercourse with the invisible world. It gives the Doctor's belief concerning God, Heaven, Hell, Inspiration, Baptism, Faith, Repentance, Judgment, Evil Demons, the Resurrection, Prayer, Immortality, etc. etc. This book of some 400 pages, consid-

BV - #0061 - 091222 - C0 - 229/152/18 - PB - 9780282409791 - Gloss Lamination